T0293727

CHINA'S REGIONAL ECONOMIC DEVELOPMENT
A Case Study of Wenzhou

WSPC-ZJUP Series on China's Regional Development

Print ISSN: 2661-3883
Online ISSN: 2661-3891

Since China's reform and opening-up in 1978, the world's most populous country has enjoyed rapid economic development. This book series sheds new light on China's phenomenal success by examining its regional development and disparity. The series starts from first few volumes focusing on Zhejiang province, one of the country's forerunners in economic, social and political transformation. These volumes analyse Zhejiang's local governance innovation, regional economic development, and social and cultural changes over the past few decades.

Published:

Vol. 6   *China's Regional Economic Development: A Case Study of Wenzhou*
          by SHI Jinchuan, JIN Xiangrong, ZHAO Wei, LUO Weidong *et al.*

Vol. 5   *Political Participation and Institutional Innovation:*
          A Case Study of Zhejiang
          by CHEN Shengyong, ZHONG Dongsheng, WU Xingzhi and
          ZHANG Bingxuan

Vol. 4   *The Belt and Road Initiative and the World's Largest Small*
          Commodity Market: Yiwu Business Circle
          by LU Lijun *et al.*

Vol. 3   *Change of China's Rural Community: A Case Study of Zhejiang's*
          Jianshanxia Village
          by MAO Dan

More information on this series can also be found at
https://www.worldscientific.com/series/wszjscrd

WSPC-ZJUP Series on China's Regional Development – Vol. 6

CHINA'S REGIONAL ECONOMIC DEVELOPMENT
A Case Study of Wenzhou

SHI Jinchuan
Zhejiang University, China

JIN Xiangrong
Zhejiang University, China

ZHAO Wei
Zhejiang University, China

LUO Weidong
Zhejiang University, China

et al.

ZHEJIANG UNIVERSITY PRESS
浙江大学出版社

World Scientific

NEW JERSEY · LONDON · SINGAPORE · BEIJING · SHANGHAI · HONG KONG · TAIPEI · CHENNAI · TOKYO

Published by

World Scientific Publishing Co. Pte. Ltd.

5 Toh Tuck Link, Singapore 596224

USA office: 27 Warren Street, Suite 401-402, Hackensack, NJ 07601

UK office: 57 Shelton Street, Covent Garden, London WC2H 9HE

and

Zhejiang University Press
No. 148, Tianmushan Road
Xixi Campus of Zhejiang University
Hangzhou 310028, China

Library of Congress Cataloging-in-Publication Data

Names: Shi, Jinchuan, 1957–   author.

Title: China's regional economic development : a case study of Wenzhou / Shi Jinchuan,
    Zhejiang University, China, Jin Xiangrong, Zhejiang University, China, Zhao Wei,
    Zhejiang University, China, Luo Weidong, Zhejiang University, China.

Description: New Jersey : World Scientific, [2020] | Series: WSPC-ZJUP series on China's regional
    development, 2661-3883 ; vol. 6 | Includes bibliographical references and index.

Identifiers: LCCN 2019057611 | ISBN 9789813279582 (hardcover)

Subjects: LCSH: Economic development--China--Wenzhou Shi--Case studies. |
    Regional planning--China--Wenzhou Shi--Case studies. |
    Wenzhou Shi (China)--Economic conditions.

Classification: LCC HC428.W46 .S55 2020 | DDC 338.95124/2--dc23

LC record available at https://lccn.loc.gov/2019057611

British Library Cataloguing-in-Publication Data

A catalogue record for this book is available from the British Library.

This edition is jointly published by World Scientific Publishing Co. Pte. Ltd. and Zhejiang University
Press. This edition is distributed outside the Chinese mainland by World Scientific Publishing Co. Pte. Ltd.

For any available supplementary material, please visit
https://www.worldscientific.com/worldscibooks/10.1142/11255#t=suppl

Desk Editors: Anthony Alexander/Lixi Dong

Typeset by Stallion Press
Email: enquiries@stallionpress.com

About the Authors

SHI Jinchuan is Professor and Doctoral Supervisor at School of Economics, Zhejiang University, and a member of the Academic Degree Committee of Zhejiang University. His research focuses on modern Western economics, macroeconomic theory and policy, regional economic development strategy, and law and economics.

JIN Xiangrong is Professor and Doctoral Supervisor of School of Economics, Zhejiang University. He formerly served as Executive Vice President of School of Economics, Zhejiang University, and President of Zhejiang Economics Association. His research focuses on the history of economic thought, industrial economics, international trade, and neo-institutional economics.

ZHAO Wei is Professor and Doctoral Supervisor of School of Economics, Zhejiang University, and Director of the Institute of International Economics, Zhejiang University. His research focuses on international economics, space economics, and foreign economic history.

LUO Weidong is Professor and Doctoral Supervisor of School of Economics, Zhejiang University, and Vice President of Zhejiang University. His research focuses on history of economic thought, economic history, and development economics.

Contents

Introduction

Since the reform and opening-up, Wenzhou, located in the eastern coastal area, has become a pilot area of large-scale institutional change and rapid economic development in China and exerted huge demonstration effects on the reform and opening-up and economic development in the other regions.

According to Yu Guangyuan, a domestic economist of the older generation, in the course of the reform and opening-up and economic development in China, a situation of "one system and multiple modes" arose. That is to say, on the premise of a stable basic economic system of China, many modes of reform and opening-up and economic development with regional characteristics have appeared in different regions and during different periods, such as the Shenzhen model, Pearl River Delta (PRD) model, South Jiangsu model, Wenzhou model, and Pudong model. Interestingly, most of these models could not do without active support and vigorous publicity by the central and local governments, except Wenzhou model. Moreover, the government has directly established some modes by intervening in the economic field. Though Wenzhou model has enjoyed a good reputation since the mid-1980s, governments at all levels hadn't popularized it in official documents until 1992. In fact, Wenzhou model has always exerted great influence on the reform of the economic system and the economic development in China. However, its influence and demonstration effects were always exerted doggedly during each key period of reform of the economic system or at each important stage of economic development by contending against social controversies about it. In other words,

Wenzhou model has always worked via informal channels instead of official channels to affect reform and development in the other regions of China. A government official, who was governor of Zhejiang Province in the mid-1980s and the late 1980s, once impressed Shi Jinchuan by saying that planned economy is for officials, while market economy is for common people. Therefore, to some degree, Wenzhou model, which first broke the planned economic system and boldly carried out the market-oriented reform in the beginning of the reform and opening-up, was created by Wenzhou people. Of course, after Deng Xiaoping's South Talks in 1992 and the 15th National Congress of the Communist Party of China, Wenzhou model became a topic that could be discussed in public and was approved by local governments at all levels. It gradually became a model of economic development for Zhejiang people and even people all over the country.

This book attempts to study Wenzhou model from a basic perspective of resource allocation of economics. Optimized allocation of resources is a core issue of economic research. From a perspective of resource allocation, economic development of a country or a region is manifested in the flow and optimized allocation of resources in different industrial sectors, namely, constant flow and optimized allocation of resources from primary industrial sectors to the manufacturing industry and the service industry in the process of economic development, which is also known as industrialization. In addition, economic development also shows the flow and optimal allocation of resources in different regional space, namely, constant flow and optimized allocation of resources from rural areas to urban areas in the process of economic development, which is also known as urbanization. Similarly, Wenzhou has undergone transformation from rural industrialization to new industrialization and from rise of small towns to modern city expansion. You may wonder what drives the economic development of Wenzhou. This book studies this problem from a perspective of resource allocation and offers an answer: One important force driving the economic development is institutional change. From a perspective of resource allocation of economics, institutional change is manifested in the change of the main body of resource allocation. In other words, common people have become the main body of resource allocation during the social development, which is privatization of the main body of resource allocation. Also, institutional change shows change of resource allocation modes. That is to say, markets have become the main mode of resource allocation by replacing plans in social economic activities, and they play an increasingly decisive role in the course of resource allocation, which is the marketization of resource allocation modes. Similarly, large-scale institutional change in Wenzhou indicates rapid development of privatization and marketization in regional economic activities.

This book studies institutional change and economic development in Wenzhou since the reform and opening-up. Research conclusions show that the most important characteristic of Wenzhou model is that it is the first to promote industrialization and urbanization by privatization and marketization. As privatization and marketization reflect reform and industrialization and urbanization stand for development, Wenzhou model promotes development through reform. Hence, Wenzhou model is not only a pattern of regional economic development, but also a model featuring prominent institutional change and integrating reform with development. In the early years of the reform and opening-up, Wenzhou people boldly took the lead in breaking through constraints of traditional planned economy, bravely explored market-oriented reform, and opened up a new path to regional economic development triumphantly. Therefore, Wenzhou model has been created by Wenzhou people and this book narrates stories of Wenzhou people.

The rise of Wenzhou model is closely related to regional natural resources, business tradition, and historical and cultural resources of Wenzhou. Though Wenzhou is located in the eastern coastal area of China, mountains account for a large proportion of its total area. A large population with relatively little arable land is always a significant characteristic of Wenzhou with respect to natural resources. After the reform and opening-up, especially after the reform of the contracted responsibility system based on the household in rural areas, farmers' enthusiasm for production greatly grew, leading to rapid increase of agricultural production and output. However, due to little arable land per capita in Wenzhou, marginal products of land soon decreased in Wenzhou, especially in mountain areas. As a result, farmers could not enhance their family income by agricultural production only. Meanwhile, due to implementation of the contracted responsibility system based on the household, farmers had real rights to dominate their own labor force. Consequently, farmers with historical tradition of business and cultural spirit of commerce started to jump out of agricultural production activities and a massive rural labor force began to move away from the agricultural production sector. Farmers either expanded their family sideline production or engaged in business activities, or they started industrial workshops in partnerships. Various private economies rose rapidly and boomed, which greatly promoted rural industrialization in Wenzhou. As China's reform of the economic system was transferred from rural areas to urban areas, people in Wenzhou who also shared business tradition took the lead in developing various private economies. Meanwhile, rural individual economic sectors poured into towns. Large-scale integration development of urban and rural private economy greatly drove the urbanization of Wenzhou. Traditional small towns expanded rapidly, while new small towns arose. Regional transportation was constantly improved and flow of various production factors became active. Regional industrialization and urbanization promoted one another, leading to a new period of economic development in Wenzhou.

Though some other regions in China were similar to Wenzhou in terms of natural resources, history, tradition, and culture, Wenzhou outshone them in the early stage of the reform and opening-up, which was closely related to the attitudes and practices of the Wenzhou government relating to individual and private economy.

First, the officials in Wenzhou were greatly influenced by local history and traditional culture, were familiar with local conditions of natural resources, and understood the true intention of local people and attributes of local human resources. Hence, during implementation of policies from the government, they paid more attention to the interests of local people and became down to earth as far as possible, leaving more scope to act during implementation. For example, in the early 1960s, Wenzhou was the first to try out the fixing of farm output quotas on a household basis, where the mode of collective labor adopted by production teams in people's commune was changed and land management rights of production teams were distributed among rural households. Also, during the "Cultural Revolution", there were still numerous individual economic activities beyond state-owned economy and collective economy in Wenzhou. Capitalism was never cut off completely in Wenzhou and many grassroots officials tolerated this situation.

Second, due to the special geographical location of Wenzhou, its historical task assigned by the central government was "farming and fishing". In other words, the central government never considered Wenzhou as a priority area for industrial development. Hence, during the period of planned economy before the reform and opening-up, the central government never considered launching an industrial project for Wenzhou to promote its economic development. As a result, regional economic development in Wenzhou was not supported by the central government for a long time. During the period of planned economy, Wenzhou didn't get much support from the central government. Naturally, after the reform and opening-up, local officials of Wenzhou seldom asked governments of higher levels for help when they tried to develop the local economy. Furthermore, they paid attention to local people. Therefore, local officials of Wenzhou held a more open-minded attitude toward the development of local individual and private economy than officials in the other regions.

The open-minded attitude held by officials of Wenzhou and the development of local individual and private economy formed a positive feedback mechanism in the course of institutional change and economic development of Wenzhou and this mechanism was constantly strengthened by interaction. Reasons for this situation are as follows: (1) With the progress of the reform and opening-up, the state held an increasingly tolerant attitude toward individual and private economy, and political risks undertaken by local officials due to support of individual and private economies reduced. (2) The development of individual and private economy drove rapid development of Wenzhou's economy, bringing great job opportunities to local officials and strengthening motivation of local officials to support individual and private economies. (3) Due to the rise and massive expansion of individual and private economy, many local families engaged in such activities, including families related to local officials, where economic interests of officials and common people were highly integrated together, affecting value orientation of officials in the process of policy development and implementation. Of course, integration of interests of officials and common people also led to some negative effects on institutional change and economic development of Wenzhou later on. Regarding these negative effects, as business activities of Wenzhou were characterized by personalized transaction, leading to close connection of public power and individual and private economy, the relationship between politics and commerce became contorted. As a result, opening-up and inflow of production factors were hindered and upgrading of the industrial structure of Wenzhou slowed down for more than ten years with intergenerational locking, impacting the development of Wenzhou's economy.

To sum up, as an order of self-expansion, Wenzhou model has been a typical example of regional institutional change and economic development since the reform and opening-up. The logic behind the rise and development of Wenzhou model is this: Resource allocation — institutional change — economic development. However, from the perspective of historical development, we should not be overoptimistic to think that as an order of self-expansion, Wenzhou model will certainly enter into the modern market economy smoothly after transition from planned economy to initial market economy. Similarly, as a pattern of regional economic institutional change, institutional change of Wenzhou is not only restricted by the course of the national institutional change but also influenced by regional culture, leading to obstruction of regional economic institutional change. Obstruction of regional economic institutional change is bound to impact vitality of regional economic development, remove the motive power of the old development pattern, and inhibit evolution of the industrial structure and growth of development power.

Based on the history of China since the reform and opening-up in 1978, this book mainly studies the economic system reform and regional economic development of Wenzhou between 1978 and 2002 and attempts to reveal the internal mechanism of formation and development of Wenzhou model from various angles.

The first three chapters mainly study institutional change and economic development of Wenzhou model from the perspective of the economic theory.

Chapter 1, Research on Wenzhou Model: Review and Prospect — It carries out a review and theoretical analysis on research literature and scholars' viewpoints about Wenzhou model with respect to connotation and development characteristics, reform of the economic system in Wenzhou, foreign research on Wenzhou model, regional cultural factors produced by Wenzhou model, and forecast on the development trend of Wenzhou model.

Chapter 2, Wenzhou Model: Institutional Change and System Innovation — It mainly applies the theory of neoinstitutional economics to research on the bold reform of the economic system in Wenzhou and its characteristics from a perspective of inductive institution evolution.

Chapter 3, Wenzhou Model: Regional Economic Development and Industrialization Path — It mainly employs the theory of neoclassical economics to study the rise of rural industrialization and regional economic development in Wenzhou model from a perspective of regional economic development.

Chapters 4–8 mainly study the growth of Wenzhou's private enterprises, evolution of industrial organization forms, development of specialized small-commodity markets and private financial markets, enterprise competitive behavior, and establishment of market order during Wenzhou's economic system reform and system transformation.

Chapter 4, Growth Path and Mechanism of Wenzhou's Private Enterprises — It primarily researches how Wenzhou broke through traditional ideological obstacles and the planned economy system and rapidly expanded private enterprises by taking the lead in innovation of enterprise systems.

Chapter 5, From a Family Workshop to a Modern Enterprise: A Case Study of Chint Group — It takes Chint Group, a famous private enterprise of Wenzhou, which developed from a family workshop to a modern enterprise, as an example, to show how family workshops in Wenzhou developed into modern enterprises.

Chapter 6, Development of Wenzhou Centralized Industrial Wholesale Markets — It researches the origin and development of specialized small-commodity markets of Wenzhou, behavior of specialized markets in local industrialization, and rise of small towns.

Chapter 7, Evolution of the Leather Shoes Industry in Wenzhou — By case study, it researches the leather shoes industry in Wenzhou, where its market was transformed from a market full of forged and fake commodities, into a regulated and orderly market attaching great importance to intellectual property protection.

Chapter 8, Family Culture and Regional Economic Development in Wenzhou — As most private enterprises in Wenzhou are family corporations, this chapter studies effects of family culture in Wenzhou on the emergence and development of private enterprises and the evolution trend of family culture and family business in Wenzhou.

The research framework of this book reflects basic research ideas and methods of the research group on Wenzhou model. The consistent dominant idea in the research thought of the group is this: Wenzhou model is not only a pattern of regional economic development but also a model of regional economic institutional change, where demonstration effects of this model are mainly reflected by its institutional change. The research group of Wenzhou model insists on the importance of both the theoretical research of Wenzhou model and attention of the real process of formation and development of Wenzhou model to explore the mechanism behind this mode, a real event in the real world. Hence, case study is adopted to help readers understand the rich connotation of this model at multiple levels. Of course, application of our research ideas and methods to this study remains to be reviewed by readers.

Hence, this book mainly studies the formation and development of Wenzhou model between 1978 and 2002 from various angles, covering the course of this model from its rise to full bloom. During the same period, this model first caused widespread concern, became controversial and then famous, and finally became a model imitated by various regions in China. However, from 2002 to 2017, Wenzhou also encountered many difficulties and problems in its economic and social development, making Wenzhou model a controversial topic again.

In the 21st century, the economic development of Wenzhou has slowed down obviously and many of its major indexes of regional economic development are worse than those of the other regions in Zhejiang, attracting much attention, especially from the academic circles. In 2003, at the International Seminar for New Political Economics hosted by Shanghai Jiao Tong University, Professor Shi Jinchuan gave a speech on historical system analysis of Wenzhou model, where a theoretical framework of comparison of historical institutional analysis put forward by Professor A. Greif at Stanford University was applied to analyzing three major problems of the model. These three problems are as follows: (1) Why did the evolution of the industrial structure in economic development of Wenzhou become slow with a tendency of intergenerational locking? (2) Why was there little external capital introduced from other regions into Wenzhou in its economic development? (3) Why did Wenzhou merchants build a commercial network across the world by massive immigration? Research of Professor Shi Jinchuan showed that the historical and cultural tradition of Wenzhou strengthened the mode of personalized transaction of Wenzhou people in business activities. Thus, it is difficult for most Wenzhou people who engage in production and marketing activities through the mode of personalized transaction in the traditional manufacturing industry to get rid of the network of personalized transaction created by Wenzhou people themselves and enter into new industries, leading to intergenerational locking of Wenzhou people in the traditional manufacturing industry. Meanwhile, as the mode of personalized transaction of Wenzhou people has gradually expanded from commercial activities to the political field, close local relationships between politics and commerce have hindered foreign investors from entering Wenzhou. As for the numerous overseas immigrants, Wenzhou merchants need to create a giant network of personalized transaction overseas so that they can focus on business all over the world.

In 2010, struck by the international financial crisis, the serious consequences of intergenerational locking of its industrial structure emerged quickly. It was hard for private enterprises in the traditional manufacturing industry to sustain with capital chain rupture, resulting in the outburst of financial risks and a financial crisis in Wenzhou. The local financial crisis in Wenzhou even made Wen Jiabao, the then Premier of the State Council, come to Wenzhou for investigation and led to direct release of an emergency policy in response to the financial crisis. Later on, he listed Wenzhou as a pilot city of regional financial reform and innovation in China. In fact, the regional financial crisis induced by the financial crisis in Wenzhou could be attributed to the mode of personalized transaction of Wenzhou. Scholars think that the main reason for formation and explosion of financial risks of Wenzhou is that implementation of financial contracts of traditional private financial activities is ensured by the mode of personalized transaction. After traditional private financial activities expanded rapidly, severe information asymmetry between the supply side and the demand side of funds in private financial activities occurred because of change in purpose and use of financing, expansion of financing scale, and sharp increase of financing subjects as well as subsequent rapid falling apart of close relations of financing subjects. As a result, personalized transaction could not play an effective role in the new private financial activities to guarantee smooth execution of private financial contracts.

Though domestic and foreign scholars have carried out various studies and offered various explanations for problems of Wenzhou model appearing in the past decade, they are relatively theoretical, logical, and convictive explanations. Of course, foreign scholars also hold different views toward explanations of the dilemma of Wenzhou model through the mode of personalized transaction. For instance, a Japanese scholar thinks that the mode of personalized transaction should not be negated, for it played an important role in forming and developing Wenzhou model. In addition, in some scholars' eyes, the personalized transaction mode can reduce transaction costs. In fact, on the premise of recognition of the personalized transaction mode, scholars have studied negative effects of this mode. In the development process of Wenzhou model, when business activities have path dependence on the personalized transaction mode, which even hinders the transformation of the market transaction mode to impersonal transaction, defects of the personalized transaction mode are revealed. Hence, the development prospect of Wenzhou model mainly depends on transformation of the transaction mode in regional economic development of Wenzhou, namely, transformation from the personalized transaction mode based on geographical and blood relations to the impersonalized transaction mode based on law. This also confirms the important role of institutional change in economic development. Modern market economy is contract economy based on legality, which is the development path that should be followed by Wenzhou model and the only road to the socialist market economy of China.

Chapter **1**

Research on Wenzhou Model: Review and Prospect

Since the reform and opening-up, due to differences in historical and cultural traditions and economic development of various regions, a "one system, multiple modes" situation has emerged in the course of industrialization and marketization in China; namely, under the precondition of an identical basic system of society, each region applies diversified economic system reforms and economic development modes. Among them, the influential ones are Pearl River Delta model, South Jiangsu model, Wenzhou model, etc. Moreover, Wenzhou model has aroused much concern for its particular high spontaneity.

Wenzhou is a city located in the south of Zhejiang Province. It has poor locational conditions, national underinvestment, and no obvious advantages in natural resources in history, and its economy developed very slowly before 1978; therefore, it was one of the economically backward regions in Zhejiang before 1978. However, since the reform and opening-up, Wenzhou's economy has been growing fairly fast, with its GDP (Gross Domestic Product) rapidly increasing from 1.322 billion yuan in 1978 to 82.5 billion yuan in 2000 and its average annual growth rate reaching 15.6%, thus promoting development of the local society and improvement of the local people's living standard, and preliminarily creating a new way to promote the rapid development of regional economy and society by taking the lead in marketization.

In the process of formation and development of Wenzhou model, there were once several strong research booms in domestic academia

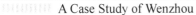
involving in-depth research of Wenzhou model from various perspectives and at different levels. For the purpose of a comprehensive summary of the characteristics of Wenzhou model, this chapter will summarize the connotation and features of Wenzhou model from the perspectives of theoretical research, review progress and the present situation of Wenzhou model related research in the past decades, and give further prospect of development and research trends of Wenzhou model in combination with the recent economic and social development of Wenzhou.

1.1 Connotation and characteristics of Wenzhou model

Wenzhou model is a kind of regional economic and social development mode formed through the demand-attract example and audacious and forward-looking partial economic system reform in the course of Chinese economic system reform and economic development, and its core lies in fully respecting and exerting demotic initiative, integrating the economic system reform and economic development organically, and making reform and development a kind of mutually promoting dynamic change process in the regional economic and social reform; it can also be said that Wenzhou model is an economic and social development mode of Wenzhou people to promote rapid development of regional economy and society by taking the lead in reforming and establishing market economic system under the guidance of the government's reform and opening-up policy.

The basic connotation of Wenzhou model includes two important aspects: On the one hand, Wenzhou model is a mode of economic and social development, especially economic development; on the other hand, it is an economic system change mode, or in other words, an economic system reform mode.

The Nobel Economics Prize Laureate Professor Simon Kuznets (1998) once pointed out that the economic development in the modern economic growth sense will cause immense change of the social economic structure, which is mainly expressed in two major aspects: One is that the product source and resource destination transfer from agricultural activities to non-agricultural production activities, which is a process of industrialization; the other is that the urban and rural population distribution changes, which is a process of urbanization. Thus, it can be seen that regional economic development is essentially a dynamic process of optimizing resource allocation, which includes two important aspects: One is the flow and optimized allocation of resources among different industrial sectors, which is expressed as the transfer of resources from the primary industrial sector represented by agriculture to the industrial sector and service industrial sector, namely, an industrialization process of economic development; the other is the flow and optimized allocation of resources in regional space, which is expressed as agglomeration of resources from the vast and dispersed rural area to urban advantaged space, namely, an urbanization process of economic and social development.

From the view of the process of Wenzhou's economic development practices, Wenzhou's economic development first benefits from the human resources within the region — all kinds of talents in the management field boasting of regional characteristic business cultural traditions. The broad environment for social and economic development created by the reform and opening-up policy led the human resources of Wenzhou to give full play to their potential advantages. Wenzhou people quickly accomplished their primitive accumulation of capital by capturing business opportunities, soon turned commercial capital into industrial capital, and had individual private industrial and commercial enterprises, and joint-stock cooperative enterprises. Incorporated enterprises and joint-stock enterprises started as family corporations and greatly developed, accelerating development of regional economy featuring rural industrialization; furthermore, they promoted the urbanization process featuring rising and rapid expansion of small towns by utilizing the creation and dramatic development of specialized markets.

Another Nobel Economics Prize Laureate Professor Douglass C. North (1999) once indicated that in the analysis of the internal relations between the economic system and economic development, efficient economic organizations are the key to economic growth, which need to make arrangements for the system and establish the ownership, so as to create a kind of stimulus to turn an individual's economic efforts into activities where the private rate of return approaches the social rate of return. The "efficient economic organization" Professor North referred to may also be understood from two aspects: One is economic organization in the view of microeconomic subject level, namely, individuals and manufacturers engaged in economic activities, e.g., individual or industrial and commercial enterprises; the other is economic organization in the view of the social and economic system as well as social and economic operation method level, namely, resource allocation method in the social and economic life, e.g., market system and market operation mode.

From the prospective of process of Wenzhou's economic system change practice, the formation and expansion of Wenzhou's "efficient economic organization" is also manifested in two aspects: One is that the diversification of microeconomic subjects, or the privatization of economic subjects, formed a pattern where individual private economy develops rapidly while multi-ownership economy components seek coexistence and common prosperity; the other is that Wenzhou quickly formed various commodity markets and production factor markets (including labor markets and non-government financial markets) with wide coverage by taking the opportunity of exuberant rising and rapid development of specialized markets, so that markets replaced the mandatory plans and became the main mode of regulation of resource allocation in the development of regional economy.

The analyses above show that Wenzhou model is a typical regional economic and social development mode utilizing privatization and marketization to promote industrialization and urbanization. The main feature of Wenzhou model is that it utilizes the first-mover advantage of reforming outside the system, and takes the lead in promoting privatization and marketization quickly, thus leading to a kind of regional economic system disparity. Besides, with the help of the "potential energy" of the economic system disparity, Wenzhou rapidly promotes the process of industrialization and urbanization and forms a regional economic development mode featuring multi-ownership economy and small town construction (Shi, 1999).

Based on the above research strategy, this chapter reviews and provides an outlook of Wenzhou model research through two main lines: One is about Wenzhou model economic development, and the other is about change of Wenzhou model system. Furthermore, in order to make the research more systematic, the whole discussion will be supplemented by two other research perspectives: One is the humanistic spirit and social order issues, and the other is the perspective of overseas scholars. The former is mainly a multidisciplinary comprehensive study, while the latter is mainly a comparative study in the international perspective.

1.2 Wenzhou model and regional economic development

In the early 1980s, with the constant promotion of the rural contract responsibility system and sustainable development of agricultural production, rural labor started to move to the manufacturing industry and commercial sector. At that time, rural industrialization of Wenzhou featuring rural household industries witnessed fast progress, which greatly boosted Wenzhou's economy. By April 1985, the number of families involved in Wenzhou household industries had reached 133,000. A large number of farmers became rich "10,000-yuan households". The rapid development of Wenzhou's economy gained widespread concern. On May 12, 1985, Sang Jinquan, a journalist, published an article titled "For Rural Industry, Look to South Jiangsu; for Household Industry, Look to South Zhejiang" in the *Jiefang Daily*, which was the first time that Wenzhou model was formally put forward by the media. The article summarized the characteristics of the development of the rural household industry in Wenzhou as follows: It was dominated by smallware production, while the distribution channels were invigorated by farmer supply, marketing clerks, and rural market trading; plus, a bunch of skillful craftsmen and trading experts ploughed their way toward wealth and prosperity. At the same time, many state leaders inspected Wenzhou, and many famous scholars also published major articles introducing and researching Wenzhou model after the inspection. For instance, in the mid-1980s, Ma Hong came to Yueqing county in Wenzhou and conducted a survey on the 10,000-yuan household, which made him affirm the positive role of the 10,000-yuan household in the rural industrialization (Ma, 1985). Fei Xiaotong summarized the main features of Wenzhou's economy as "'small commodity and large market' with commerce driving industry" (Fei, 1986). However, Wu Xiang summarized the basic features of Wenzhou's economy as follows: "Its foundation is the household industry managed by farmers, and its link is the specialized market with the farmer purchase clerks as backbone and its support is the small town built and developed by farmers' fund." (Wu, 1986) Although Dong & Zhao (1986) didn't directly mention Wenzhou model, they highly praised the development of Wenzhou's economy. Shanghai Academy of Social Sciences even set up a research group to conduct a systematic survey on Wenzhou, and published a book named *Wenzhou Model and Path to Prosperity* in 1987. Zhang Renshou, a local scholar in Zhejiang, has continued to conduct comprehensive and systematic research on Wenzhou model since the mid-1980s, and the work *Research on Wenzhou* by Zhang & Li (1990) became the most profound and systematic economic work on the research of Wenzhou regional economic development mode.

Fei Xiaotong was one of the first scholars to turn his attention to Wenzhou. He visited Wenzhou three times, and published three articles in the *Outlook*, the first of which had the greatest impact. In his articles, Fei Xiaotong firstly vividly summarized the basic features of rural economic development of Wenzhou as "'small commodity and large market' with commerce driving industry". From this view, he indicated that Wenzhou model had gone beyond the region, and it had a universal meaning. One important feature of Wenzhou model was not its development of household industry, but the "small commodity and large market" of spontaneous folk worldwide, which directly built an all-pervasive circulation network between producers and consumers (Fei, 1986). Here, "small commodity and large market" was the most vivid and straightforward demonstration of the product mix and commodity circulation mode in Wenzhou, and the "commerce driving industry" highly summarized the mode marketing driving industry, which was an institutional change and economic development interaction in Wenzhou's economic development. However, people paid more attention to the regional economic model in the midst of researching Wenzhou model, which lacked a thorough discussion of the institutional change and its role in the regional economic development in Wenzhou.

The scholars, including Dong Fureng and Zhao Renwei, summarized the characteristics of the Wenzhou rural commodity economic development as follows: The private industry managed by households and joint households was combined with professional market, farmer salesmen, and private credit. They believed that the successful experiences of Wenzhou could be summarized as follows. First, in comparison with township enterprises initiated by rural organs of political power at all levels, the private industries managed by the individual household and the joint household had the following advantages: The private industries had enough autonomous right; the management result and the producers' benefit were closely linked, which was conducive to exerting the enthusiasm of practitioners; the private industries were easily established because they required little equipment and small investment, and had a quick beginning; they could also utilize the humble rural houses for production, which had the advantage of low cost and high profit rate on funds; the production skills were easy to master, and spread fast; the scale of the private industries was small and they could change their business quickly; and so on. Second, remedying and filling the market gap as the direction of production and management were conducive to gaining room for the existence and development of enterprises. Third, the commodity circulation network structured by specialized market and widespread farmer salesmen played a significate role in promoting, regulating, and organizing the production of private industries.

Wenzhou Model and Path to Prosperity, written by Yuan Enzhen who worked in the Economic Institution of Shanghai Academy of Social Sciences, was the first work researching Wenzhou model. This book summarized the contents of Wenzhou model as follows: The main feature of Wenzhou model was individual economy, and the basic form was household industry and specialized market, making farmers acquire wealth through developing commodity economy. The local cadres and the masses described the generation of Wenzhou model as "decentralized", "pushed", "innovated", and "supported" (Yuan, 1987). Besides, Yuan Enzhen put forward insightful views on some problems in the course of Wenzhou marketing in his book. It was believed that the root cause for fake, shoddy products and deceiving was more the insufficient development of commodity economy than the development of commodity economy itself. With the further development and universalness of commodity economy, every commodity producer was bound to pay attention to the product quality and maintain his business reputation so that he could strive to develop in the marketing competition. Besides, the abnormal situations in which some people in certain government organs and enterprises let the organization buy inferior goods in bulk and suffer loss for their personal gains would disappear as the reform of economic system progresses.

In *The Research on Wenzhou Model*, Zhang Renshou and Li Hong pointed out that Wenzhou model was mainly an economic development pattern transferring the natural economy in rural areas to commodity economy. The book summarized the features of Wenzhou model as follows: the household management as its foundation, the market as its guide, small towns as its support, and rural able people as its backbone. They believed that the generation and the development of Wenzhou model were the result of the interactions of a series of factors including realistic and historical factors, internal and external factors, and objective and subjective factors. Specifically, the causes of Wenzhou model were mainly divided into four aspects: First, the contradiction of a large population with relatively little arable land between laborers and land resources, the limited geographic location (no big urban agglomeration nearby), the weak rural collective economic strength, and commune- and brigade-run enterprise foundation, plus the small state investment, made the household industry become an inevitable choice of Wenzhou to develop commodity economy and solve the outlet problem of rural labor. Second, the farmers in Wenzhou who had the tradition of regional trade culture improved labor skills, increased knowledge, mastered technology, and quickly accumulated initial funds of household industry through various channels including commercial activities and operational labors. Third, Wenzhou possessed a regional lax policy and public opinion environment. Fourth, there was a huge demand for low-end goods for everyday consumption in the 1980s, which provided favorable market conditions for the household industry of Wenzhou (Zhang & Li, 1990). *The Research on Wenzhou Model* had three distinct characteristics. In the first place, the main author could conduct an empirical study after he got firsthand materials because he was a scholar in Wenzhou. Many crucial research conclusions could be analyzed from multiple perspectives by deeply observing economic activities. In the second place, although the authors mainly researched Wenzhou model as a pattern of regional economic development, they deeply analyzed the interactive relationships between regional economic institution reform and regional economic development by researching the ownership and enterprise system, specialized market, and market system, which started to involve the institutional transition in the regional development in all directions. In the third place, the authors concluded that Wenzhou model was more typical than South Jiangsu model and Pearl River Delta model in the vast underdeveloped rural areas by comparing different development patterns in rural industrialization.

In conclusion, from the mid-1980s to the early 1990s, domestic academic circles mainly discussed Wenzhou model as a regional economic development pattern, and the main contents and points were the development methods and characteristics. The economic system and institutional transition in the course of generation, formation, and development related to Wenzhou model were mostly involved in research on the causes of Wenzhou model, but not as a relatively independent "subject". After that, with Deng Xiaoping's South Talks, the convening of the 14th National Congress of the Communist Party of China and the establishment of the reform target of the socialist market economy system, the "hot topics" related to Wenzhou model research started to turn to the economic system reform and economic institutional change.

From the perspectives of personalized transaction and impersonal transaction, scholars started to study the development prospect of Wenzhou model. Employing the theoretical analytical framework put forward by Professor A. Greif, a famous economist, Professor Shi Jinchuan researched the extremely slow evolution of the manufacturing structure in Wenzhou and proposed the concept of intergenerational locking in the industrial structure of Wenzhou. Research conclusions show that since the reform and opening-up, in Wenzhou, two generations of entrepreneurs have grown up with the same cultural background of regional industry, and have had similar local knowledge and engaged in production and trade in the same or similar industries, constructing a grid of personalized transaction of Wenzhou people. This relatively closed grid of personalized transaction resulted in path dependence on the evolution of the industrial structure of Wenzhou, leading to intergenerational locking (Shi, 2004).

After Professor Shi's paper was published, Wenzhou model turned into a controversial topic again. Professor Zhang Shuguang from the Institute of Economics, Chinese Academy of Social Sciences, holds that, though the industrial structure of Wenzhou is not transformed from traditional industries into high and new technology industries, it cannot be denied that it is transformed from low technology into high technology, from low working into high working, and from low additional value into high additional value within traditional industries. According to the framework of historical institutional analysis conducted by Professor Shi, it's too early to define the industrial structure of Wenzhou as intergenerational locking (Zhang, 2004).

Major divergences of views of different scholars are as follows: whether there's intergenerational locking in the evolution of the industrial structure of Wenzhou, and causes for certain intergenerational locking in the evolution of industrial structure of Wenzhou. Thus, the great discussion on historical institutional analysis of Wenzhou model triggered by Professor Shi is no longer a simple study of Wenzhou model from a perspective of its development. Instead, it starts with industrial development of Wenzhou model and discusses institutional factors behind the development of Wenzhou model.

1.3 Wenzhou model and economic institutional change

After the 1990s, with the reform being deepened constantly, the research on Wenzhou model faced many new problems. At the same time, with the broadcast of neoinstitutional economics, the domestic scholars began to pay attention to building the transition economics in economy transition in China. Under this background, many scholars began to deeply research angle of economic institutional change and economic transition. Ma Jinlong first tried to analyze the formation of Wenzhou model by the concept of neoinstitutional economics in the research of joint-equity cooperative enterprises (Ma,1993). Zhang Jun researched the rural financial market structure in Wenzhou with the incomplete information theory of information economics and the relation between the interest rate level and risk in the informal financial sector (Zhang, 1997). Xu Minghua did research on the institution of different development phases in Wenzhou through transition economics (Xu, 1999). Jin Xiangrong comprehensively analyzed the path and method of the institution in the formation of Wenzhou model by the institutional transition theory of the neoinstitutional economics (Jin, 2000).

In the subject "study on the construction of the cooperative enterprise systems in Wenzhou", Ma Jinlong was the first person to use the concept of compulsory institutional transition and inductive institutional transition in neoinstitutional economics to research the enterprise system evolution problem in the formation course of Wenzhou model. He believed that the compulsory institutional transition made it easy to intensify the social conflict and give rise to social unrest, and the transition cost, also named "transition fee" in the institutional transition, was above normal. However, the inductive institutional transition was a relatively steady formation of institutional transition because of its cushion process. Wenzhou model was a typical formation of establishing market economy through inductive institutional transition in the course of reform. Wenzhou's joint-venture company was the combined effect of the economic approach and the political approach, according to both the farmers' choice and the government's choice.[1] The aspect of economic approach in the farmers' choice was as follows: On the one hand, the constant improvement of the technology required

---

[1]Joint-equity cooperative enterprises are a form of enterprise organization that rose in the 1990s in Wenzhou. Just as the name implies, they are enterprise organizations integrating joint stock with cooperation. In fact, they belong to joint-equity enterprises and reservation of the cooperative system is for catering to ideology and political protection.

enterprises to quickly expand the investment scale, but the joint-stock cooperative system was relatively conducive to collecting scattered capital. On the other hand, the various regulations of accumulation and distribution of the enterprises related to different ownership formalities gave joint-equity cooperative enterprises more favorable development conditions than private enterprises. For instance, the capital stock of joint-equity cooperative enterprises and the shared provident fund of shareholders according to their shareholdings could disburse dividend before taxes, but the owned capital of private enterprises could not acquire earnings. The effective tax of joint-equity cooperative enterprises and the loan interest rate were also lower than those of private enterprises. As collectively owned enterprises, joint-equity cooperative enterprises could enjoy favorable treatments in the aspects of derating revenue, acquiring the land use right, competing for the advanced unit prize, and getting a license. The aspect of political approach in the farmers' choice was as follows: As a sector of socialist economy under collective ownership by the working people, joint-equity cooperative enterprises were in the dominant position of socialist public ownership in law, and their development was not limited by the government policy then. On the contrary, private enterprises usually met with legal crisis. The aspect of the economic approach in the government's choice was as follows: Seeking political achievement from local productivity development out of the consensus on economic construction, all levels of government tipped the scales toward the standard of the economic approach at the time of choosing the form of enterprises. Because of the weak foundation of state-owned business and big collectively owned enterprises, Wenzhou had no choice but to set up household enterprises. The choice of the government is politically oriented: The basic principle of patterns of ownership of the primary stage of socialism was the public ownership as the main form, but the proportions of state-owned business and collectively owned enterprises of Wenzhou constantly decreased, which created a huge political challenge for the local government. Therefore, conducting part of the individual private enterprises to gradually transfer to the new form of enterprise organization which had the public economic sector became the conscious choice for the Wenzhou government. In the mid-1980s, the "joint stock" managed with the share formation in Wenzhou rural areas was popularized, which provided objective conditions for this choice. Hence, on the foundation of respecting the individual property right, the Wenzhou government adapted the formation of joint-stock partnership, gradually conducting demutualization renovation on the basis of "shareholding" and "joint possession" to the existing joint-stock enterprises. The former was to guarantee the property right of legal persons and build limited liability systems through establishing a new system by supervision. The latter was to establish standards through building the common accumulated system owned by the staff. According to the research conclusions of Ma Jinlong, as a new-type "mixed economy" with the share factor and cooperation sector, the development tendency of joint-equity cooperative enterprises was gradually decreased but the share sector was gradually increased. Joint-equity cooperative enterprises would probably become a widespread form of enterprise organization with the cooperation sector to some degree and with the foundation of the shareholding system, and would exist for a long time in the course of rural industrialization and modernization (Ma, 1993).

On the basis of the attention given to the important role of Wenzhou's informal finance in the development of regional economy, Zhang Jun used the information economic theory to research the structure change, property, and influence of Wenzhou's rural financial sectors. From the perspective of information asymmetry, Zhang Jun regarded the rural credit rate as having a function of regulating the credit crisis profile and filtering credit crisis. He believed that the segmentation of the rural credit market and the steady interest rate in the informal credit sector always higher than that of the formal credit sector were rational reactions of the severely unsymmetrical distribution of loan returning risks in the rural financial market among households and household organizations (family enterprises). In developing counties and regions, the credit was extended from relatives, friends, and neighbors. The reason was that the problems of asymmetric information and contract fulfillment were not severe in general, which could lower the risks of credit. In the relationship of debit and credit among relatives and friends, the interest of credit was always low and free because of the less-severe screening. With the accelerating of the regional industrialized process and the expansion of household production management scale, the demand of capital was increased at the same time. With the constant extension of the relation chain of credit, the informal rural credit gradually developed as a market. In this process, the interest rate had gradually begun to exert the functions of filtering and preventing credit risk. Therefore, Zhang Jun believed that the government should actively guide instead of weakening the rural informal financial sectors to enter into the market while it reformed the formal financial sectors. Meanwhile, when the government gradually opened the rural financial market, it should loosen the control of rural credit cooperatives and make them accessible to market as an independent player. The role of the government was to govern the whole rural financial market and make it open to a more organized competitive pattern (Zhang, 1997).

In recent years, research on private financial development in Wenzhou carried out by scholars in Zhejiang has increased. In a study of private finance, Pan Shiyuan and Luo Deming analyzed the operating mechanism of private finance and its active role in regional economic development (Pan & Luo, 2006). Zhang Xiang studied private financial markets in Wenzhou and Taizhou during the reform and opening-up, started with the information mechanism of private financial contracts to research financial contracts of three types of private financial activities in private financial institutions (Zhang, 2016). Focusing on regional financial risks emerging in Wenzhou from 2010 to 2011, Shi Jinchuan revealed the rapid expansion of private financial markets in Wenzhou, where failure of the execution mechanism of private financial contract was characterized by personalized transaction, leading to concentration and outburst of financial risks in private financial markets (Shi, 2012).

Xu Minghua researched the institutional transition of different development phases in Wenzhou in a framework of the transition economics, and he believed that the generation and development of Wenzhou model not only conformed to the target and direction of China's market reform but also conformed to the internal logic of China's market development. First of all, he analyzed that the origin of Wenzhou model was a large population with relatively little arable land and insufficient state investment. The traditional culture of Wenzhou was emphasizing utilitarianism, industry and commerce. The people of Wenzhou were hardworking and full of the spirit of adventure. Hence, Wenzhou carried out marketing management activities which were regarded as illegal activities "illegal marketization" before the reform and opening-up. After the reform and opening-up, due to the relatively high trade cost and efficiency loss brought about by "illegal marketization", people tried to seek legal protection for the main part of these market management activities. On the one hand, the main part of "illegal marketization" was made legal through the formation of "reform". On the other hand, local government always connived and even publicly supported market activities and protected them. In all these courses, the rural independent innovation was the major impetus to the Wenzhou economic development, and the government also played a crucial role in the directive standard of the rural independent innovation in turn. Both interworked and mutually promoted one another, which pushed the expansion of Wenzhou economy marketization as a whole. The process of marketization could be seen as a broadcast process about the knowledge of the market system. Wenzhou had a stock of human capital with knowledge of the market system, so the marketization could be pushed and developed quickly by rural independent innovation.

Meanwhile, any reform comes with a cost. The reform cost could not only be shown as friction cost resulting from benefit conflicts but also be shown as implementation cost of searching for knowledge, learning new systems, and resigning for the reform system. Both the friction cost and the implementation cost were shown as the obstruction of reform. Under the influence of the starting condition on friction cost, the reform possessed strong impetus and small friction cost because people in Wenzhou almost did not receive the "benefit of planned economy" in the planned economy. Under the influence of the starting condition on the implementation cost, although the reform of the new system in Wenzhou cost a lot, it would confront the survival crisis without reform; by contrast, the relative high implementation cost of reform was acceptable to most people. Meanwhile, the occurrence and development of Wenzhou model exactly followed the so-called "extended order of human cooperation" mentioned by Hayek, and started by the individual initiative, individual innovation in the unplanned space. Therefore, as long as the top policymakers could understand and respect the individual innovation of the people, as well as the correct guidance, some order would probably be established and constantly extended (Xu, 1999).

Jin Xiangrong used the method of new institutional economics to conduct a relatively comprehensive and deep research on Wenzhou model from the perspective of demand derivative system innovation, and he believed that Wenzhou model was the first to form a "space pole" of "institutional innovation" in Zhejiang Province and even the whole nation through demand derivative local system innovation. Wenzhou was the first to carry out institutional innovation nationwide, it accomplished the institutional transition from the traditional planned economy to the market economy, and established the property system with the main distinct and exclusive sector of non-state-owned and non-public economy. Unlike the other type of institutional innovation enforced by the government and leading type of supply, Wenzhou model was generated in the institutional competition between the initial demand derivative institutional innovation and the compulsory innovation of the leading type of supply. In the development process, Wenzhou model formed a progressive innovation method with the minimized friction cost and quasi-demand derivative institutional change as the principal, which brought Wenzhou and then Zhejiang more advantages of institutional imbalance than the other regions, and promoted the rapid and sustainable regional growth. From the aspect of regional institutional innovation and system transition, Jin Xiangrong pointed out that Wenzhou basically completed the transition from planned economy to the primary market economy ("the first institutional transition"), and it was in the economic transition period from the primary market economy to the modern economy — "the second institutional transition" from the property institutional transition to the management revolution being its main content. The key point was to achieve the transformation from the traditional enterprise system to the modern enterprise system. It was a period when the "revolution" replaced changes in the enterprise and the market boundary. If the government wanted to realize the phased institutional transformation, it would have to lay emphasis on the factor market construction, change the traditional market organization and market trading methods, and relieve the accessible regulation of the sector of non-state-owned and non-public economy at the same time. Therefore, Wenzhou model manifested as people in Wenzhou actually choosing a low-cost and high-return reform path, which coexisted with multiple institutional transition methods and progressive transformation, and could achieve the institutional transition in a timely manner, so that the "North Paradox" in the inefficient property right structure could be eliminated or decreased to the minimum range. Therefore, in comparison with other regional economic patterns, Wenzhou model had more referential values in the reform and development nationwide (Jin, 2004).

In the "Wenzhou Power", Zhao Wei summarized the characteristics of Wenzhou model as "clear ownership, source accumulation and intersectional trade." The first characteristic was building an enterprise system with clear property rights, the second was the formation of capital totally depending on the individual accumulation of regional people, and the third was the market mainly depending on the domestic market. Meanwhile, Zhao Wei pointed out that, due to the fact that wealth in Wenzhou was mainly owned by individuals and private enterprises, the expenditure of the government was mainly derived from the revenue handed in by enterprises. Grassroots officials began to widely realize that only if the enterprises developed could the government function well, and the concept of government working for businesses could become well reasoned. In order to retain investment and maintain economic prosperity, the government should try to create a favorable investment environment. In addition, in such a regional environment, if the township government would like to adopt a significant decision, it would be difficult to implement without the general acceptance of private enterprises. If this tendency continued, it would probably form a reversed democratic system. In addition, Zhao Wei pointed out that Wenzhou model belonged to a growing regional industrialized pattern after all, and some latent defects emerged, such as those of the industry structure, the product level, and the enterprise culture. But all of these were secondary. As long as the pattern itself constantly expanded, the latent defects could gradually be overcome. The biggest challenge brought about by further development of Wenzhou model would come from the external, and that was the lag caused by the economic institutional reform at the intermediate level. The lag of financial institution and farmland institution reform would probably directly restrict the further development of this pattern (Zhao, 1999). In Zhao Wei's research on the combination of economic institutional transition and economic development path in Wenzhou, the problems related to institutional transition not only lay in the economic institutional level but also began to involve the political institutional level.

Above all, the research on economic system transition of Wenzhou model possessed two relatively distinct characteristics: First, the research on concrete economic system transition (such as the enterprise system and the financial system arrangement) was gradually expanded to the research on the overall process and transition methods. Second, the research on the economic system transition was expanded to the influence of it and the economic development changes on the political system, which greatly enriched and deepened the research on Wenzhou model.

1.4 Humanistic perspective of Wenzhou model

With the fast expansion of Wenzhou model in the 1990s and the in-depth discussion of the research related to it, many scholars began to realize that the economic prosperity of Wenzhou was closely related to the regional humanistic spirit of Wenzhou people in fact except for the various factors revealed by the analysis of economics. Scholars such as Zhang Renshou had already discussed the influence of history on the emergence of Wenzhou model in the mid-1980s. They pointed out that the traditional industry and commerce passed down from generation to generation gave Wenzhou people a distinct advantage in managing industry and commerce. Meanwhile, Wenzhou had a regional cultural tradition advocating "utility" and "mercantilism". Wenzhou people were deeply edified by "Ouyue Culture", and the mental burdens of "justice outweighing benefit" and "agriculture outweighing commerce" were light, which made Wenzhou people utilitarian, aggressive, assiduous, adventurous, and competitive, paying attention to industry and commerce, being hardworking and industrious. The cultural tradition was consistent with the concept and spirit required in developing commodity economy, and became the major spiritual strength accelerating the prosperity of rural commodity economy in Wenzhou (Zhang & Li, 1990). In the 1990s, many scholars began to realize that the formation and development of Wenzhou model were not only an economic phenomenon of specialized regions but also an economic and social phenomenon possessing specialized cultural characteristics of specialized regions, so they further analyzed the characteristics of Wenzhou people and the influence exerted by their characteristics on Wenzhou model from the perspectives of sociology and humanism. Thereinto, many scholars such as Zhou Xiaohong and Wang Chunguang specialized in the Wenzhou people who were perennially out on business, especially the phenomenon of "Zhejiang village" in Beijing (Zhou, 1996); Wang Chunguang *et al.* also studied the Wenzhou people in Paris concerning how to integrate into the local society. However, Li Minghuan specialized in the migration of Wenzhou people to Europe (Li, 1999). Wang Xiaoyi conducted comparative research on the impact of the village industrialization on the family system of Guangdong and Wenzhou through a survey of Xiangdong village, Qianku town, Cangnan county, Wenzhou City (Wang, 1996).

Based on comparative research on Yantian village of Guangdong and Xiangdong village of Wenzhou, Wang Xiaoyi pointed out that the rural family system and concept of grassroots society were local, and the impact of local culture on the regional economy and society was related to the big social system and cultural background. The role of the family system was depressed in the places strictly controlled by the state. Conversely, the family system would probably be relatively active in other places. The family system of Wenzhou before the reform was relatively more active than that of other places, but was limited on the whole. After the rural reform, because the state controlled the family system less, the local family system recovered to some degree, and meanwhile the family system and the family concept developed. The impact of the family system in Xiangdong village was manifested in the establishing of a large number of family corporations, and even the emergence of the first rural corporation by means of the families. But the performance of rural corporations of this village was not good after this period. However, the rural joint-equity enterprises gained a good development momentum. With the increase of the rural opening degree and the external population, rich villagers moved to nearby towns and reduced contact with the village. In this state of development, kinship circles centering on family were reduced, and the economic community with the core of the family and with close relatives (such as brothers and sisters) as members was intensified. Rural industrialization needed the support of the family system, especially in the primary stage of development. However, with the promotion of industrialization and the change of property relationships and organizational forms, the role of the family system would be different. In another aspect, the role of Chinese rural industrialization on the Chinese family system was much more important than the role of land reform or the people's commune (Wang, 1996).

In the analysis of the cultural causes of Wenzhou model, Zhu Kangdui believed that to figure out the development history of Wenzhou rural economy we must deeply analyze the role of family culture in the process of rural industrialization. In the production of small commodities, the household production method had an incomparable strength that the large-scale production could not match. On the one hand, the household production divided the integrated industrial production and integrated it into the distributed household production. On the other hand, it integrated the distributed household production to have certain advantages of regional integration, which could reduce the whole trade cost of the rural community and enhance the competitiveness of the regional economy. Therefore, the main characteristics of the Wenzhou rural economy with the small-commodity production as the main content and with the household industry as the main formation were composed in the process of Wenzhou's rural industrialization. Although Wenzhou possessed more than 30,000 joint-equity cooperative enterprises and some limited liability companies and enterprise groups built on the basis of private and joint-equity cooperative enterprises, the family-oriented enterprises owned by couples, fathers and sons, or relatives still existed. Some enterprises revealed a modern style from their names and forms, but their internal operation and management mechanism were still the reproduction of household enterprises, and their development depended fundamentally on the inner aggregation force of the family. Therefore, the household enterprises built on the foundation of familialism had remarkable advantages to some degree, but the inner defects would finally hinder their further development. At present, the scales of Wenzhou enterprises are generally small and it is difficult to form a powerful scale advantage, which exactly proves this. At that point, related enterprises were badly in need of breaking through the family shackles, carrying out thorough institutional innovation, building a modern enterprise system for regional economic development, and fundamentally transcending the rural culture (Zhu, 1999).

Cai Kejiao believed that Wenzhou's humanistic spirit was generated from its history, geography, economy, and culture. Wenzhou is a commercial city renowned for its handicrafts (Cai, 2000). Wenzhou people always pay attention to commerce and utility; they yearn for family but do not remain in one place, and they could adjust themselves at any moment, try their best to cater to any environment, and strive for survival, while pursuing benefits and development by the most effective methods. Wenzhou has a distinct regional culture in its thinking mode, value concept, lifestyle, and behaviors: Wenzhou citizens have independent subject consciousness affected by the theory of cause and contribution of Yongjia. Affected by the doctrine of work, Wenzhou citizens have more independent subject consciousness. Effected by the industrial and commercial management, Wenzhou people are hardworking. They believe that "people are diligent by strength and win by strength", and have a competitive spirit. Additionally, they are ingenious and honest, and are extremity interested in the new things and have strong imitation abilities and acceptance capabilities. The Wenzhou people working on handicraft and small-commodity production and operation have a strong independent consciousness as demonstrated by the saying "better be the head of a dog than the tail of a lion". From the perspective of cultural history, Wenzhou humanistic spirit has a tendency of secularity. In addition, their strong mental structure and the advocation of a vigorous and humanitarian attitude toward life play an important role in the formation of their humanistic spirit and economic and social development in Wenzhou (Cai, 2000).

Li Qingpeng also placed emphasis on explaining the role of Wenzhou's humanistic spirit in the regional economic and civic society from the perspective of history, and he believed that the rise of temporary commercial industry had a profound and original relationship with the historically developed industrial and commercial tradition of Wenzhou, such as the agricultural and commercial culture, migration culture, maritime civilization, and the theory of cause and contribution of Yongjia. He used the view of "truth" (1999) to conclude that the essence of "Ouyue Culture" was a typical "agricultural and commercial culture" on the premise of survival. As for Wenzhou, the sensual culture in history was a typical "agricultural and commercial culture" and the rational culture in history was the inheritance of Yongjia school and its concept. From the perspective of the social influence of the two cultures, the effect of ancient sensual culture on farmers was more obvious. Actually, Yongjia school came up with the agricultural and commercial culture to a large extent. Therefore, it can be said that Yongjia school was the result of agricultural and commercial culture for one thing. For another thing, the tradition of mercantilism of Yongjia school continues to the present and broadly penetrated into the consciousness of people, which constituted the specific "culture gene". The contributions of Yongjia school to Wenzhou culture, especially the reform of economic concepts, mainly have three aspects: The first one is coming up with a new idea of morality and profit, the second one is coming up with the theory of laying equal emphasis on industry and commerce, and the third one is affirming the employment values (Li, 1999).

Wang Chunguang *et al.* further expanded the research view on the influence of Wenzhou's humanistic spirit on the economic and civic society of the regions outside Wenzhou, and conducted deep research on the social network features of Wenzhou and its effects on the economy expanding capability. They conducted long-term investigations into "Zhejiang village" in Beijing successively in 1993, 1994, and 1997, and conducted a survey on "Wenzhou City" in Paris from September 1998 to January 1999, for a period of up to 4 months. After the deep research and analysis through firsthand materials, Wang Chunguang *et al.* believed that the "big market" of Wenzhou model was not only limited to the top 10 famous specialized markets emerging in Wenzhou in the 1980s but also included the economic association network worldwide, and that was the social network of the Wenzhou people. Wang Chunguang made the regional social network as the main focus of his investigation, and paid attention to how Wenzhou people utilized, updated, and supplemented the social network in the course of movement, migration, and integration for the purpose of enlarging the economic strength and influence. From the aspect of comprehensive quality, he found that Wenzhou people both in "Zhejiang village" in Beijing and in "Wenzhou City" in Paris had no more particularities or advantages than people in other places of China, and even had more drawbacks in some fields. But why could Wenzhou people trade all around the world and establish enterprises? The reason was that there was a huge social network dominating the movement and migration of Wenzhou people. Wenzhou people assembled together again through the flow of the interpersonal relationship chain and migration. The social network is the major weapon and social capital of Wenzhou people existing, developing, and integrating in other counties and cities. As for many Wenzhou people of "Zhejiang village" in Beijing and "Wenzhou City" in Paris, the individual resources were pretty limited, which was not enough to support their survival and development. Their survival and development were more dependent on clansmen, relatives, and friends, and they built their social network on this foundation. In other words, such a social network made the new environment accessible to them and provided them with the opportunity of survival and development, and their survival and development could expand their social network in turn. Their social network was mainly organized by relatives, friends, and neighbors who could provide support for their movement and migration, employment, financing, emotional connection, and so on. In short, the social network could significantly help Wenzhou people reduce the cost of production and management, and reduce the risks of survival, existence, and development in foreign countries. It is the social network that made Wenzhou people find jobs, survive, and even develop well in the new situation of being ignorant of the local languages and customs.

Above all, research related to the relationship between humanistic spirit and Wenzhou model actually includes two important aspects. One is research on the role of the Wenzhou humanistic spirit in the local economy and social development. It is done mostly by local scholars, who are familiar with the environment of Wenzhou. The other is the analysis of the effect of the humanistic spirit on the economic activities. The analysis on the research of regional Wenzhou model actually was extended to the research of economic behaviors of the Wenzhou group, which made people observe Wenzhou model from various points of view and deepened their understandings of it. Meanwhile, research on Wenzhou model related to the views of humanities also created a more favorable condition to comprehensively research Wenzhou model from multidisciplinary views.

1.5 Research on Wenzhou model from an overseas perspective

In the mid-1980s, Wenzhou model became famous in a short time, and gradually gained attention from foreign press circles and scholars. With the constant increase of reports made by foreign press (Lin, 1990), some foreign scholars and ethnic Chinese scholars began to investigate the economy and social development in China, and wrote about it. For example, Professor Nolan Peter, an English economist, and Professor Dong Fureng, a Chinese economist, co-edited and published *China's*

Marketing Strength: Competitiveness, Small Business and Argument about Wenzhou in 1990 (Nolan & Dong, 1990). Additionally, when Doctor Yan Shanping, a scholar traveling to Japan, studied the rural industrialization of China, he also focused on Wenzhou model with the feature of individual private economy (Yan, 1992). Among so many works of research literature related to Wenzhou model abroad, the research results of K. Parris, associate professor at Washington State University in America, and Alan P. L. Liu, professor at University of California, Santa Barbara, were most influential on the Chinese academic circles.

K. Parris's *Local Initiative and Reform: The Wenzhou Model of Development* conducted relatively comprehensive research on Wenzhou model (Parris, 1993). Its English version was published in *Documentation and Information of Shanghai Municipal Party*. K. Parris believed that Wenzhou model was the results of the mutual contradiction, compromise, and long-term negotiation between common people, the local government, and China's state organs, and the local cadres played a crucial role. The new economic institutions, optional values, and the appearance of organization all reflected the boundary transformation of the current nation and society and the redetermination between them. Although K. Parris did not introduce the analysis methods of "game theory" of modern economics, actually he regarded Wenzhou model as the result of the competitiveness among regional common people, local officials, and the central government when he investigated the reasons for the success of Wenzhou model. For example, when K. Parris stated the characteristics of Wenzhou model, he specialized in the "registration" of individual or household industry and public-owned commercial enterprises, and also studied the "reform" phenomenon where the private enterprises registered to the collectively owned enterprise, and called this phenomenon "creative deceitful trick". The practice of Wenzhou's economic development indicated that, in certain historical conditions and development environments, the "creative deceitful trick" played an active role in mitigating the conflicts that the private employment had with the central departments, and reduced the crisis of the ideology in the efforts of local officials maintaining the development of individual private economy. In addition, "registration" and "reform" could help individual private enterprises receive investment funds from nationalized banks and official credit agencies and get some preferential treatment in rate paying. As a result, "the new economic institution comes into being on the foundation of local requirements and positivity". When he investigated the institutional transformation, K. Parris took the example of "individual industrial and commercial labor association", studied the relationship between the voluntary association of private entrepreneurs and local governmental organs and state organs, and revealed how the private entrepreneurs were prevented from being the challengers of ideological principles and at the same time aligned with governmental organs and the officials so that the private entrepreneurs could spontaneously organize and become the "strength" of the national socialist system. This process also indicated how the antecedent national systems and ideology adapted to the local behaviors, and finally promoted the development of local economy in the course of the limited increase of legitimacy of private interests. K. Parris's research indicated that reform not only took place in an up-down manner but was also initiated from bottom to top by individuals, households, and communities who responded to satisfy their needs due to the insufficiency of state-operated economy. Not only could these ordinary individuals utilize opportunities allowed by the state but they could also create their own chances together with local governmental officials. Therefore, it is better to construe China's "great reform" as a combination of bottom-up reforms.

Alan P. L. Liu conducted a relatively comprehensive and deep study of the secrets, lessons, and significance of the success of Wenzhou model in his article titled Pros and Cons of Wenzhou model[2]. Alan P. L. Liu believed that Wenzhou model was the most "representative" and "typical" mode of China's regional economic and social development, and the key to its success lay in "changing the traditional system to fit into the modern situation".[3] Specifically, the secret of Wenzhou's success can be summarized as an excellent combination of "3M" and "1I", i.e., mass initiativeness, mobility, markets, and interstice of China's economic structure. Alan P. L. Liu laid great emphasis on the important influence that regional economic traditions of Wenzhou had on the generation of Wenzhou model. He believed that the formation of such regional economy was related to the unique response of Wenzhou people under environmental pressure in history; thus, the development of Wenzhou's economy during the reform and opening-up can be viewed as a continuation of Wenzhou people reacting to the pressure of the social environment through immigration and long-distance trading like they did in history. Therefore, in Alan P. L. Liu's opinion, as the mode "sailed the furthest" among many development modes of China's socialist economy from the realistic perspective, the main driving force of Wenzhou model undoubtedly came from the enterprises and personnel of private sectors, as well as flexible policies of the local Party and government departments and the political support of the grassroots organizations; it was also closely related to the strong political support in some regions (such as Shanghai). More importantly, Wenzhou model obtained the active support of the state leaders advocating bold reforms during its course of development. For example, the State

---

[2]See details in "Pros and Cons of Wenzhou Model" by Alan P. L. Liu, originally published in Volume 8, 1992 of *Asian Survey*, and later published in Western Experts Diagnosis of China's Economy edited by Zhang Minjie, 1997 version of China Economic Publishing House.

[3]Alan P. L. Liu, "Pros and Cons of Wenzhou Model", originally published in Volume 8, 1992 of *Asian Survey*, and later published in Western Experts Diagnosis of China's Economy, edited by Zhang Minjie, 1997 version of China Economic Publishing House, p. 217.

Council announced the establishment of the Wenzhou "Pilot Zone" in 1986, allowing Wenzhou to reform while unrestrained by traditional systems and the then current policies of China. When elaborating on the significance of Wenzhou model, Alan P. L. Liu pointed out that Wenzhou's economic and social development had a profound impact on China's modernization; if Wenzhou model had been widely advocated in China, sooner or later, it would have promoted the rationalization of China's politics, culture, and institution. As a "bottom-up" regional economic and social development mode, Wenzhou model possesses the characteristics of "comprehensive independence" and "open independence". Its significance will no longer be "small commodity and big market" only, but may even generate profound significance of "small independence and big democracy".

In addition, Steven N. S. Cheung, a famous economist of the neoinstitutional school also commented on Wenzhou model after his field investigation of Wenzhou in September 1987 (Lin, 1990). Steven N.S. Cheung believed that Wenzhou was the front-runner of China's opening-up, and Wenzhou's accomplishments represented China's opening-up. One of the most important reasons for Wenzhou's development was as follows: At the beginning of the opening-up, the proportion of state-run enterprises in Wenzhou was small and the degree of government monopoly was low; many gaps available for development existed at that time, and the new property right system was thus generated. Besides, from the perspective of the market, at the beginning of the reform and opening-up, China possessed great market potential; residents had great demand for goods for everyday consumption. Wenzhou's enterprises focused on sales of domestic goods since the very beginning and thus, compared to enterprises of other regions, Wenzhou's enterprises acquired the advance chance to explore the market and expanded the space for regional economic development. The "openness" emphasized by Steven N. S. Cheung not only referred to the opening-up in the general sense but also the cross-regional openness, i.e., the regional economy jumped outside the closed development pattern and actively interacted with the other regions of China, and utilized the vast domestic market to promote development.

Since the 21st century, overseas scholars have paid attention to possible influences of Wenzhou model on future political transformation of China. Hemant Adlakha from Jawaharlal Nehru University, India, thought that in the regional, provincial mode of good governance in China, Wenzhou model characterized by special functions was becoming an increasingly promising example of civil society, but it still required more research. Wenzhou model is known as the first model of rural governance in China based on rural or civil society rising in the grassroots class. Recently, Chinese academics referred to this new model governing rural society through rural commercialization or urbanization as civil society from the grassroots rural areas. Hemant Adlakha also pointed out that it was regarded as the theoretical basis for constructing national social dynamics (driven by markets) and was poles apart from the concept of a free, independent, and autonomic "civil society" (Adlakha, 2004).

Joseph Fewsmith, professor of politics at Boston University, paid attention to the development of the Wenzhou Chamber of Commerce for a long time. In the fourth chapter of his book, *Logic and Limitations of China's Political Reform*, published in 2013. He pointed out that due to accumulation of social capital in families, clans, and other social relations, Wenzhou people developed family enterprises in the local area, in the country, and even in the world. Social networks offer investment opportunities, production possibilities, and information of business dealings. With the expansion of these networks from Wenzhou to the world, it is easy for them to establish the most extensive network of industry associations in China, a country with clear preference of vertical relations in the government. Wenzhou model is in great contrast with the planned economy dominating China's reform era and large state-owned enterprises in recent years. In China, only Wenzhou has a chance to establish an increasingly politically neutral legal system of capitalist economy due to industry interest and pressure put by the chamber of commerce. Wenzhou entrepreneurs not only grew up ahead of schedule but also grew beyond the "neutral zone" put forward by Zou Tang. In addition, it created a clear boundary between the state and society and built a new system. However, it failed in the end. Wenzhou Chamber of Commerce failed to become a platform to create a civil society or a democratic transition between the state and society. In the end, his conclusion was as follows: As the government still controlled the development of private economy in Wenzhou and other regions, economic change did not bring about political change (Fewsmith, 2013).

1.6 Prospect of Wenzhou model

After entering the 21st Century, the academic world remained pretty enthusiastic toward the study of Wenzhou model. Wenzhou model is also a hot topic attracting attention from domestic and foreign media. One important event was the great discussion of Wenzhou model triggered by historical institutional analysis of it by Shi Jinchuan in 2004. Another important event was the seminar titled 30-year Economic Transition of China initiated by Professor Coase at the University of Chicago in 2008. Professor Coase invited scholars of Wenzhou model and local officials and entrepreneurs of Wenzhou to discuss the development prospect of Wenzhou model. At the advent of the new economy, against the grand background of China's new round of the reform and opening-up, deep research on Wenzhou model may center on the following questions: (1) What's the true inherent vitality of the development of Wenzhou model? Or, would Wenzhou model get "pinned down"? (2) How great is the reference significance of the reform and development process of Wenzhou model in China to other regions? (3) Will Wenzhou model pose any influence on the political structure and organizational framework of society in the sense of "expanding order"?

The problem of the inherent vitality of the development of Wenzhou model is related to the development prospects of Wenzhou model in the new century; it is a hot topic in the domestic academic world, including Zhejiang scholars, and also an issue catching much attention from the local Party committee and the government of Wenzhou.

Zhejiang scholars pointed out in their studies of Wenzhou model that the reform and development of Zhejiang economy represented by Wenzhou model has completed its task of the first stage (Jin, 2000; Shi & Zheng, 2000). From the perspective of the economic system reform, this is a stage transiting from planned economy to primary market economy. At this stage, the emergence of abundant individual and private-run economies quickly changed the pattern of the relatively singular system of ownership and greatly pushed the privatization process of the economy. At the same time, the rising and prosperous development of specialized markets greatly promoted the marketization of the regional economy. From the perspective of economic development, in this stage, under the forces of privatization and marketization, the industrialization featuring rural industrialization and urbanization featuring development of small townships advanced promptly, promoting the economic development from the initial stage of industrialization to the middle stage.

At the beginning of the new century, the economic development of Wenzhou and even Zhejiang would confront the same stage change — how to move from the primary market economy to the modern market economy, how to advance from the middle stage to the later stage of industrialization and even basically realize modernization of regional economic and social development. If the economy of Wenzhou had to successfully accomplish the phase transformation task of the above reform and development, it had to make arduous efforts in the following four aspects: (1) Transform the traditional business organization to the modern business organization, build and develop a batch of enterprises or enterprise groups of the modern corporation system in the foundation of a large number of individual private enterprises or family-owned enterprises. (2) Transform the traditional and laggard market organizational form and market trading mode to the modern market organizational form and market trading mode. (3) Gradually update labor-intensive products and industrial structures with low degree of low additional value to capital- and technology-intensive products and industrial structures with high degree of high additional values. (4) Transform the urbanization process featuring the extension of small towns, accelerate the construction of big and small cities, and strengthen the cohesive force and radial force of the central city in the regional economy.

In the new stage of the reform and opening-up and economic development, if the reform and development of Wenzhou could gain new developmental breakthrough, the strong vitality of Wenzhou model would be proved undoubtedly. However, if the reform and development of Wenzhou could not gain new developmental breakthrough in the stage transformation process, and basically stuck to the original economic organization and the industrial structure of Wenzhou model, it would be faced with the danger of "pin down". The question, "what's the true magnitude of Wenzhou's development potential", raised by some domestic scholars is, in fact, a worry for the future of Wenzhou model. Meanwhile, some domestic scholars believed that the "Wenzhou model" nowadays is no longer the "Wenzhou model" of the 1980s, but the "new Wenzhou model". "The new Wenzhou model" has broken through the traditional limit managed by joint households of Wenzhou model, and developed the joint-equity cooperative economy and enterprise groups. It adjusted the operating mode solely oriented by the market and rerouted to the path of comprehensive development integrating asset operation and capital operation. It changed the marketing mode solely supported by small towns, and rerouted to the path of online marketing and transnational operation. Wenzhou model drew the regional economy close to the modern market economy, and began to catch up with the international community.

On the referential value of the economic system reform and economic development in other regions of China, Wenzhou model actually involved the cognition of the capability extending to the outside of the region. The great attention paid to this issue from scholars of Jiangsu and Zhejiang originates from the fact that this issue was raised in conjunction with the background of the comparative study of South Jiangsu model and Wenzhou model.

The American scholar Alan P. L. Liu elaborated the significance of Wenzhou model for China's moderation, and pointed out that the rural industrialization of Wenzhou was developed under the background of low deposit, and low technique and relying on household industry in comparison with the south Jiangsu depending on the big city and technology and talents of state-owned enterprises, so Wenzhou model was more suitable in the Chinese rural development than South Jiangsu model (Alan, 1992). However, he also believed that the factors for the success of Wenzhou model such as creativity, flowability, and skills in distance trading were closely linked to the history and culture of Wenzhou. The question of how many rural communities in China possess such qualities is worth a discussion.

In fact, the present differences in opinions on the referential significance of Wenzhou are derived from the diversities of the research perspectives of researchers. The scholars holding affirmative opinions always regard the demonstration effect of Wenzhou model from the formation and development of the institutional evolution and market economy. They believed that Wenzhou model is, in fact, the epitome of the development history of the market economy in China, and that Wenzhou model actually revealed a method of institutional transformation, which represented derivative system transformation. Hence, the summary on the mechanism of the generation and development of Wenzhou model can provide economic institutional reform and economic development with a beneficial revelation. Additionally, some scholars further emphasized that the formation of Wenzhou model is the connection of China's modern industry and modern commerce, and the intrinsic regional development type is consistent with the major economic development type in China to a great extent. Therefore, Wenzhou model is a good reference for the other regions of China.

From the objective perspective, the issue of referential values of Wenzhou model should be investigated from the aspects of economic institutional transformation and economic development. It should be mentioned that Wenzhou model is a good reference in institutional transformation and economic development for some relatively underdeveloped regions in China at present. This fact is reflected in the high enthusiasm of some domestic governments and entrepreneurs while inspecting Wenzhou. However, for coastal regions of China with pretty developed economies, the reference value of Wenzhou model is mainly in the aspect of institutional transformation; even from the angle of "clear and clarified ownership", Wenzhou model still possesses great reference significance. Certainly, from the angle of development, the reference significance of Wenzhou model depends on its own development to a large extent, i.e., whether there is truly a new "Wenzhou model".

Whether further development of Wenzhou model could evolve to a general "expanding order" mode and what influences such "expanding order" process would generate on the political structure and organizational structure of the community are the two connected questions attracting wide attention from scholars in the fields of economics, sociology, and politics.

Feng Xingyuan is one of the early scholars who explored Wenzhou model from the angle of the relationship among cultural traditions, institutional transformation, and "spontaneous order model". He pointed out that the so-called Wenzhou model is a development mode dominated by the development of individual and private economy. Zhejiang model is the upgraded and expanded model of Wenzhou model; in its essence, it is a market solution mode, and in other words, a spontaneous development mode and self-organizing mode. In these, the functions of the government are important, but they are more of the promoting, assisting and advocating roles, instead of economic management. The core of Zhejiang model is the spontaneous and endogenous development with strong self-organization characteristics. Its driving force comes from the folk strength and traditional cultures of Zhejiang. Especially in Wenzhou, institutional innovations were proposed from time to time before the reform and opening-up (such as "fix farm output quotas for each household"), and it formed the famous Wenzhou model through its reform process. Informal systems drove these developments, including the cultural tradition of mercantilism of Zhejiang, especially Wenzhou. Feng Xingyuan believed that Wenzhou model and its expanding mode (Zhejiang model) are expandable; they can be expanded to South Jiangsu and the other regions of China, and may also become a "Hayek expansion order pattern" or "Hayek spontaneous order pattern"(Feng, 2001).

Li Junhui from Sun Yat-Sen University focused on the comparative research between local "autonomy" of Wenzhou and local "autonomy" of Shunde, Guangdong. He believed that Wenzhou model could be viewed as a "folk autonomy" mode from an economic angle or a social angle; it offers a possibility for regions already practicing "autonomy" to develop a route different from the current national institution (Li, 2000a). In addition, Zhao Wei, a professor at Zhejiang University, studied the influences of Wenzhou's economic development on local governments' behaviors and local grassroots democratic system from the angle of "reversed democratic system" (Zhao, 1999).

In fact, the economic development of Wenzhou has had some influence on the organizational structure of Wenzhou's community and grassroots governments. Such influence is largely positive; it is manifested as the emphasis of local governments on entrepreneurs developing the local economy, the great attention paid to improving the internal environment of the local economy, as well as the enhancement of local governments' awareness of transforming their own functionalities and awareness of democracy. However, such influences also possess some negative attributes. Such negative influences, in fact, more or less reflect the backwardness of the political system reform against the economic system reform. From this perspective, whether or not Wenzhou model could become a true "expanding order" mode not only depends on the development of Wenzhou's local economy and society as well as modernization of Wenzhou people but more importantly on the deepening of nationwide economic system reform and promoting of political system reform. We believe that further development of Wenzhou model would offer more new revelations and references to China's comprehensive reforms, and contribute new and precious experiences to China's socialist modernization construction, socialist democracy, and legal system construction.

Chapter 2

Wenzhou Model: Institutional Change and System Innovation

Two kinds of reform costs exist in the course of transforming from planned economy to market economy: implementation cost and friction cost. Implementation cost includes all the efficiency loss arising from the "incomplete information", "incomplete knowledge", and instability of system prospects when the reform starts; friction cost includes the consumption of time and materials caused by the social friction during the reform (Fan, 1993). Reform means the readjustment of the interest pattern; its essence is "non-Pareto change". Therefore, the circumstances in which some people get benefits and some people suffer losses is inevitable, thus causing reform resistance and frictional cost. In China's institutional environment which was long dominated by the ideology and philosophy of planned economy, it is necessary to divide the frictional cost into political cost and adjustment cost for the progressive reform of the economic reform. Political cost refers to the risks of making "political mistakes" for breaking through the ideology and philosophy of planned economy in order to push forward the marketization reform. Adjustment cost refers to the compensation that the "non-Pareto" feature of the reform requires for the "victims" of the reform, characteristics of the reform to reduce reform resistance. Once the political cost of "freeing the mind" is introduced, the demand-induced institutional transformation will become the "quasi-demand-induced institutional transformation" (Jin, 2000a). Wenzhou model was a product of the progressive reform featuring quasi-demand-induced institutional transformation pushed forward in the course of pursuing the reform plan with minimized frictional cost (political cost), regarding "freeing the mind" as the national institutional environment evolved. The difference between the institutional transformation characteristics demonstrated by Wenzhou model and the traditional demand-induced institutional transformation was as follows: The microeconomic unit of Wenzhou model was used to seek benefits in promoting the institutional transformation in the institutional environment long dominated by the ideology and philosophy of planned economy; it must "free the mind" to break through the political cost barrier caused by the ideology and thinking inertia of planned economy. Therefore, the significance of Wenzhou model lay in exploring a reform path with minimum friction cost (i.e., political cost) of "freeing the mind".

2.1 Initial conditions of regional economic institutional change

Wenzhou model is a "space pole" of "system reform" of Zhejiang and even the entire China formed through demand-induced regional system reform during the progressive reform of the nationwide economic system, or something similar to a "reform pole" in the sense of development pole (Jin, 2000a). Wenzhou takes the lead in the institutional change of quasi-demand-induced type throughout the country, which is closely related to a series of factors that were achieved before the reform of Wenzhou. These factors constitute the initial condition of the market-oriented reform in Wenzhou, and decide the direction and strength of the market-oriented reform.

2.1.1 Cultural tradition

Rules are a kind of behavior codes which cover social, political, and economic behaviors. These rules include formal constraints, such as laws, decrees, regulations, as well as informal constraints, such as culture, habits, taboos. Once a behavior restriction is universally accepted and internalized into people's value system, it becomes the engine of economic parties' spontaneous behavior and forms a lasting intrinsic incentive factor. Cultural tradition is one of the basic factors in explaining why Wenzhou takes the lead in promoting institutional change over other parts of the country. The Yongjia school of Wenzhou in the Southern Song Dynasty raised the "utilitarian" banner, criticized the idea of "attaching importance to agriculture and suppressing development of business", and put forward propositions of "combining benefit with righteousness and promoting benefit and righteousness simultaneously". In the Southern Song Dynasty, Wenzhou's business was extremely developed, and Yongjia county's business tax alone reached more than 2,500 penetration, equivalent to 7 times that of the national average in the business tax. Businessmen rushing to Wenzhou from around the country included not only Chinese businessmen but also Japanese businessmen (Xie & Ren, 2000). The historical accumulation of the utilitarian philosophy of the Yongjia school had a subtle influence on Wenzhou people's consciousness of enhancing the commodity economy. In modern times, Wenzhou developed into a commercial port in 1876 with more frequent foreign economic exchanges. The collision and fusion of Western commodity economy consciousness and the Yongjia school of utilitarianism shaped the unique "spirit of Wenzhou", which is adventurous, pragmatic, and innovative. It is difficult to bridge the rift between Wenzhou's "utilitarianism" commercial culture tradition and the traditional planned economy thinking. Once the traditional planned economy thought and thinking inertia are repressed, they will find a breakthrough for their own development, forming a "departure" from the traditional planned economy thinking. This is an important implementation of quasi-demand-induced institutional change in Wenzhou.

2.1.2 Population pressure

Douglas North and Robert Thomas found when inspecting the economic history from the tenth century to the sixteenth century that with the growth of population, the land became increasingly scarce, thus forcing people to continue to change the ownership of land to more intensively use the land. "In addition, since the best land was gradually extended, further population growth forced residents to more intensively farm on the existing land, or to farm on the comparatively barren land". Before the reform and opening-up, there was a long-lasting tension between the population and the land (cultivated land) in Wenzhou. In 1978, the per capita cultivated land area of Wenzhou was only 0.53 mu, and the per capita net income of farmers was only 113 yuan.[1] In 1985, the People's Government of Zhejiang Province issued a policy supportive to five poverty-stricken counties in the province, of which three counties (Taishun, Yongjia, and Wencheng) were affiliated to Wenzhou.[2] In the rural areas of Wenzhou, the pressure caused by the tension between population and land forced people to try to break through the land use system under planned economy, so as to obtain the benefits outside the system. "As early as 1956, when the Chinese rural cooperative movement was in the climax occasion transiting rapidly from primary service to senior agency, the Party Committee of Yongjia county, set Liaoyuan agricultural production cooperatives in Sanxi area as a pilot unit, promoting an organized experiment of 'household responsibility system', creating the precedent of family contract management in rural areas of China. By 1957, there had been as many as 1,000 cooperative households and 178 thousand members, accounting for about 15% of the total households" (Xie & Ren, 2000).

2.1.3 Geography and traffic

Wenzhou is located on the coast. Before the reform and opening-up, the investment in Wenzhou was limited. After the founding of People's Republic of China to 1981, the country's total investment

---

[1] *Wenzhou Statistical Yearbook 2000*. Beijing: China Statistics Press, p. 21.

[2] *Zhejiang Economic Yearbook 1986*. Hangzhou: Zhejiang People's Press, p. 62.

in Wenzhou was only 655 million yuan.[3] The bad traffic conditions of Wenzhou, one side by sea and three sides by river, got improved because of the Jin-Wen railway that did not officially start until 1992 and did not become functional until 1997. Before that, there existed large traffic barriers between Wenzhou and the other parts of the country. Poor geographical and transportation conditions led to a very weak economic base in Wenzhou. In 1978, the total investment in fixed assets in Wenzhou was only 37,620,000 yuan, of which 35,990,000 yuan was invested by state-owned units and 1,630,000 yuan by collective units.[4] Under the underdeveloped condition in the public sector of the economy (state-owned and collective economy), there were not many expectations for public sector employment in the resettlement areas, so it was urgent to find other chances. However, Wenzhou's specially closed and isolated economic environment provided a test bed for high political risk.

2.2 Basic features of quasi-demand-induced institutional change

The essential features and links of change is "non-Pareto change", and some people will benefit from it, while others suffer damage, forming the driving force and hindering force of institutional change. As far as Wenzhou model is concerned, the resistance to the reform of this partial institutional change includes external resistance and internal resistance. The external resistance refers to the interests (including social organizations, some government agencies, the public, etc.) of the reform except the participants (force), because they thought reform brought direct losses (relative decline in income loss, indirect interests, conflict of values, etc.), forming an opposition alliance against reform and

---

[3] *Zhejiang Non-public Economy Yearbook 2000*. Beijing: Zhonghua Book Company, p. 112.

[4] *Wenzhou Statistical Yearbook 2000*. Beijing: China Statistics Press, p. 313.

exerting pressure on the group of participants in the reform. The internal resistance of the reform refers to the uneven distribution of the reform dividend among different participants due to the difference in the ability to acquire the benefits outside the system. The reform participants with relative income decline are dissatisfied with the reform, and are transformed from the participants and promoters to the bystanders and opponents of the reform. The success of Wenzhou model lies in the fact that it explores the reform path of "freeing the mind" by way of political cost minimization, namely, changes agents through the "backdoor" and "compensation" and other ways to successfully resolve the internal resistance and the external resistance of the reform, and pushes forward the market-oriented reform. This reform path, costing less to avoid the traditional thinking on microeconomy cooperation of the contractual arrangement of access restriction, is a response to the microeconomy the lag of traditional planned economy thought and thinking adjustment.

2.2.1 Resolving external resistance
(1) Striving for the right to reform: Microsubject behavior

Under the traditional planned economy system, the microeconomic entities of the current system in a non-equilibrium state, and each signing cooperative contractual arrangements to promote institutional change "from top to bottom", would encounter entry barriers (Yang, 1998). The traditional planned economy ideology limits the cooperative contractual arrangements between microeconomic entities, and causes the demand-induced institutional change to be "distorted" and "twisted". The significance of the "Wenzhou model" as a model of institutional change lies in the "adapted adjustment" of the microeconomic entity through the cooperative contract arrangement (reformation plan) to avoid the "political risk" brought about by the lag of traditional ideology

adjustment, thereby gaining the "entry right" of reform. The
evolution of enterprise organizations in Wenzhou profoundly reflects
the efforts of microeconomic entities to break through the rigidity
of traditional ideology so as to obtain the access to reform. The
evolution of enterprise organizations in Wenzhou's history and
the history of the evolution of enterprise organizations in Western
countries are different in the following ways: first, the early "hanging
a management"; second, the emergence of joint-stock cooperative
enterprises; and third, grassroots party organizations for non-public
enterprises. In the early stages of reform, cooperative contractual
arrangements between members of the family (family business) and
other non-public sectors of the economy was not authorized by law,
and the cooperative contractual arrangements of microeconomic
subject had to be grafted in the public sector of the economy to get
the license into the "reform". In essence, "operations of enterprises
run by individuals but attached to public institutions" refers to
microeconomic entities seeking political asylum for cooperative
contractual arrangements to avoid political risks caused by
ideological rigidity. In the "nature" of traditional ideology, rather
than "freeing the mind" by the external forces to accept this "new
thing", it is better to have the legal status of the interest groups (such
as collective enterprises) to pay a "guakao fee", to impersonate the
public sector of the economy and system innovation of the entry
right. This approach follows the principle of minimizing costs. When
the scale of family enterprise expands, the capital supply within the
family cannot meet the demand for the expansion of the enterprise
scale due to the strong demand for capital. However, under the
shackles of traditional planned economy, the "political identity"
of family enterprises makes it difficult to obtain financing in the
formal financial sector. The private lending market in this aspect
of the informal financial sector, on the contrary, forced the family
enterprise, through the disguise of the joint-stock cooperative system

with the public ownership economy nature, to get the factor market alternative "access". Obviously, the establishment of "provident fund" in joint-stock cooperative enterprises is an important manifestation of the "political risk" of microeconomic entities, avoiding the delay of traditional ideology adjustment. After the 15th National Congress of the Communist Party of China, the legal status of private enterprises was confirmed, which made many joint-stock enterprises in Wenzhou rapidly switch to private enterprises or limited liability companies through equity repurchase. This phenomenon fully shows that the reform costs of microeconomic entities are lagging behind the adjustment of traditional ideology. In Wenzhou, non-public enterprises' avoidance of the political costs of traditional ideology also shows that non-public enterprises establish Party organizations. In a sense, for the establishment of the Party organization of the non-public enterprises, especially that of large-scale private enterprises, is a response to the microscopic economic subject of the traditional ideology lagging adjustment, and also a rational choice of minimizing political costs to follow the principle of "freeing the mind".

(2) Defending the fruits of reform: Local government behavior

Along with the reform of fiscal decentralization strategy and the implementation of the financial "eating separately" system, local governments have independent behavioral goals and behavioral patterns, thus playing the role of "first action group" in actively advancing the net income of potential institutions in the gradual transition to a market economy (Yang, 1998). In the diffusion pattern of institutional change of Professor Yang, the local government functions as institutional change "first action group", and in the quasi-demand-induced institutional change within the framework, the local government functions as institutional change "secondary action group". On the path of reform of Wenzhou model, local government and microeconomic entities share potential system benefits, and also want to break the shackles of the traditional ideology, to reform the traditional ideology. The rapid increase in fiscal revenue is a reflection of high performance of the system in the microeconomic system (especially the property rights system), which is directly related to the central government's tolerance for the local institutional innovation of the creators of the Wenzhou model. Within the fiscal framework of the tax-sharing system, the growth of local fiscal revenue is directly related to the enthusiasm and support of local governments for institutional innovation within the government's jurisdiction. Before the implementation of "eating separately" in finance, Wenzhou's budget total fiscal revenue grew rapidly from 1978 to 1992, and the average annual revenue growth rate was 16.83%. After the implementation of "eating separately" in finance, Wenzhou City budget revenue exceeded the central local fiscal revenue, and the gap was widening (see Figure 2.1).

The institutional change in Wenzhou has brought about a high growth of fiscal revenue, which makes the central government adopt a more tolerant attitude toward this part of the system. The continuous growth of local fiscal revenue and the continuous expansion of local government revenue share also make local governments play a positive role as an interpreter of their own

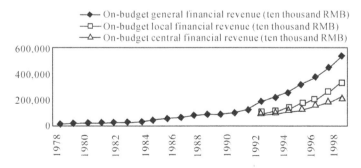

Figure 2.1.   Wenzhou on-budget financial revenue: Central and local financial revenue.
Data source: *Wenzhou Statistical Yearbook 2000*, China Statistics Press.

interests. Every year Wenzhou receives tens of thousands of central and local government inspection groups and delegations. The local government should explain Wenzhou model from a "positive" position, in order to eliminate any "misunderstanding" or prejudice that the central and local governments might have. Among them, the payment of "business entertainment fee" is considered the political cost of "freeing the mind". From 1998, in Wenzhou City, government expenditure and business expenses were at a proportion of 16%–17%, and the business expenses accounted for the proportion of 5 per thousand to 6 per thousand of GDP (see Table 2.1). Although Wenzhou's state business expenditure by local government is regarded as "freeing the mind" and eliminating the external resistance of a far-fetched reform cost, in fact (including the local government and enterprises) the cost of expenditure compared with this data will only be heavier. Therefore, for the local government of Wenzhou, to protect and defend the efficient property rights system for the "sacrifice" is a rational choice in order to pursue the maximization of fiscal revenue.

2.2.2 Resolving internal resistance

Quasi-demand-induced institutional change of Wenzhou model is the result of the fact that the microscopic economic subject obtained great potential profits indicated by the system's non-profit equilibrium, and the transition to establish an efficient property right system at the micro level can promote high economic growth in Wenzhou. Wenzhou's GDP increased from 1.32 billion yuan in 1978 to 82.5 million yuan in 2000, an average annual growth rate of 15.6%. High performance that has been reached in the reform shows that reform dividend was reasonably distributed within Wenzhou between different interest groups. On the one hand, the relative income of vested interest groups is not spoilt due to the reform, reducing the resistance to reform; on the other hand, the income increment of the reform facilitator is high enough to keep the momentum for reform. The quasi-demand-induced institutional change of Wenzhou model follows the principle

Table 2.1.   Wenzhou state organ expenditures: 1998–1999.

Item	Income and welfare expenditures (ten thousand yuan)	Social insurance expenditures (ten thousand yuan)	Official business expenditures (ten thousand yuan)	Equipment procurement expenditures (ten thousand yuan)	Operating expenditures (ten thousand yuan)	Other expenditures (ten thousand yuan)	Total expenditures (ten thousand yuan)	Operating expenditures/ total expenditures/ %	Operating expenditures/ GDP/ %
1998	58,302	10,477	32,917	14,463	34,388	47,880	208,698	16.48	5.08
1999	70,955	13,241	38,465	16,549	40,664	51,437	240,841	16.88	5.54

Data source: Wenzhou Statistical Yearbook 1999, Wenzhou Statistical Yearbook 2000, China Statistics Press.

of minimizing the political cost from the view of the external resistance and follows the principle of minimizing the cost of adjustment in terms of the internal resistance.

Regarding the first internal resistance of the state-owned interest group and the non-state interest group, by breaking through the shackles of traditional planned economy thinking, Wenzhou model takes the lead in establishing an efficient exclusive property right system in the non-state-owned sector of the economy, and realizes the incremental reform in the marginal sense. The non-state-owned sector's growth will inevitably break the original pattern of interests, and the state-owned sector of the economy as the vested interest group may benefit from the perspective of "slander" of the new force, especially by taking advantage of the traditional planned economy ideology's high disapproval of non-public sectors of the economy; the state can very easily use the traditional ideological power to discredit the non-state-owned sector (for example, at the beginning of the reform, street voluntary organizations were treated as such by the state-owned and collective economy), and rely on local government forces to impose a "ban" (for example, the individual and private enterprise's economic activities were accused of "speculation" and other such charges). In this case, the non-state-owned sector must share the benefits of reform with the state-owned economic sector or bear more of the cost of reform, to maintain the relative income of the state-owned sector of the economy as vested interest groups remain unchanged, so that the market reform continues. Wenzhou model makes Wenzhou become the institutional innovation center of "diffusion", forming a larger "gap" of system with the other areas; large inflows of foreign labor are the inevitable result of the "gap" of system to promote Wenzhou's economic growth. Because of the restriction of the household registration system and the barriers of layoffs of state-owned enterprises, it is difficult for the foreign labor force to obtain employment in the state-owned economic sector, and instead they seek profit opportunities from the non-state-owned sectors. The non-state-owned sector of the economy bears the resettlement costs of the laid-off workers in Wenzhou's local state-owned enterprises and the inflow of foreign labor force, thus diluting the reform gains of the workers in the non-state-owned sector of the economy. Therefore, the state-owned sector with high entry barriers makes effective internalization of state-owned sector reform's profit, and the non-state-owned economic sector with low barriers to entry barriers gains greater spillover effect. According to statistics, the average wage level of workers in state-owned economic sector in Wenzhou over the period of 1978–1999 was higher than the average wage level of the workers in the collective economic sector. The average wage level of workers in the non-public sector of the economy was higher in the initial stage, which was caused by "institutional gap" concealment and elements of the "institutional gap" perception and reaction lagging; but with the development of non-public economic growth, "institutional gap" gradually became dominant and the elements of perception and reaction system of "gap" became flexible, and the rushing in of the laid-off workers and foreign labor caused the average wage level of workers of the non-public sector to fall (see Figure 2.2). The change of average wage in Wenzhou state-owned and non-state-owned economic sectors shows that the non-public sector of the economy has achieved great reform gains in the early stages of reform to maintain the momentum for reform, while the state-owned sector of the economy in the process of reform has always maintained a high income growth, weakening the discontent and resistance to the non-public sector of the economy and

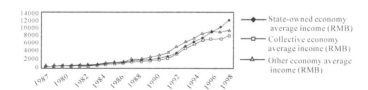

Figure 2.2.   Annual income of staff in Wenzhou state-owned and non-state-owned economic sectors: 1978–1999.
Data source: *Wenzhou Statistical Yearbook 2000*, China Statistics Press.

the reform, thus reducing the adjustment cost of quasi-demand-induced institutional change.

The second internal obstruction is urban and rural interest groups. Wenzhou institutional change first occurred in rural areas. Trials of "fixing farm output quotas for each household" were carried out in Sanxi District, Yongjia county, in 1956, and the Jinxing Dadui Stationery Factory was founded in Jinxiang, Cangnan county, in 1979 (with 30 production units assuming sole responsibility for one's own profits or losses). These cooperative contracts among microeconomic units in rural areas offered huge reform profit to farmers, greatly changed economic appearance in rural areas, and increased actual income of farmers. All of a sudden, many 10,000-yuan households appeared. By 1985, there were more than 7,000 10,000-yuan households in Yueqing, Wenzhou. With the development of industrial economy in rural families of Wenzhou, some rich families in rural areas gathered in cities to obtain marketing information and technical support. These rich families brought capital and employment positions to urban areas and played an important role in raising funds for city construction. In fact, these rural rich families exchanged a part of reform bonuses brought by rural institutional change for admission to cities in this process. The "farmer town" in Longgang is a typical case in this respect. According to statistical data, in the initial stage of reform (1981–1985), the growth rate of income of farmers was higher than that of urban residents, ensuring the impetus for reform. With the proceeding of reform (1986–1990), the growth rate of income of urban residents started to exceed that of farmers. For a long time (1981–1999), growth rate of income of urban and rural residents was similar (see Table 2.2). By combining "start first" and "advance together", institutional innovation benefits of reform impellers were guaranteed and the impetus for reform was maintained. In addition, the benefit distribution structure before reform was basically preserved and benefit distribution on a higher level was realized, reducing the voice of vested interests against reform and adjustment costs of quasi-demand-induced institutional change.

Table 2.2. Wenzhou urban resident and rural resident per capita income growth
condition: 1981–1999.

Item	Rural resident per capita income annual growth rate (%)	Urban resident per capita living expense annual growth rate (%)
1981–1985	22.01	14.46
1986–1990	19.51	19.62
1991–1995	25.16	30.51
1996–1999	9.48	8.59
Total	18.31	18.77

Data source: *Wenzhou Statistical Yearbook 2000*, China Statistics Press.

2.3 Transformation of quasi-demand-induced institutional change

Marked by the approval of Constitutional Amendment (1999),
the legislature carried out flexible adjustment of traditional ideology
of planned economy. The argument that the non-public economy is an
important part of the socialist market economy has been recognized
by the country's fundamental legal system, and the development of
the non-public economy has gained a good institutional environment.
Cooperative contractual arrangements among microeconomic units
can be conducted under the condition of zero political cost (or nearly
zero political cost) with respect to ideological emancipation, resulting
in complete release of inhibitory needs of institutional innovation and
transformation of quasi-demand-induced institutional change into
demand-induced institutional change. Therefore, Wenzhou model is a
pattern of institutional change and its meaning is as follows: When a
market-oriented reform is hindered by ideology of traditional planned
economy, microeconomic units successfully break through the barrier
of ideology of traditional planned economy and get the permission to
participate in reform to promote the market-oriented reform by seeking
political cost minimization with respect to ideological emancipation. Due

to the approval of Constitutional Amendment, institutional innovation carried out by microeconomic units is no longer restricted or seldom restricted by ideology of traditional planned economy. Elimination of political costs of institutional change made Wenzhou model meaningless and the institutional change was transformed into completely efficiency-oriented demand-induced institutional change. So far, Wenzhou has basically established a microcosmic system foundation with clear property rights required by normal operation of market economy, but micro-enterprises, market organizations, and industrial organizations in Wenzhou are characterized by classical market economy. Essentially, Wenzhou only realizes the transformation from traditional planned economy to classical market economy, which is the basic task of Wenzhou model. Moreover, the transformation from classical market economy to modern market economy is the basic task of the new Wenzhou model. The new Wenzhou model is characterized by gradual transformation from quasi-demand-induced institutional change to demand-induced institutional change, and dual tasks of incremental reform and storage reform must be completed with the new Wenzhou model.

2.3.1 Deepening the incremental reform

Under the condition of zero political cost with respect to ideological emancipation, microeconomic units can draw up cooperative contracts freely in accordance with market opportunities and internalize external economic profits that cannot be obtained through existing institutional arrangement, promoting further change and innovation of the institution. Main sources of these external economic profits include the following: (1) economies of scale and scope; (2) internalization of externalities; and (3) saving of trade costs. The new Wenzhou model is basically characterized by gradual transformation from quasi-demand-induced institutional change to demand-induced institutional change, where microeconomic units get the permission of reform participation. When they draw up cooperative contracts, they no longer bear political costs with respect to ideological emancipation. Besides, inhibitory needs of off-institutional economic profits will be released completely.

(1) Economies of scale and scope: Economies of scale and scope are important for inducing innovation of enterprises and organizations for off-institutional profits. Most microenterprises founded on Wenzhou model are at the stage of primitive accumulation of capital. These enterprises are small and most of them are family corporations without separation of ownership and management, clear division of labor, or paid managers. In addition, stock right setup of these enterprises is not complete with low equity liquidity and most of them are companies of unlimited liability. Obviously, these enterprises are the so-called "classic enterprises" defined by Chandler. During transformation from quasi-demand-induced institutional change to demand-induced institutional change, cooperative contracts among microeconomic units will certainly promote conversion from classic enterprises to modern enterprises to accommodate production function characterized by modern technology and obtain interests of economies of scale and scope. According to development and evolution of business organizations in Wenzhou in recent years, property relations of enterprises have become increasingly clear, and enterprises with clear property relations, for example, private enterprises and individual business with clear property relations, constantly increase, while enterprises without clear property relations, including state-owned, collectively-owned, associated, and stock cooperative enterprises, show an obvious downtrend (see Table 2.3). Meanwhile, in Wenzhou, 4,386 private limited liability companies accounted for 66.53% of total private enterprises in 1998, and 6243 private limited liability companies accounted for 72.37% of total private enterprises in 1999. In terms of size, Wenzhou had 186 enterprise groups, including 181 state-owned limited liability companies and 5 private enterprise groups, in 1998; Wenzhou had 198 enterprise groups, including 191 state-owned limited liability companies and 7 private enterprise groups, in 1999.[5] It indicated that both quantity and scale of microeconomic units with clear property relations, such as private limited liability companies,

---

[5] *Wenzhou Statistical Yearbook 1999.* Beijing: China Statistics Press, p. 277; *Wenzhou Statistical Yearbook 2000.* Beijing: China Statistics Press, p. 275.

Table 2.3. Registration of industrial and commercial enterprises and individual industry and commerce: 1998 and 1999 (Unit: family).

Year	Type							
	State-owned	Collectively owned	Associated	Stock system	Stock cooperative system	Private	Foreign invested	Individual
1998	6,110	18,583	217	13,697	28,380	6,590	915	203,440
1999	5,328	13,390	185	14,105	24,990	8,627	857	210,444

Data source: *Wenzhou Yearbook 1999*, China Statistics Press.

were enhanced, manifesting an intense impulse of extension to obtain interests of economies of scale and scope.

(2) Internalization of externalities: Counterfeit and shoddy products are of high negative externality. Wenzhou was famous for counterfeit and shoddy products. For a long time, many malls in the other places put up the slogan "We refuse to sell products from Wenzhou" to show that they sell genuine products, making lots of Wenzhou enterprises suffer a heavy blow with respect to product marketing. At the stage of primitive accumulation of capital, classic enterprises could not eliminate negative externality resulting from counterfeit and shoddy products. Moreover, with the conversion from a seller's market to a buyer's market in China, it marked transformation of the market structure from perfect competition to monopolistic competition. Product competition among micro-enterprises changed from homogeneous competition to diversified competition. Classic enterprises and the professional market system established on Wenzhou model were short of technical innovation and necessary means of protection. In particular, it was difficult to remove profit spillover caused by product imitation resulting from spillover of specific technology and knowledge. Institutional innovation required by microeconomic units was bound to drive brand management, eliminate negative externality brought about by counterfeit and shoddy products, and obtain spillover benefits caused by knowledge spillover. Chint Group in Wenzhou was transformed from a classic enterprise into a modern enterprise through the process of internalization.

(3) Saving of trade costs: Wenzhou model finished the transformation from planned economy to classic market economy and established classic enterprises that were mainly promoted by inverse replacement of enterprises by markets. In order to complete transformation from classic market economy to modern market economy and classic enterprises to modern enterprises, the new Wenzhou model had to depend on replacement of markets by enterprises. Classic enterprises saved their expenses of product marketing through specialized market organization. By concentration of similar products, specialized markets allowed classic enterprises, which could not build up a marketing network independently, to obtain concentration of demands and information, leading to saving of trade costs and high transaction efficiency. In order to complete transformation from classic market economy to modern market economy and from classic enterprises to modern enterprises, the new Wenzhou model could not do without support of factor markets. In recent years, expansion failure of enterprises and outflow of mature enterprises in Wenzhou have been the major results of obstruction of cooperative contracts among microeconomic units caused by inadequate development of factor markets. The important difference between transformation from classic market economy to modern market economy and transformation from planned economy to classic market economy is that the former attaches importance to replacement of product markets by business organizations, while the latter pays attention to replacement of enterprise extension organizations by product markets. Through the replacement, revolutionary change of the boundary between enterprises and markets occurs. The replacement of product markets by business organizations manifests as longitudinal and transverse enterprise integration, enterprise conglomeration, and enterprise strategic alliances, and it must rely on support of developed factor markets. Objectively speaking, Wenzhou model hasn't developed perfect markets of factors, including talents, capital, etc. Furthermore, it is very likely that Wenzhou will stagnate at the stage of classic market economy and even have a risk of deindustrialization caused by migration of mature enterprises resulting from inadequate development of factor markets. Therefore, in order to get rid of path dependence caused by inertia of Wenzhou model, the new Wenzhou model should focus on direction and intensity of saving of trade costs for evolution of micro-enterprises brought by reform and perfection of factor markets.

2.3.2 Promoting of storage reform

The possible approaches of storage reform induced by incremental reform are as follows: (1) developed increment outside the system annexes stock in the system to complete storage reform; (2) as the power center perceives competitive pressure of stock in the system caused by increment outside the system, it carries out storage reform proactively (Yang, 1994). According to development experience of Wenzhou, Wenzhou model has built a micro-system basis with clear property rights, and non-state-owned and non-public-owned economies have developed properly and absorbed 90% of the working population.[6] In the new Wenzhou model, the main approach of storage reform is non-public-owned economies carrying out assets reorganization, distribution of redundant personnel and organ resetting of state-owned economies through participation, holding, merger, and acquisition to establish a modern enterprise system with clear property rights, well-defined power and responsibility, separation between government and enterprises, and scientific management, where establishment and perfection of corporate governance structure in a company are the top priority in this process. Delixi Group of Wenzhou attempted to conduct storage reform and obtain reform profits. At the end of 1999, Delixi purchased Hangzhou Xizi Group Corporation through merger and acquisition. Six months after the merger and acquisition, Hangzhou Xizi Group Corporation

---

[6]*Wenzhou Statistical Yearbook 2000*. Beijing: China Statistics Press, p. 393.

made up the deficit and got surplus through reform. With the approval of Constitutional Amendment, the legitimate status of non-public-owned economy is established and the discriminatory ideological obstacle is gradually removed. Participation, holding, merger, and acquisition of state-owned economies conducted by non-public-owned economies will become the main way of storage reform in the new Wenzhou model. However, state-owned economies still dominate in Wenzhou. In 1999, state-owned infrastructure investment and state-owned non-infrastructure investment accounted for 24.04% and 10.68% of total investment in fixed assets of Wenzhou, respectively.[7] It was difficult to fulfil reform tasks through annexing of public-owned economies by non-public-owned economies only. Meanwhile, as Professor Yang Ruilong said, competitive pressure of state-owned economies caused by rapid development of non-public-owned economies forced interest groups relating to state-owned economies to deepen storage reform, leading to enterprise transformation. During the initiative market-oriented reform of state-owned economic stocks, the following was a feasible reform path: During the first stage, partial transfer of residuals claim and control from the government to enterprises was conducted through expansion of the enterprises' decision-making power, contract system, and stockholding system; in the second stage, shareholding of operators was realized by stock option incentive plans; and during the third stage, shares of operators increased properly by MBO until completion of storage reform. The reform was confronted with some political risks and costs. Government-dominated compulsory institutional change could solve the problem of entry barriers effectively, which was in favor of low-cost storage reform. When operators held major shares, fundamental change of institutional basis occurs, where ambiguous property rights and traditional ideological obstacles disappear. As a result, profit-oriented institutional innovation of microeconomic units develops toward demand-induced institutional change.

---

[7] *Wenzhou Statistical Yearbook 2000*. Beijing: China Statistics Press, p. 313.

Chapter 3

Wenzhou Model: Regional Economic Development and Industrialization Path

3.1 Issues of regional economic development

The 20 years of rapid industrialization progress in China has witnessed several unique regional industrialization modes. In the mid-1990s and late 1990s, there were three most notable regional industrial modes: The first was the industrialization pattern created by the South China area, which is usually called "Pearl River Delta model"; the second is the mode that rose in Suzhou, Wuxi, Changzhou, and the other regions next to Shanghai at the Yangtze River Delta, which is academically recognized as "South Jiangsu model"; and the third mode was the mode created in the coastal area of south Zhejiang and it is called "Wenzhou model" in the academic circles. The academic opinions may vary a lot about the prospects of these three regional industrialization modes. For Pearl River Delta model, the commonly accepted point of view is that such a mode was born in a special geographical environment as a neighbor of Hong Kong and Macau where the capitalist market economy rules. The region was increasingly interacting with the economy of Hong Kong and Macau. Therefore, as long as Hong Kong and Macau maintained the capitalist market economy system, their economy kept prospering and Hong Kong continued to run as one of the freest markets in the world. By contrast, South Jiangsu model is often criticized for the form of property on which it relies. A general opinion is that this mode may lack the momentum in the late stage, considering its ambiguous property subject of the collective economy that the mode depends on. As for Wenzhou model, both the government and scholars were not sure about this mode for a very long time and only acknowledged it somehow within two or three years after the 15th National Congress of the Communist Party of China. Even now, it can still be heard from officials and scholars that this mode is only applicable to Wenzhou and not suitable for the other areas. Zhao & Huang (1997) took Pearl River Delta model as a foreign capital-oriented industrialization mode and South Jiangsu model as a local (collective) enterprise-oriented industrialization mode. These names are based on the following facts. Pearl River Delta model rose up with a series of beneficial policies offered by the central government in the 1980s. Its distinct characteristic is the extensive utilization and high independence on foreign direct investment and the global market. South Jiangsu model was developed on the reutilization and transformation of the "collective enterprises" established during the planned economy period as well as the system innovation. Its prominent feature lies in the rapid growth of local collective enterprises and their unconstrained attempts and moves. One of their key points was to investigate the external structural features of these two modes and they arrived at a conclusion based on the quantitative analysis and comparison of the economic external dependence. Here is the conclusion: By the external structure, since the late 1990s, South Jiangsu model started to look up to Pearl River Delta model. Specifically, as the South Jiangsu region launched the "three-foreign" policy (foreign investment, foreign trade, and foreign economy) and the strategy of "foreign breeds domestic", dependence on foreign resources in this area was growing rapidly. By the end of the 1990s, in several typical towns and cities implementing South Jiangsu model, more than 40% of GDP was contributed by the global market. Meanwhile, over 1/3 of the social capital of the whole South Jiangsu region relied on foreign investment. However, by the transformation of the internal enterprise system, the South Jiangsu region was looking up to Wenzhou model, marked by a trend of local enterprise transformation with a focus on the property clarification in this area since 1997. Many collective enterprises were transformed into private enterprises or "shareholding enterprises" controlled by private capitals, showing consistency with the major enterprise system in Wenzhou (Chang, 2001).

The approach of changing from South Jiangsu model to Wenzhou model by its internal characteristics somehow supports the feasibility of Wenzhou model and encourages researchers to reexamine this mode. To put it objectively, since China's economy is undergoing a dual or "doubleization" transformation, i.e., marketization in the economic system and industrialization of economic society, the inspection and study of Wenzhou model could be continued as a paradigm of systematic transformation or regional industrialization. In this book, the mode is mainly reviewed as a paradigm of regional industrialization with an attempt to discuss the following four intertwined questions: (1) definition of Wenzhou model as a paradigm of regional industrialization; (2) main features of Wenzhou model as a paradigm of regional industrialization; (3) future prospects and trends of the industrialization under this pattern; and (4) major obstacles to the further development of Wenzhou model.

The previous industrialization experiences of developed countries indicated that the industrialization of major countries usually started in several areas and then spread to the whole country. This rule clearly also applies to China. Over 20 years of industrialization experience in China suggests that, if not all, at least a majority of the good reform and development modes are created by the grassroots in specific areas. The earliest production responsibility regulations in agriculture as well as the recent successful mode of regional industrialization proves it. It can be said that the breakthrough and final completion of industrialization and modernization both rely on the grassroots and progress on the regional level. Therefore, economists should all pay attention to the regional industrialization modes in China.

3.2 Neoclassical regional industrialization mode

Reviewing the formation of Wenzhou model in a vertical way, this mode could somehow be compared with European classical industrialization beginning in Lancashire in the northwest of England. It is not hard to agree, after comparison, with the following opinion raised by Zhao (1999): The evolution of this mode has the major features of the early development of European classical market economy industrialization. To be more specific, the mode shares a similar experience with European classical industrialization in four aspects.

The first aspect is the acquisition of start-up capital or preliminary capital. Just like what happened in developed countries, Wenzhou also underwent a difficult time of primitive capital accumulation, which is different from the situation in other regions in China, especially Pearl River Delta and South Jiangsu region. By comparing the capital formation paths of the three regions in the early 1980s, the differences could be clearly noticed: The original capital for the industrialization of Pearl River Delta was mainly contributed by merchants from Hong Kong and Macau and overseas Chinese. For South Jiangsu region, there had been active "collective enterprises" since the planned economy period and the regional industrialization had built a solid basis, which allowed the accumulation of considerable original capital. Unlike these two regions, Wenzhou wasn't dealing with many state-owned enterprise issues left from the planned economy period in the beginning of industrialization. Out of 1,112 million yuan of industrial production value in 1978, state-owned enterprises only contributed 35.6%, which was significantly lower than the ratio of the whole Zhejiang Province (61.34%). Among non-state-owned enterprises, there was 9.3% industrial value belonging to the "non-public but private-owned" domain, which was rarely seen in China. In fact, according to the data of Zhejiang industrial production value at that time, public-owned (state-owned and collectively-owned) enterprises' production value accounted for more than 99.99%. It was the pioneering and demonstrative role of the 9.3% private owners that led a not long but extremely effective preliminary accumulation in Wenzhou in the early 1980s. Its process surely couldn't rival Western countries but its microcosmic subjects and difficulty of the preliminary accumulation were just like the experience of developed countries. The economic history study reveals that the microcosmic subjects of the preliminary accumulation in Europe were individuals pursuing business benefits and the process is long, legendary, and adventurous with both legal and illegal means. Compared with the early experience of Europe, though the process of preliminary accumulation in Wenzhou was on a small scale, the experience was still legendary and adventurous with "ugliness" to some extent. Many approaches in the early stage were also swaying between legal and illegal.

The second aspect is the development of the enterprise organization form. Private enterprises of Wenzhou start from the scattered workshop-scale family business and the modern private enterprise system originates in the family industrial system. This evolution process is very similar to the early industrial experience of Europe but different from the experience of Pearl River Delta and South Jiangsu region. The economic history study indicates that the industrialization in Europe, especially in the first industrial society (Britain), originates from family workshops or the "family industrial system". The first organizational form of family industry is mostly so-called "scattered workshop" where workers or small businessmen work in their own homes and proceed with the orders of production according to the middlemen. It was those workshops scattered in the houses of workers and small businessmen that bred the intensive workshops, which later evolved into the modern "factory system". The early family factories in Wenzhou share some similarities. The joint-stock cooperative enterprises in businesses such as the OEM in Cangnan, woolen sweaters in Changqiao and Rui'an, and low-voltage electronics in Liushi and Yueqing were mostly born in family workshops in the beginning. They developed in the form of "being attached to public institutions", which is mostly close to the classic scattered workshops in the incubation stage. Take the stationery business in Cangnan as an example. In the beginning, the stationery in this county was produced and sold by families. In 1980, a village of the town (Jinxing village) first realized organizational innovation. The brand of "Jinxing Village Stationery Factory" used the same factory name, bank account, and taxation account to submit management fee but the production was distributed to households, which is called "operation by individual households but attached to the public institutions". Such a kind of organizational form is adaptive to the internal private property ownership relationship and meets the social need preferred by the collective outside (public-owned). Therefore, it was imitated by the surrounding areas. Within a year, plastic label and artifact manufacture industries in this county were running more than 2,500 public institution-attached operation enterprises. By contrast, the South Jiangsu region and Pearl River Delta skipped the stage of family industry to some extent. The former was based on the "collective enterprises" that were taking shape at the time and the latter directly introduced the foreign capital to establish non-state-owned companies with distinct "modern" features. Regarding the classical industrialization, the progress from the family industrial system to the modern "factory system" brought the technological evolution from handmade to machinery production in Europe that took a century or even centuries. The industrial revolution in Britain also lasted nearly a century. But in Wenzhou, since family production was already equipped with machines in the very beginning, the technology underwent a leaping growth. As a consequence, it only took less than two decades to evolve from the family industrial system to the factory system and then to the newly emerged modern joint-stock company system. The time spent on company expansion was so short and the growth rate was extremely fast.[1] Due to the accelerating transformation, even now, there are still many kinds of enterprise organizational forms under different enterprise systems in the whole growing process.

The third aspect is the institutional environment in the development process. We all know that before the 15th National Congress of the CPC, the best treatment of private economy was only being considered as the "supplement to the socialist market economy", positioned at the lowest level "outside the system", and constantly challenged by the state-owned and collectively-owned companies "within the system",

---

[1] In Wenzhou and even many other areas in Zhejiang, we often hear that successful private entrepreneurs introduce themselves in the following way: Our enterprise started from a small workshop with only several people and little money. After only 20 years, the small workshop has grown into a group company with assets worth billions of yuan and thousands of employees.

"three types of investment", and collective companies "outside the system". The enterprises mentioned above either are the monopoly in certain industries, or enjoy the protection from divisions or regional governments, or have the access to the beneficial policy or official financing channel. Their operation environment is much better than that of private-owned enterprises. We know that there were once abundant privileged enterprises in Europe. These enterprises used their close relationship with the government to obtain the operation franchise in many industries and their operation environment was also superior to the small-scale private enterprises. Objectively speaking, in the first 19 years of the reform and opening-up in China, the differences between the operation environment of private-owned enterprises and private sector economy and that of "system-insider" enterprises and "three kinds of investment" enterprises were rather similar to the differences between those two types of enterprises in Europe. The "state-owned" and "three kinds of investment" enterprises are generally similar to franchised enterprises in the late middle ages of Europe. The industrialization in Wenzhou was driven by the private power, and the private sector took the leading role. Therefore, the industrialization of Wenzhou model didn't gain the acknowledgement and support from cross-regional governments for most of its development time. The best policy launched by the provincial government for this mode was actually a kind of "governing by non-inference".[2] It is an ironic result that in Wenzhou and even the whole Zhejiang Province, the private economy ignored and even inhibited by the governmental policy gained the best growth momentum while "system-insider" enterprises specially favored by the governmental policy either underwent a downturn

---

[2] Some have carried out feature studies identifying that in the first 19 years of the reform and opening-up, from 1978 to 1996, the provincial governments never released any document concerning the issue of encouraging the development of private sector economy. But they did issue abundant papers for building up the enterprises "inside the system", especially the state-owned companies.

or fluctuated a lot. This situation is also similar to the falling of the franchised and specially protected enterprises and industries (e.g., wool industry in England) in the previous era of Europe. In the meantime, those countryside industries ignored by the government (e.g., textile industry in England) survived in the fierce competition and bred the modern corporate system and big-industry machinery.

The fourth aspect is the factors encouraging the rapid rise of industrialization which are similar to those that motivated classical industrialization in Europe. The economic history has revealed that the development of the cotton spinning industry in Lancashire, England, was associated with two factors: One was that the abundant surplus labor in the rural areas suddenly forced those people to leave their land to participate in "non-agricultural" industry; the other was the formation of a giant business interest group which, along with its employees, formed a huge marketing group and a marketing network spreading across the country and overseas. It was this network that connected the rural industries in England with the global market. On the contrary, the enormous demand of the world market facilitated the historical change of rural industries in Lancashire and brought the wave of industrialization (Mantoux, 1983). Objectively speaking, the beginning of the rural industries in Wenzhou was also closely related to these two interlinked factors: One was the regional factors' unique features. The most prominent one was the richness of labor and farmland supply. The second was the organic composition of regional cultural environment. Wenzhou folks have long been carrying the urge for certain commercial preference. It was the simultaneous release of these two factors that brought a great leap of the Wenzhou family industry: the sudden release of abundant rural surplus labor, forcing people not to make a living by agriculture. The release of private commercial urge rapidly formed a rising marketing group and the growing marketing group connected the rural industries in Wenzhou to the far commodity market and non-labor element sources. It is shown that in the mid-1980s, the ratio of Wenzhou manufacturing industry's insiders to the supply and marketing personnel was as high as 5:1. As the "shortage economy" environment in the mid-1990s shows, once an area possesses the advantage in commercial marketing, there will be unlimited business opportunities. It is easy to draw the conclusion that the European classical industrialization over 200 years ago and the recent Wenzhou industrialization were both inseparable with two factors in the beginning: One is the sudden release of surplus labor and the other is the establishment of extensive business relations and exploitation of a huge market. But it is worth noticing that the reasons behind the release of these two factors are completely different in the two regions. In the source place of European classical industrialization, the rural surplus labor was caused by "the movement of enclosures". The extensive business network was an output of governmental long-term policy of mercantilism. But in modern Wenzhou, these factors were rapidly released as the rise of the institutional reform, where the release of the rural surplus labor was directly associated with the launch of production responsibility system. The release of private business urge has something to do with the new explanation of "commodity market" (market economy later) by the ideology. It is undeniable that Pearl River Delta and South Jiangsu region both had similar conditions as Wenzhou. However, due to the location of these two regions, the above factors, especially the establishment of commercial network, were largely pushed by certain "external force". For example, South Jiangsu region could benefit from the "radiation" effect of its neighbor Shanghai which is the biggest manufacturing center in China[3], while Pearl River Delta could enjoy both "demonstrative" effect of foreign investment and businesses as well as the exploited overseas market as it sits next to Hong Kong and Macau.

However, the analogy could only end here. Compared with the rise of European classical industrialization, Wenzhou's regional

---

[3] In fact, South Jiangsu collective enterprises were handling certain upstream small-product businesses released from state-owned enterprises in Shanghai in the beginning.

industrialization had a lot of other conditions during its occurrence and growth. There are three clearest differences:

The first is the different external conditions in the beginning. European classical industrialization started in the area of agricultural economy. Wenzhou industrialization is different as it belongs to the industrialization of a limited area in the half-industrialized economy, rising in the narrow space between the domestic and big global industry. However, due to the supply shortage of industrial products caused by the special planned economy in China, the market environment in the beginning of Wenzhou industrialization was different from that in regions in some other developing countries.

The second is the different internal political system. European classical industrialization was launched after the establishment of a solid capitalist private property right system while Wenzhou industrialization was launched on the premise of insisting on the socialist public ownership system. Therefore, the latter was always doubted, challenged, and even suppressed at the initial stage of its formation and progress.

The third is the different economy system arrangement before their ascent. Before the European classical industrialization, the market power had played a fundamental role in resource allocation. The industrialization didn't go against the free market system. On the contrary, Wenzhou industrialization was launched when the planned economy was still dominating the market, so the industrialization went hand in hand with the systematic transformation.

Since the major characteristics of Wenzhou's regional industrialization are similar to those of classical industrialization with differences only in the time and internal and external environments, to some extent, Wenzhou model could be called "the paradigm of Chinese neoclassical regional industrialization".

3.3 Characteristics of regional economic development

As a regional industrial paradigm, Wenzhou model has characteristics which are worthy of extra attention. The major features of Wenzhou model could be found by regional horizontal comparison. Horizontally, we should take several other regional industrialization modes along China's coasts as references, considering that there was no big difference in macropolitical and macroeconomic environments and location conditions shared by Wenzhou and other coastal areas in forming their modes. However, they are completely different from those of inland regions. If we compare Wenzhou model with other typical coastal regional industrialization modes, it would be easily noticed that before the end of the 1990s, it had four distinct mode features.

The first characteristic is concerned with the property right structure of microcosmic industrial unit (enterprise). To be more specific, it has a clear property right system. The basic mark of clear property right is that the enterprises with premises for clear property right — non-public-owned enterprises — dominate the industrial value. Statistical data reveal that by the end of the 1990s, in the total gross industrial value of Wenzhou, the proportion of "public-owned" enterprises (state-owned and collective-owned) accounted for only about 15% (where the proportion of state-owned industrial production value was less than 4%) while non-public-owned industrial value (private-owned and joint-stock enterprises) accounted for as high as about 85% (see Figure 3.1).

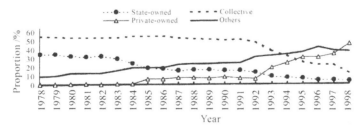

Figure 3.1. Wenzhou's industrial gross output composition change of companies with different ownership systems: 1978–1998.
Data source: Wenzhou Statistics Bureau (1999).

According to the national data in the same period, the public-owned enterprises' production value accounted for over 63% of the total while only "state-owned and state-joint" enterprises' production value already took up more than 28%. These two figures in Zhejiang were, respectively, 38% and 11%. According to the comparative studies of provinces, autonomous regions, and direct-controlled municipalities, the proportion of "state-owned industry's production value" to Zhejiang's total industrial production value was the lowest in China. The comparison between areas in Zhejiang also reveals that Wenzhou had the lowest proportion in the whole province. In Wenzhou, the non-public-owned enterprises with clear property right consisted of three types of enterprises: The first was the growing private enterprises in the process of the reform and opening-up, the second was the "red-hat enterprises" taking off the "red hat" since the late 1990s (private enterprises attached to the label of "collective"), and the third was the sold state-owned enterprises in the process of "transformation". By the end of the 1990s, the property rights of these enterprises were completely or basically clear. This point was especially prominent in the industries of manufacturing, product retail, and highway passenger and cargo transportation. In comparison, in many other coastal areas, especially the South Jiangsu region two or three years ago, the ambiguous property rights under "collective ownership" were usually a basic characteristic of the enterprises' property right structure (Chang, 2001).[4]

The second feature is reflected in the capital composition structure. By the proportion of domestic and foreign capital, an obvious characteristic is that the capital in the process of Wenzhou industrialization is clearly from an internal source. Specifically, from the start of Wenzhou's industrialization to the recent development, capital was mainly obtained through internal channels (district, provincial, or national) without little

---

[4]Local officials in South Jiangsu generally consider that "unquestionably, the core implication of South Jiangsu model is to develop non-agricultural economy, especially rural industry, in collective ownership" (Chang, 2001).

introduction of foreign capital. Even when nearly all places in China were boldly introducing foreign investment after Deng Xiaoping's South Talks in 1992 and many coastal places (including representative counties and cities of South Jiangsu model) significantly increased their dependence on foreign investment, such kind of dependence remained low in Wenzhou. According to statistical data, from 1995 to 1998, the proportion of introduced foreign capital to the total fixed asset investment in major cities of Pearl River Delta model was 47% at the lowest and above 55% for most of the years. The average in the South Jiangsu region was no lower than 30%. But this figure was less than 3% in Wenzhou. The highest ratio was only 2.79% in 1997 and this number reduced to 1.5% in 1998. Such kind of proportion was not only rare in the coastal areas but also significantly lower than the national average level (the proportions of actual used foreign capital in the national fixed asset investment in 1997 and 1998 were, respectively, 15.06% and 13%). It could be easily inferred that the key factors in the industrialization process of Wenzhou, capital, were basically from the domestic area (see Figure 3.2). It has been also noticeably revealed that the domestic capital was mainly obtained through cross-regional business activities between private enterprises rather than official financial channels like banks or capital markets as these official financial channels were usually far beyond the reach of small-scale private-owned enterprises.

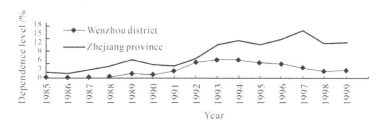

Figure 3.2.   Comparison between Wenzhou and the other regions in Zhejiang Province in foreign investment dependence level: 1985–1999.
Data source: Zhejiang Statistics Bureau (2000).

The third feature is about the market structure. What makes it special is the inter-region of the trade flow and extremely high dependence on the domestic market. By horizontally investigating the market structure of the economic development in Wenzhou, it could be easily concluded that in the economic development by the end of the 1990s, the commodity market of Wenzhou was mainly domestic rather than overseas. Therefore, it could be considered that the inter-regional trade rather than global trade was the main drive for its growth. According to the statistical data, in the second half of the 1990s, Pearl River Delta region's dependence on foreign trade and export (export amount/GDP) was close to 100% and this figure in typical cities of South Jiangsu model was also above 40%. However, Wenzhou long kept it below 10%. Even in the late 1990s after the market enhanced the foreign trade work, the total proportion of export and import of Wenzhou to its GDP, namely, the so-called national economy foreign trade dependence, was lower than 15%. Before the early 1990s, the figures were below 5% in most years. Such numbers were extremely small no matter compared to Jiangsu where South Jiangsu model grew and Guangdong where Pearl River Delta model thrived (see Figures 3.3–3.5).

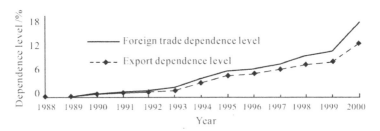

Figure 3.3.   Change of Wenzhou's economy and foreign trade dependence levels: 1988–2000.

Data source: Wenzhou Statistics Bureau (2000).

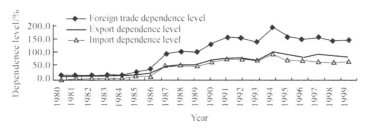

Figure 3.4.   Change of Guangdong's economy and foreign trade dependence levels: 1980–1999.
Note: The foreign trade at Pearl River Delta region accounted for more than 80% of Guangdong's total amount, suggesting higher dependence.
Data source: National Statistics Bureau (2000).

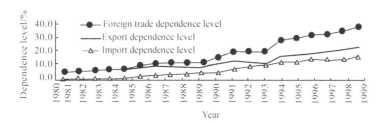

Figure 3.5.   Change of Jiangsu's economy and foreign trade dependence levels: 1980–1999.
Note: South Jiangsu region's foreign trade dependence level was generally much higher than the total amount of Jiangsu.
Data source: National Statistics Bureau (2000).

The fourth characteristic is shown in the industrial and technological choices of the industrialization. Wenzhou's industrialization was basically driven by the private investment and the investment scale was growing gradually in the development process. Consistent with the private small-scale investment, the invested industrial choices were mostly made in the traditional manufacturing industry with short payback periods and small risks. Meanwhile, the choices of industrial technology were mostly limited to the low-barrier technological industries. According to the data, until 1998, the major industries of Wenzhou's manufacturers were mostly the leading industries that had developed in the first and second industrial revolutions in Western countries. These industries usually posed low barriers to technology and investment, which was suitable for the growth of small private businesses. Investment in the high-tech industries or mid-to-high-level technological fields in Wenzhou is still very rare today (see Table 3.1).

The conclusion could be easily drawn based on the four characteristics of the development of Wenzhou model presented above: As a regional industrialization paradigm, Wenzhou model maximally absorbed or motivated the public to participate in the development process, maximally utilized the domestic resource and domestic market, and it started from and expanded around traditional manufacturing. In this sense, it is obvious that Wenzhou model could be seen as a regional industrialization paradigm based on the internal market and resources as well as the traditional manufacturing industry to make the advancement from the bottom to the top.

Table 3.1.   Main industries in Wenzhou manufacturing sector: 1998.

Industry	Output	Technical level
Shoemaking	Leather shoes output accounted for 20% of the country	Traditional low technology
Clothes (including leather clothes)	Suit output accounted for 10% of the country	Traditional low technology
Lighter	Wind-proof lighter manufacturing and export accounted for over 90% of the country and created profits of over USD 300 million	Traditional low technology
Lamp	The proportion in the country was unclear	Small amount of new technology

Table 3.1.   (*Continued*)

Industry	Output	Technical level
Valve	33,100-ton output	Medium technology
Automobile (motorbike) parts	Around 6 million bearing output	New technology to some extent
Button	Largest production and sales volume in the country	Traditional technology + modern design
Stationery	20 million stationery cases and 1,600 million pens	Low technology+new design
Low-pressure electrical appliance	Over 35% production and sales volume in the country	Medium technology
Glasses	Over 80% production and sales volume in the country	Traditional technology + new design
Printing (printing machine)	1,136 printing machines	Certain new technology
Plastic product	Trademark and badge accounted for over 40% of the country	Certain new technology

Data source: Arranged according to Wenzhou industry analysis results (printed manuscripts and informal publication materials).

3.4 Trend of regional economic development

Objectively speaking, till the early 21st century, Wenzhou model as a regional industrialization paradigm had clearly formed some internal factors driving the continuous expansion of industrialization. Among all factors, the following three factors are worthy of special attention:

The first factor is the solid basis of capital formation. One of its important marks was the extensively growing private savings as well as the growing importance of private investment payback in the regional capital formation. It has been reported that since the late 1990s, Wenzhou's saving rate, especially private saving rate, was surging up all along and ranking high in the whole Zhejiang Province for many consecutive years. By the end of 2000, the saving balance of the financial institutes sharply rose by 22.1% where the growth rate of corporate saving was not impressive but the private saving's growth rate hit 22.3%, nearly 5% higher than the average level of the whole Zhejiang Province. After all, the growth rate of private saving rate in Zhejiang already stayed high across the whole country. The constantly growing private saving, along with the "wealth effect" of private accumulated saving and investment, kept driving the expansion of the source of the private capital formation. Moreover, this source was further amplified by the merchants from Wenzhou who went to all economic centers and even remote cities and counties in China.

The second factor is the scattering and public participation of investment decision-making as well as the private dominance of the microeconomic decision-making that came along, internalizing the drive of economic growth. This is directly associated with clarifying the corporate property right system. It has been revealed in the analysis that in the social fixed asset investment in Wenzhou, the proportion of private investment always topped, which was over 10% higher than the figure of the whole province (see Figure 3.6). In the meantime,

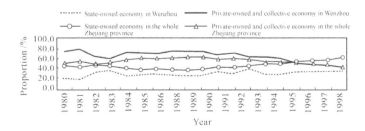

Figure 3.6.   Comparison between Wenzhou and the whole Zhejiang Province in the investment structure: 1980–1998.

the private investment's share to the total investment in Wenzhou also ranked high among the coastal provinces. We all know that by the investment decision-making mechanism, the biggest difference between private investment and state-owned investment lay in the fact that the former was scattered while the latter was more concentrated. The former binds the investors and decision-makers together while the latter separates the two roles. The former comes from the internal urge of investors for pursuing profits while the latter relies on the motivation of government and community. The dispersive investment decision-making mechanism and its mutually interdependent clear property right enterprise system somehow changed the dominant participants of Wenzhou's economic development, transforming from the traditional government-leading mode to the real market and private power-leading mode. Therefore, its economic growth escaped from the traditional mode of relying on the governmental motivation. We know that in the traditional government-leading economic mode, the major force for the economic growth is extraneous and the governmental decision is the biggest extraneous variable. Therefore, the "malfunction" of government, the loosened supervision over the leaders of the public-owned economy, or the wrong public investment decision might cause serious damage to the local economy. On the contrary, in the economy led by market and private power, the drive for the economic growth is endogenous. The temporary lassitude or malfunction of the government won't inhibit the private investment flow and the role of entrepreneurship, which means its negative influence on the economic growth is much weaker.

The third factor is the inter-regionalization of market distribution and element absorption which enables economic development to maximally avoid the influence of global unstable factors. It has been mentioned that one of the most important characteristics of Wenzhou model is the inter-regionalization of trade and the endogenous feature of capital formation. This mode is basically aligned with the general characteristics of regional development of a big country's economy.

Since it effectively seizes the advantage of cross-regional flow of inter-regional trade and element in a big country, mainly the domestic inter-regional commodity market and element market expansion, its economic growth is less likely to be affected by external factors. This is especially highlighted in the frequently shaking global economic environment after the East Asian financial crisis. The study of Zhao (2001) also undoubtedly reveals that according to the general law of the externalization of regional economy in the industrialization process, the regional opening in the industrialization of a limited area could either start from inter-regionalization or globalization. But for the internal limited area in a big country, inter-regionalization and then closely connecting the capital formation and market distribution with other domestic areas could not only obtain favorable benefits from inter-regional cooperation but also avoid the influence from the global unstable factors in the early stage of industrialization. To some extent, Wenzhou's industrialization has already closely connected its capital and market with the rapidly expanding domestic inter-regional economy today and the drive for its further development is undoubtedly solid.

Based on the three factors above, it could be considered that as a regional industrialization paradigm, Wenzhou model's development drive is still growing today and the momentum of its advancement is irreversible. But it should also be realized that the next step of Wenzhou's industrialization is certainly to shed a new light on the future direction.

According to the development trend, in the next few years of industrialization progress of Wenzhou model, there are two new trends worthy of attention.

One of the trends could be seen from the industrial structure change in the industrialization progress, namely, the transition from "secondary-industrialization" to "tertiary-industrialization". The historical experience of developed industrialized countries has proved that, in a full industrialization process of an economy, although the changes in the industrial structure generally show a "non-agriculturization" trend, the focus of the non-agriculturization varies according to the depth and width of industrialization. Generally, in the early stage of industrialization, the "non-agriculturization" focus in the industrial structure is on manufacturing. Therefore, the so-called "non-agriculturization" is embodied as manufacture orientation or "secondary-industrialization". As the industrialization deepens, especially in the middle to late stage of industrialization, the focus would shift to the service sector. In this stage, the characteristic of the changes in the industrial structure is that the proportion of the secondary industry or manufacturing industry to the total output stops rising and then starts to fall. By contrast, the tertiary industry centering on the service sector grows rapidly and gradually replaces the manufacturing industry to become the main contributor to GDP. Therefore, the "non-agriculturization" in this stage shows a clear trend of "tertiary-industrialization" or service-oriented feature. It could clearly be seen through analyzing the evolution of Wenzhou's GDP industrial source structure that the change in the focuses of "non-agriculturization" could be divided into two stages by the year 1996: Before that, the focus of "non-agriculturization" lay on the manufacturing with strong tendency of "secondary-industrialization". The added value of secondary industrialization is increasing its proportion in GDP, first from 35.8% in 1980 to 43.2% in 1986 and 58.5% in 1993, then finally to 59.2% in 1996. In the same period, the first industry dropped from 42.2% to 31.3% and then 13.4%. In 1996, the figure further dropped to 9.4%. After that, the proportion of the secondary industry to total GDP grew no more and began to slow down. In 1999, the figure fell to 57.4% and further to below 56% in 2000. In general, the proportion of the tertiary industry in the whole process kept rising stably. The figure climbed slowly before 1996. From 1986 to 1996, the number only rose by over 4%. But after 1996, the growth started to accelerate. Only within three years from 1996 to 1999, its share grew by nearly 4% (see Figure 3.7). It could be easily seen that the focus of "non-agriculturization" of Wenzhou's industrialization has gradually changed. It could be inferred

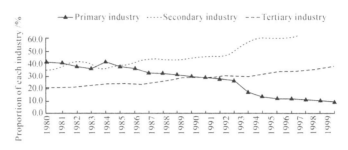

Figure 3.7.   Change of Wenzhou's Industry Structures: 1980–1999.
Data source: Wenzhou Statistics Bureau (1999).

that in the next few years, the focus of industrialization is going to gradually move to the tertiary industry and the service sector is heading for an unconventional development period. According to the developed industrialized countries' experience, the ratio of added value of the tertiary industry to the total GDP would at least reach 50%. Therefore, for Wenzhou's economy, in the further advancement of industrialization, there is still huge space for the "tertiary industrialization".

The second trend can be concluded from the market structural change in the industrialization process, i.e., the expansion from the trade inter-regionalization to globalization. It has been discussed that one of the key features of Wenzhou model as an industrialization paradigm is the inter-regionalization of trading. Its domestic trading, especially the cross-regional trading, dominated the total trading volume. But this cannot cover another trend that the proportion of global trading is rising though still remaining low. The foreign trade dependence that reflects the importance of global trading (total amount of export and import to GDP) was only 2.39% in 1993 and climbed to 7.43% in 1996. After 1998, the growth started to leap forward, reaching 10.75% in 1998, 12.43% in 1999, and nearly 7% more in 2000, which breaks 20%! The export dependence also reached 14% (see Figure 3.3). Although these two dependence levels were both far lower than that of South Jiangsu region, let alone competing with Pearl River Delta, the rapid growth since the late 1990s suggests that the market and the trading structure of Wenzhou's economy are changing from the dependence on the overwhelming advantages of the domestic inter-regional market to equal attention to inter-regional and global markets. This trend is generally consistent with Britain model among the regional economic opening modes revealed in Zhao (2001a, 2001b). As is analyzed, the regional opening started from inter-regionalization and grew into globalization. Coincidentally, Wenzhou model pattern shares similarities with English classical model. It could be foreseen that further progress of industrialization would surely improve the trend concerning market structural evolution.

For the authors of this book, the two trends above are inevitable in the industrialization process and they are the necessary conditions for Wenzhou model as an industrialization paradigm to expand in depth and width. With the reinforcement of the two trends, the neoclassical features of Wenzhou model would be further highlighted.

3.5 Challenges in economic development

After all, Wenzhou model is still a growing regional industrialization paradigm. Therefore, its future developments are still facing many challenges and obstacles. But we consider that some existing internal problems presented are mostly secondary. This mode could overcome all these internal problems step by step as long as it expands continuously. The biggest challenge posed to the future of this mode comes from external rather than internal factors. The biggest external restriction is the lagging mid-level institutional reform. The lagging of reform should be explained by both economic system reasons and non-economic system reasons. By economic system reasons, there is a factor that will affect the normal progress of Wenzhou's industrialization and then distort this mode.

It is the lagged financial system reform. Objectively speaking, Wenzhou's manufacturing industry did undergo a deepened institutional reform. Its mark is that in the manufacturing industry, most production values and employment opportunities are provided by non-state-owned enterprises with clear property rights. However, in a strong contrast to the institutional transformation in manufacturing, there is serious backwardness of the financial system reform beyond the control of the regional government. Its important mark is that commercial banks are still a state-owned monopoly industry. We know that state-owned commercial banks mainly serve state-owned companies and governmental bodies traditionally, and they are separated from non-state-owned enterprises. Such separation is presented in the detached relationship between non-state-owned enterprises and state-owned banks. On the one hand, as the reform of state-owned manufacturing enterprises and competition of non-state-owned enterprises are proceeding, state-owned commercial banks are losing their traditional loan targets — state-owned enterprises with good return, which leads to the overstock of money and they are in urgent need of finding new loan targets. On the other hand, non-state-owned manufacturing enterprises, especially small- and medium-sized enterprises, pay a heavy price to interact with state-owned banks, forcing them to form the habit of not relying on the banks.

The detachment of banks and private enterprises would bring about two problems. One is the "limited size" of non-state-owned enterprises. According to relevant data, from 1978 to 1998, Wenzhou's industrial production value grew 123.7 times and the number of enterprises increased 30.3 times. However, the average scale based on a single enterprise's average production value at the same time only increased twofold. It could also be seen from a vertical examination that the average output scale of Wenzhou's industrial enterprises underwent two backspins in the early 1980s and the mid-1990s. From 1980 to 1985, the average production scale shrunk from 255,000 yuan to 65,000 yuan; from 1992 to 1994, the average production scale fell from 446,000 yuan to 345,000 yuan (see Table 3.2). The other problem is the financial

Table 3.2.   Change of company sizes in Wenzhou: 1978–1998.

Year	Number of industrial companies	Number of state-owned companies	Gross industrial output (10,000 yuan)	Average company output (10,000 yuan/ per unit)
1978	4,085	294	111,000	27.2
1980	6,477	302	165,000	25.5
1985	65,045	321	421,000	6.5
1990	41,741	336	951,000	22.8
1991	34,034	332	1,234,000	36.3
1992	41,021	330	1,830,000	44.6
1993	96,740	314	3,434,000	39.6
1994	152,688	295	5,273,000	34.5
1995	117,829	296	7,195,000	61.1
1996	127,253	278	10,040,000	78.9
1997	121,253	232	12,424,000	102.5
1998	127,980	168	13,846,000	108.2

Data source: Wenzhou Statistics Bureau (1999).

chaos. Since small enterprises mainly rely on private financing channels, as they are very active in Wenzhou. However, private underground and half-underground financing activities are illegal and not professional at all in their operation. The operational cost and transaction cost are both higher than those through formal financing channels. The financial participants of private financing activities are facing larger risks than the formal financial industry.

The above two problems are actually two sides of the same question. On one side, objectively speaking, to solve the problem of the limited size of non-state-owned enterprises, financial reform needs to make some breakthrough. It has never been too clear that it is hard for non-state-owned enterprises to expand by reinvestment based on their own internal capital accumulation and profits. Even if it works, the whole process is time consuming. To cultivate non-state-owned enterprise sectors that are able to participate in inter-regional competition and even global competition, it is necessary to leverage the power of finance and resort to mergers and acquisitions. In this respect, the previous industrialized economies also offer examples. Based on the vertical examination of American enterprises' merging history, we totally agree with Stiegler that all big American companies grow through certain ways of merging. Almost no big company simply relies on the internal expansion. But we also notice that in the wave of manufacturing merging in the U.S., banks and especially non-banking financial institutes (mainly investment companies) played a critical role. Although America is implementing a strict bank segregation system, the quasi-banking investment companies are always playing an important role. According to the research of American economic historian Scheibe, Vatter & Faulkner (1983), "giant financial companies" played the role of "broker" in mergers and acquisitions. Some economic historians also found that Morgan Financial Group grew up in a form of investment company. In the formation of a series of giants from the 1970s to the 1980s, the Morgan Group played a huge role. But in Wenzhou, due to the common detached relationship between banks and enterprises, it is hard to start the wave of company merger.[5] Therefore, it could be believed that if we could make a breakthrough in financial reform and

---

[5]There is an explanation of why the reasons for the difficulty in starting the merging wave among private enterprises in Wenzhou lie in the local idea of "rather be the head of a chicken than the tail of a cow". We don't identify this idea as a main reason because its idea is not limited to the private entrepreneurs in Wenzhou but also occurs in the Western market economy. It is widely known that American culture teaches its people the idea of independence since a very young age. The Western corporate culture long teaches people to start their own company. Without such ideas and concepts of independence, Bill Gates wouldn't have thought about starting "Microsoft" when facing the competition of giants and many other new enterprises wouldn't have been started. But in America, with the backup of highly efficient and free-access financial departments, successful enterprises could usually use the financial leverage to merge and eliminate some low-efficiency "chicken-head" enterprises.

establish real and organic relationships between financial institutes, especially non-banking financial institutes, and non-state-owned enterprises, it is possible to motivate the merger of Chinese non-state-owned enterprises and mergers could largely solve the "limited size" issue troubling the non-state-owned enterprises. However, the systematic reform of state-owned financial institutes, especially the transformation of the property right system, is beyond the reach of the local government.

The other side is the lagged transformation of the farmland system and its closely related agricultural operation system. The history of early European industrialization and the industrialization experience of Japan and Taiwan (China) both show that the farmland reform and agricultural revolution are the prelude of industrialization. Without good farmland revolution, it is impossible to establish a farmland system aligned with the modern market economy and the industrialization process would become hard and slow. This was somehow proved by France after the French Revolution. Looking at the system changes in Wenzhou in an objective way, it is easy to see that the major breakthrough in the system of Wenzhou model mainly lay in one and a half industries. "One industry" is the secondary industry and "a half industry" refers to some industries of the tertiary industry. The clear corporate property right system now only exists in the manufacturing industry in the secondary sector and the non-leading industries in the tertiary sector, such as commodity retail and food and beverage service. As for the agriculture in the first industry and the leading industries in the tertiary sector — finance, insurance, and commodity wholesales — they don't show much difference from those in other regions. If we say the lagged transformation of the financial system in the tertiary industry would directly restrict the company scale and product level in the secondary industry, then certain institutional problems in the first industry would negatively affect the industrialization and urbanization process of Wenzhou and even Zhejiang. Specifically, since rural areas are still maintaining the property right relationship under the production responsibility system and the land property right is ambiguous along with the restriction of current land laws and the household registration system, the "non-agriculturization" of labor and urbanization of population cost a huge amount and carry huge distortion.[6]

The lagged farmland system also brings about many problems: Many farmers have left the village for years but it is still hard for them to abandon the land as it is not completely useless. Some people that are good at farming have no stable property right or use access to the farmland, so they are unable to expand the production and implement long-term investment in the land. As a consequence, the land is deliberately wasted. The extremely scarce land resources are even abandoned repeatedly in some villages. The phenomenon of the land for industrialization and urbanization being restricted by the existing land laws is very commonly seen.

The problem that rises together with the lagged economic system reform is the lagged non-economic system reform, especially the lagged administrative system reform that determines the relationship between the government and the market. Since Wenzhou model was formed under the old governmental management system facilitated by the planned economic system, the non-interference of the government in the early and middle stages of its growth could well avoid the inappropriate intervention. But as the market economic system is gradually established across the

---

[6]In many villages of Wenzhou, farming has become a matter of complete loss. Local governmental cadres revealed that by the end of the 1990s, many villages were facing the situation that farmers would have no revenue at all if they distribute their own responsible farmland to be farmed by others and they even needed to submit a fee of 600 yuan/mu. It should be noticed that since 2001, with the adjustment of agricultural production structures in Zhejiang, the agricultural operation rights have been loosened and the sublet scale of land rentals has been growing, which might be a tendency benefiting the process of Wenzhou's industrialization and urbanization.

country and Zhejiang's economy is growing rapidly in the marketization of resource allocation, the "malfunction" of the government is becoming increasingly prominent. Since Wenzhou has a large proportion of non-state-owned economy, the market power plays a significant role. Therefore, the governmental "malfunction" is most easily occurring. There are two demonstrated facts to support this point. One is that the government is not engaged in offering public products, which is reflected in the lack of thoroughly long-term planning of urban construction and the serious phenomenon of "constant changes in policies". The other is the insufficient governmental role in the market regulation, so that the issue of forged and fake commodities couldn't be effectively solved for long. This problem seems to be caused by the "local protectionism" on the surface, but actually reflects the governmental "malfunction".

If the breakthrough in the lagged economic system reform is out of reach of the local government, the local government could surely do something to overcome the "malfunction". Likewise, if the lagged mid-level economic system reform would affect the scale, revenue, and competitiveness of Wenzhou's enterprises, the local government's "malfunction" might worsen the investment environment and lead to the investment outflow and larger negative influence.

Chapter 4

Growth Path and Mechanism of Wenzhou's Private Enterprises

The most significant thing in modern economic systems is the formation of rational market subjects. There was once an influential debate in the domestic economic circles. One side held that the establishment and perfection of the socialist market economy should focus on defining the property rights of enterprises, while the other side thought that the perfection of the market system, especially the competition order and the rationalization of the price system, was more important. Although there were great differences between the two sides, there was not much difference between the two sides of the argument regarding the shaping of the rational market subject being the key to the establishment and perfection of the socialist market economy system. Differences mainly focused on how to shape a reasonable market subject.

From the point of view of reality, economic growth is often more healthy and sustainable in the region where enterprise growth is more smooth. The intensity of the discussion on the three major models of socialist economic development and reform in China fluctuates, and the progress is slow. The reason is that the research on the growth of enterprises in the areas covered by these models is relatively weak. There is a tendency to highlight the commonness of township enterprises in these areas and ignore the differences in the growth paths of enterprises in different regions and their consequences. The result is that the essential characteristics of different models are uncertain. Therefore, the question we are interested in is: In the developed coastal areas of China, what are the paths and characteristics of enterprise growth in different regions, and how significant are these characteristics for depicting different economic models?

This chapter attempts to describe the growth path and mechanism of Wenzhou's private enterprises.

The private enterprises here refer to the business organizations whose actual owners of property rights are individuals or families. Unlike collective enterprises or state-owned enterprises, these enterprises cannot completely avoid the interference of government regulation, but can exercise the final disposition of their assets. According to the standard of property right economics, whether an enterprise property right is complete or not depends on the size of the residual claim. A striking feature of private enterprises is that business owners can use their assets and their earnings to exchange with the owners of other resources. So the final disposition of the property or residual claim is relatively complete. However, for state-owned enterprises and collective enterprises, the disposal right and residual claim of the enterprise assets by the actual person in charge of the enterprise are restricted by laws and policies. The folk enterprise here is similar to the free enterprise described in Western economics. The reason why we do not use the names of the private enterprises that are currently used in China is that the term "private enterprise" includes not only the real non-public enterprises (individuals and private enterprises) but also public-owned enterprises with part of the management of its property rights being contracted out to private individuals. The latter has no substantive significance for Wenzhou's economy, nor does it mean much to our research. The reason for not using the term "private enterprise" is that it is easily understood narrowly as a form of ownership provided by law, making it difficult to include a large number of individual enterprises and the emerging joint-stock system of the cooperative economy in the study. We try to define the enterprises whose assets are entirely derived from individuals and households (monetary capital, human capital, and material capital) on which the development of the enterprise is based by the term "folk enterprise" no matter what legal form this enterprise takes.

4.1 Background and origin of private enterprises

4.1.1 Disintegration of commune- and brigade-run enterprises and publicity of "underground economic organizations"

Different from South Jiangsu model, the logical starting point and historical starting point of the growth of Wenzhou folk enterprises were not the commune- and brigade-run enterprise in the people's commune period. Compared with the Hangzhou, Jiaxing, and Huzhou areas in northeast Zhejiang, Wenzhou's rural collective enterprises were insignificant both in scale and quality. With the implementation of the household contract responsibility system, such small commune- and brigade-run enterprises quickly collapsed. In Wenzhou, because the commune- and brigade-run enterprise was underdeveloped, the influence was insufficient, and the relationship with agricultural production was not straightened out, the comparative advantage of the collective production organization was not as obvious as in the north-eastern region of Zhejiang. There have long been doubts about the superiority of collective agricultural and industrial production.[1]

---

[1] In fact, as early as in 1956, Wenzhou Yongjia County Party Committee organized trails for fixing of farm output quotas for each household, and in September the county convened the Senior Community Directors' Meeting, requiring the district party committee and the township party branch to strengthen the agricultural production responsibility system. This led to 200 high-level communities of the county to implement the practice of fixing of farm output quotas for each household. For the fixing of farm output quotas for each household, the members at that time summed up "Five Goods" (clear responsibility is good, labor quality is good, pooling everybody's wisdom is good, relationship between cadre and mass is good, and convenient work point recording process is good), "Five Highs" (high quality of farm work, high grain yield, high enthusiasm for learning technology, high prestige of model worker, and high living standard), and "Six Mores" (more accretive soil fertilizer, more live pigs, more people learning technology, more people concerned about production, more harmony and unity, and more people working on cultivated land). The county's practice of fixing of farm output quotas for each household quickly received positive responses from the other rural areas in Wenzhou. By the spring of 1957, the total number of cooperatives in the whole Wenzhou area had reached more than 1,000, with 178,000 commune members, accounting for about 15% of the total number of peasant households (Zhang & Li, 1990).

According to statistics, from 1973 to 1976, more than 70% of the state-owned and collective enterprises in the city stopped production, and the total industrial output value decreased by 60% compared with those in the 1960s, and more than 60% of enterprises often failed to pay salaries.

On the contrary, civil economic activities were very active even in the traditional system under very strict policy restrictions, and the "underground economy" was difficult to ban. For example, in the Yishan area of Pingyang county, between 1957 and 1970, handweaving was suppressed many times, but survived stubbornly. This area became known as the national regenerated cotton processing base. According to the survey, the number of unlicensed vendors in Wenzhou was 5,200 in 1970, 6,400 in 1974, and 11,115 in 1976. Underground contractors, underground transportation teams, private markets, and a black market for means of production were also widespread. In 1976, the private market accounted for 90% of the retail sales of social commodities. Table 4.1 lists the economic structure of Zhejiang Province on the eve of the household contract responsibility system. In the table, in the row of

Table 4.1.   The ownership structure of investment and industry in Zhejiang Province in 1982.

Categories of industry	Hangzhou	Ningbo	Wenzhou	Jiaxing	Huzhou	Shaoxing	Jinhua	Quzhou	Zhoushan	Taizhou	Lishui
Non-state-owned collective units to the fixed assets investment in the whole society.	17	NA	49	42	29	29	33	21	22	39	18
The non-state collective industry to the total industrial output value (%)	NA	NA	13	0.1	NA	NA	NA	0.7	0.6	15	2

Source: Zhejiang Bureau of Statistics, *Compilation of Statistical Data of the 50 Years of New Zhejiang*, China Statistics Press.

the non-state-owned collective units to the fixed assets investment in the whole society, Wenzhou was up to 49%, which was the highest in the province, and was 2.88 times that of Hangzhou, the most economically developed region in the province at that time. The non-state collective industry accounted for 13% of total industrial output, second only to Taizhou, which was far ahead of other parts of Zhejiang Province. This showed that even under the traditional economic system, the vitality and scale of Wenzhou's private economy were not negligible. It can be said that the private economy of Wenzhou grew based on this.

4.1.2 Household contract responsibility system and family industry

(1) The various forms of family industry

Understanding the logical starting point and the historical starting point of the mode of rural industrialization in Zhejiang is impossible without understanding the unique industrial form of the family industry. This form of industrial organization is based on the possession of the means of production of the household (individual), relying on the family's own labour force, supplemented by a small number of helpers, and using housing as a place of production to develop the processing industry. This form mostly uses locally produced raw materials to process commodities.This kind of production doesn't require high technologies, doesn't require too much, capital and is suitable for production in a household.

The family industry was originally developed as a form of labor force utilization in the slack period. In traditional agricultural society, family industry was the main complement of rural economy. In areas with relatively developed coastal commodity economies, such as the Mediterranean coast of the 15th century and the coastal areas of the south of the Yangtze River during the Ming and Qing dynasties, the household industry was more developed. The decline of household industry in China was mainly due to the import of cheap industrial products after China opened its doors in the late Qing dynasty. But the decline of the family industry was by no means a disappearance. Although the products of the family industry had been squeezed out of the market by foreign goods, its roots still survived in the form of a latent force, and once the environment permitted, it was revitalized and rejuvenated.

The family industry in rural Wenzhou can be divided into three kinds: peasant household by-business, family workshop, and family work house. Peasant household by-business was a primary form of family industry. It refers to the production of some industrial products by farmers' families in addition to land labor and the production of agricultural products. The extent of the by-business is different in different regions and seasons. Therefore, the scale and income of peasant household by-business were difficult to estimate. It can also be divided into domestic collaboration and internal division of labor.[2] Domestic collaboration refers to a situation in which all members of

---

[2] This is a division by us. According to our observation, in many areas of rural China, the by-business of peasant households is mainly a collaborative by-business. This kind of by-business is not very dependent on the specificity of human capital, but the dependence on market demand and rural production conditions is obvious. For example, farmers weave hats and brooms on rainy days, as long as two conditions are available: The first is the need for such products, and the second is the slack time. This kind of labor does not need special skill and everyone can be competent. But it takes three years of apprenticeship and almost the same length of time to assist a master in his work before starting one's own business. The farm work of the craftsman who makes articles from bamboo strips is generally borne by the other members or the apprentices who follow him, and the craftsmen themselves are basically no longer working. The difference between an ordinary farmer weaving hats on a rainy day and a craftsman specializing in bamboo products is clear. The former is the domestic collaboration by-business while the latter is the division of labor.

the family are engaged in the production during the slack season or when other opportunities that are conducive to industrial production are available. The domestic division of labor refers to such a situation: The family members of peasant households are divided into two fixed roles, one is basically engaged in agricultural production, and the other one is basically engaged in industrial production. The boundary between the two is relatively clear. These two specific forms are different for the evolution and development of rural industrial production forms. Domestic collaboration is one of the most primitive forms of instability. It has the potential to transform into a variety of other forms of production, such as returning to land labor when the market shrinks, or exporting labor, or remaining idle.[3] The significance of family division by-business for rural industrialization is much more important than that of family collaborative by-business. Due to the division of labor, the professional producers make faster progress in industrial production skills, so that they can grasp industrial production and other related information fully. The comparative advantage of division of labor in industrial production is also increasingly consolidated.

When the by-business is not to solve its own direct consumption demand but to make a profit, whether the farmers choose the collaborative by-business or the division of labor by-business depends on the following factors: first, the market size of industrial products; second, the ratio of the

---

[3] In his book *Farmers' Economic Organization*, Chayanov makes a detailed study of farmers' economic choices. The book is the representative work of the peasantry, which proves the stability and the inherent inevitability of the family economy of small-scale peasant economy or self-employment. It is also of great significance to analyze the industrial labor of peasant households. In his book *Small Peasant Families and Rural Development in Yangtze River Delta*, Huang Zongzhi tries to build a new model of rural economic operation beyond the Chayanov and Smith Doctrine. But it can be seen that in many parts of the book, it is deeply influenced by Chayanov's theory.

opportunity cost of choosing agriculture to industry (this opportunity cost includes the production and transaction costs of each of the two categories of products); and third, the existing specialized production of skills and knowledge endowment. These factors together determine the efficiency of by-business and the comparative advantages of the two forms of by-business.

The rural areas of Zhejiang, especially Wenzhou, developed a more common family division of labor from the beginning, which was because the region had the above three conditions. From the perspective of the market demand of industrial products, after the reform and opening-up, with the improvement of income level of urban and rural residents, the expanding demand for household consumer goods became the important reason for the family by-business. The psychology of consumer compensation, which had long been the cause of consumer repression, began to play a role in the market. Urban workers increased their household disposable income by a relatively large margin in a short period of two years, resulting in a rapid increase in household disposable income. The consumption compensation psychology and the ability to pay constructed a rapidly expanding market for consumer goods in urban areas. Demand for leather shoes, high-end fabrics, leather clothing, and other commodities reached an inexplicable high level in the early 1980s. For rural areas where the system of contracted responsibility linking remuneration to output had been implemented, as a result of successive bumper harvests in grain and the increase in grain purchase prices by the state, household monetary income had increased by a large margin, purchasing power had risen, and the market for consumer goods had expanded. The huge expansion of the consumer goods market in urban and rural areas, which was a very favorable situation, kept the market in a structure that was short of supply for a long time. This kind of market structure played an immeasurable role in the rural households industry. On the one hand, it provided a powerful external cause for industrial expansion and upgrading of rural households; on the other hand, it significantly reduced the transaction costs borne by farmers during the clearing process of the industrial product market.

All of these significantly consolidated the comparative advantages of the family division of labor, enabled the newly recovered household industrial production to change smoothly from the collaborative by-business to the division of labor by-business, and further evolved to the family workshop. This, of course, was the demand factor for the shift from the rural household industry to specialization.

On the supply side, knowledge endowment on commodity production and management skills played an irreplaceable role in this period. As we all know, the regional culture under the influence of Confucian tradition mostly divided people into two classes according to the labor type, advocating that those headworkers govern people. A headworker should be a gentleman who only used his mouth and did not do anything. Business was regarded as a "cunning, failing morality", and industry was an insignificant skill. In short, industry and commerce were disregarded when compared with scholars and peasants. Wenzhou, on the fringes of the mainstream culture, did not have such a strong sense of hierarchy and discrimination against industry and commerce. On the contrary, it formed a strong tradition of doing business and working. Here, the concept and mode of doing business have been handed down from generation to generation. Farmers can create markets as soon as they meet the right opportunities. Moreover, the production of household sideline has been relatively developed, and skilled craftsmen are everywhere. A large number of handicraft products, such as pottery, lacquer, shipbuilding, paper making, carving, embroidery, paper umbrellas, and leather, made in Wenzhou are sold at home and abroad. People are familiar with industrial production and have no psychological barriers. When the time comes, they can quickly transform into a new generation of household industrial owners. This is rare in areas like Wenzhou with such a high degree of industrial and commercial human capital intensity. The existence of special industrial and commercial human capital stock helps explain why in the middle of the 1980s, when the national consumer market rebounded, Wenzhou's products were able to move rapidly to the whole country, and the supply elasticity of consumer goods was higher than that of other regions. The historical stage into which Wenzhou's rural industry entered and completed the primitive accumulation of capital is closely related to this kind of human capital endowment. Most of the first generation of homeworkers were farmers with some kind of handicraft or business experience. Such a fact is often overlooked, and today we need to reevaluate their historical function.[4] The first choice of products in

---

[4] Professor Huang Zongzhi was puzzled by such a phenomenon when he studied the rural development in North China and the south of the Yangtze River: That is, areas such as the Yangtze River Delta, where agricultural productivity is very high and farmers' by-business is more common, once had a very high rate of commercialization, but in recent times there has been no evolution of developed rural industry. His explanation is that farmers in these regions are not choosing to produce goods for the profit above the subsistence level, but when the population density is too high, they have to do it in order to survive. In this case, the by-business of farmers cannot go to the development track of benign interaction of marketization and industrialization. It is of great significance to compare the reasons of different household management directions in rural areas before liberation and after liberation, especially after the reform and opening-up to the outside world. The population density did not decrease, but increased sharply after liberation. In the period of collectivization, by-business of peasant households was accepted into the formal political system. Individual and private workers had to send out letters of introduction from communes and brigades to work outside the country, and submit one year's income to the brigade in exchange for converted work points. So it could no longer be said to be a kind of individual labor. As for centralized enterprises, they were organized by the brigade. Huang Zongzhi believes that the land system and the level of rent borne by farmers are the main reasons for explaining the fact that the marketization under high-density conditions cannot lead to modernization. For this explanation, it seems necessary to analyze the farmers' burden level (Huang, Z. *Small Peasant Family and Social Development in Yangtze River Delta*. Beijing: Zhonghua Book Bureau, 2000).

Wenzhou's rural industry is small commodities required by urban and rural residents or production units that the industrial sector of the city will not produce.

To be exact, it is recycled products, such as recycled cloth, recycled plastic, reclaimed glue, and recycled wool. The operator first collected old materials from the city and the countryside and reprocessed them, and then made daily necessities such as woven bags, plastic shoes, and recycled cloth. The industry in Yishan town in Pingyang county developed from the production of recycled handwoven cloth, recycled acrylic shirts, and children's shirts, and then gradually made the transition to the production of high processing products such as carpets, lace, and jacquard. Another kind of rural industry mainly supplemented the urban industrial production, namely, the hardware, small appliances, small accessories, small buttons, and so on required for daily life of the urban and rural residents that the large industry could not produce or refused to produce. The raw materials needed for the production of these products were also mostly leftover scraps or substandard goods left over from the urban industry. Yueqing's low-voltage electrical appliances, Yongjia's valves, and Ruian's auto parts belong to this class. For recycling or supplementary production, the funds and venues needed were limited for the convenience of one household. The farmers could rely on the domestic labor force and the housing for the production and processing activities. If there was no problem with the sale, the market could guarantee that the family industry could gradually transform from the collaborative by-business to the division of labor by-business.

Different forms of family by-businesses were the starting point of the historical process of Wenzhou's rural industrialization and the premise of the reform of the form and system of rural industrial organization. At the beginning of the reform and opening-up, the number of rural farmers in Wenzhou who entered into by-business was very large, with some engaged in sideline business, and some others engaged in business. The form of by-business was convenient for farmers to make full use of all kinds of labor force and time among family members. For example, about a third of the farmers in Yishan town in Cangnan county had textile machines and looms, and have long had a tradition of handwoven spinning. In accordance with the market demand for all kinds of clothing and plastic woven products, while being engaged in agricultural production, they set up a family processing point. According to statistics, before 1986, 23,302 households of 25,863 households in the district entered the textile processing business, accounting for 90% of the total number of households. By-business farmers had 33,000 sets of flowering machines, spinning machines, weaving machines, and products including recycled cotton cloth, recycled knitted clothing, patchwork clothing, lace trademarks, recycled acrylic blanket, rabbit wool knitwear, and the plastic woven bags. In 1986, the total output value reached 1,600 million yuan. According to incomplete statistics, in 1985, in only one region of Wenzhou, the income of by-business peasant households was 490.85 million yuan. This number increased to 638.14 million yuan in 1986, with an increase of up to 30.01%. Among them, the increase rate of urban areas in Wenzhou was 54.68%, and in Yongjia county, 72% (Zhang & Li, 1990: 45). The household by-business income became an important source of income for the farmers. For example, in 1986, the industrial production value of the farmers in Wenzhou City accounted for 29.05% of the total agricultural output (Zhang & Li, 1990: 45).

If the home-based rural industry was unstable and at a low level, then the family workshop was the basic organization form of the rural industry. The family workshop was the natural development of family division of labor. In the form of the family workshop, industrial production became the main industry of the family, and the income of farmers from the family industry accounted for a higher proportion of the total income. Most farmers only worked in the cultivation and harvest season. Some farmers transferred the land privately to others to manage or hired others to run it. Family members spent most of their time and energy on industrial production. Unlike family workshops, the family workshop labor was still dominated by family labor or discontinuous hiring of a small number of helpers. The technical means and labor tools used were still mainly manual tools. The main products were labor-intensive daily commodities, such as a variety of clothing, toys, and construction materials of small quantities with low technology and capital content. At that time, for example, the production of elastic belts and shoelaces in the town of Tangxia in Ruian was very simple. Housewives and elderly people could take care of the machines while doing housework.

When it came to the form of family workshops, the rural industry became the dominant industry of the rural economy relatively firmly. Unlike by-business of family workshops, the production capital and technical content of family workshops increased. Some non-traditional production processes and production equipment were adopted, and some family workshops even had some advanced equipment. At this stage, the family industry began to employ domestic workers more often, and the role of the workers was no longer like the apprenticeship in the workshop, but became that of a more obvious wage laborer. In the family workshop, the residence and the processing places had been separated, and there was a strict division of labor between each link of production and the process. Production was organized entirely according to market demand. This kind of family workshop took a variety of forms such as family enterprises, joint household enterprises, employee management enterprises, and stock enterprises. Li (2000a) conducted a survey of 31 household employees, including 10 proprietorships, 20 partnerships, and 1 joint-stock enterprise. These companies employed a total of 1,560 workers, with an average of 50 employees per enterprise. The largest number of employees in enterprises was 110.

These three forms developed very quickly in areas with early rural industrialization such as Wenzhou. In 1982, Wenzhou's family industry began to take shape. In 1984, the number of farmers reached over 80,000 and increased to 110,000 in 1986. The number of people employed was 300,000, and the output value of the rural industry accounted for 50%, which was several times higher than that in the initial stage of 1982 (Li, 2000a).

The three forms of family industry in the early stage of rural industrial development had the time of succession, developing from by-business to family workshops. This change in the organizational form reflected the deepening of industrialization. To a certain extent, the industrialization model developed by the family industry is similar to that of European classical industrialization.

(2) Analysis of the advantages of the family industrial system

The reason why the family labor-based industry was revitalized and naturally evolved into a modern industrial enterprise should have its own special conditions. Why the family industry, the ancient form of industrial production organization, can take on great vitality is worthy of deep consideration. Especially when we observe the reality that cannot be ignored that most of the micro production units in Wenzhou industry are still household enterprises, the importance of the problem becomes even more obvious. During the whole process of economic transformation, although we can often see from newspapers and other media that such family enterprises have rid themselves of the barriers of the family system and have fit into a modern enterprise system, many people will get the illusion that private enterprises are already changing their systems, but if we look closely at the statistical yearbook, we will find that the household industry that truly completes the transition to the modern enterprise system accounts for a very small proportion of all industrial enterprises. Joint-stock cooperative enterprises, joint ventures, private enterprises, or de facto family enterprises are no more than expanded family enterprises. The extended family or the proposed family business is widespread and completely entrenched in the economy, and has certainly not been paid enough attention to the economic literature so far.[5] We believe that the seed of rural industrial innovation was embedded in various forms of family industrial enterprises, which also set up the space for institutional innovation.

The institutional advantages of the family industrial organization are rooted in the effective reduction of the coordination cost based on the interpersonal relationship based on blood ties, and internalization of interests is realized. It should be said that the existence of the family-owned industrial production and operation mode is not an unreasonable phenomenon. What needs to be studied is why farmers tend to choose the family industrial enterprise system. Assume that there are two producers, A and B. A and B produce the same products, use the same production technology and other factors, but one of them hires their family members and the other hires members from other families. Thus, is the productivity of the two households the same? In the framework of traditional neoclassical economics, there can be no difference in the output between the two.

The reality is much more complex. We believe that the existence of family industrial enterprises can be considered from the following factors.

First, we need to consider the technical nature of the product. It is a product that can be continuously produced with a high degree of standardization, or a product that is less standardized and thus difficult to produce on a large scale. The former has the obvious increasing trend of scale return, while the latter is the product of decreasing scale return.

---

[5] The Chayanov School is an important exception in this respect. Through the firsthand materials obtained through investigation of the Russian countryside, Chayanov proved the rationality of the existence of small-scale peasant economy by using the principles of Austrian school economics. Although this does not directly prove the stability and rationality of the existence of household industry, its analysis of the problem of by-business is instructive.

The family industry is suited to the latter and not to the former. Second, we need to consider whether the products can be sold evenly through standardized market networks or can only be sold in unstable markets in which a single order does not guarantee long-term continuous production. Third, we should consider whether the mechanization of the production process can effectively reduce the supervision cost. If it's a streamlined production, it is a production activity in which laborers are highly subordinate to machinery and require little coordination of interpersonal conflicts, so it does not cost too much to monitor the cost of production. In other words, it can encourage endogenous production through piecework wages, and this production can be externalized to non-family enterprises. On the contrary, if the artificial degree of production is high, labor-intensive nature is highlighted, and labor process measurement supervision is difficult, it needs a production process with more supervision cost and it is more suitable for family enterprises to organize. Fourth, we need to consider the family preference or risk aversion psychology. From the chooser himself, if in the midst of interpersonal relationship, when the chooser doesn't have sufficient knowledge and skills to cooperate with a person other than the family, or is sensitive to the risk perception of cooperation with outsiders, he will tend to choose the production organization form of family business. On the contrary, if there is no psychological discomfort in cooperation with outsiders, the psychological cost of interpersonal communication is lower, or the risk expectation is more optimistic, then such people will choose the non-family cooperation mode. Finally, the higher the legalization of a society, the more favorable it is for inter-family cooperation; the lower the legal level, the more people tend to cooperate within the family. Therefore, farmers' evaluation of the family industrial production organization depends on the technical characteristics, market conditions, personal preference, and political and legal environment of the industries they enter into.

Most of the reasons for Wenzhou people choosing the form of family industrial organization after the reform and opening-up are among the several aspects analyzed above.

Primarily, it is the industry entered into. As mentioned earlier, before the reform and opening-up, there were all kinds of household industries in the coastal areas of China. At that time, the household industry was mainly for the farmers' daily consumption, not for the market production, or only to exchange a small amount of money to subsidize the household.

This type of household industry was not as closely related to the market as it is today. Even if the product was not sold, it would not have a substantial impact on people's daily life. Naturally, the smooth sale of products would not immediately lead to the expansion of production. In short, the supply flexibility of this kind of household industry was relatively low, and the scale of production was limited to their own basic living needs. It was a case of small production of so-called "men tilling the farm and women weaving". Such small primitive home industries entered into fields such as spinning and weaving or making household utensils. The daily necessities' production had many varieties, and it was difficult to organize large-scale standardized production. In other words, the increasing trend of scale income of large-scale standardized production was not significantly higher than that of the household industry. Therefore, when other conditions were the same, the choice of the production industry would automatically be locked in the organization of the production system and the mode. The industry into which the household industry entered at the beginning determined to a large extent the advantages of the family as a production unit. For example, for the production of leather shoes, the more numerous the styles and varieties, the more efficient the market. But for production organizations, it was difficult to be uniform. The processing equipment of different styles of leather shoes was different in terms of specifications and performance, and it was unlikely to be produced through the standard streamlined operation model, which was commonly used in large production plants such as refrigerator and washing machine factories. Therefore, in the production of leather shoes, family enterprises had a comparative advantage.

The characteristics of this industry and the institutional conditions at that time formed specific market characteristics. Although after the reform and opening-up, the consumption compensation psychology in urban and rural areas led to a great expansion of the demand for consumer goods, the transmission mechanism of this expansion to rural industry was seriously distorted. The reform of the state-owned or collective (cooperative) commercial system obviously lagged behind that of the rural industries, the commercial sector of the public sector controlled the distribution network and purchasing channels of commodities, and the development of non-public commerce was still relatively fragile. Rural industries had to find consumers or suppliers of raw materials directly by themselves to sell their products. Therefore, the sales channel or network was an extremely important economic resource, and market-oriented production in most cases was directly consumer-oriented production. For the commercial enterprises in the system, it was often necessary to take the informal means to infiltrate the rural industry, such as taking the form of high rebates or other additional benefits. This method not only had the political risk of destroying the socialist economic order but also had the financial risk of the enterprise. How was one to do things skillfully? It requires the supply and marketing personnel to have the corresponding qualities, and the people with these qualities are harder to fnd than the simple processing and production personnel. Therefore, for an enterprise, the importance of supply and marketing personnel must be above the production personnel. Supply and marketing personnel and production personnel must be integrated into a unified community to manage and coordinate to ensure the continuity of production activities. In this case, the cohesion of the household or family is extremely advantageous in resolving the possible contradiction between production and marketing.

In fact, many of the collective industrial enterprises at that time ended up being unable to form a good institutional arrangement to coordinate the relationship between the supply and marketing personnel and the production staff. This inability couldn't stop the enterprise's production function from being abandoned by the sales function which caused enterprise collapse. This is rarely the case in family industrial organizations. In the family industry, if you need to open up your own sales channels, it is inevitable that the main family members of the parents will be running the supply and marketing themselves, or the male adult offspring of the extended family will go out for marketing. It is necessary for the members of the family industrial enterprises to control the mode of distribution channel, which is necessary for the stability and efficiency of family production. The sense of responsibility and life experience of the family helped keep the balance between supply and production. Later, with the expansion of production scale, the early industrial production of these families also began to have functional differentiation: Some families gave up the production function altogether and concentrated on the marketing of goods; some families withdrew from the business of traditional commodities and focused on developing new products.

Another factor related to the production of products is the monitoring cost. The production of clothing, toys, and other daily necessities is not highly specialized. As a labor-intensive product, the value of the product depends greatly on the quality of labor. Therefore, to make a profit through such production activities, there must be better control of quantity or quality. Whether the time wage or the piecework wage is implemented, supervision and inspection procedures are indispensable. But the cost of monitoring and testing depends on the strength of the producer's opportunistic tendencies. The stronger the opportunism, the greater the cost to the business owners of monitoring and testing activities; the weaker the opportunism, the lower the cost. In general, the tendency of opportunism among members of the community or family is the weakest. Some uncontrollable production activities are produced within the family, which can save monitoring and testing costs. This is also the natural selection of farmers who do not have the choice of advanced monitoring technology or testing equipment conditions. When the scale of production of the original product continues to expand and the number of workers who need to be employed is far greater than the number of members of the family, the supervisory function of the family business will be replaced by the function of specialized management. At the same time, the enterprise will be able to introduce more advanced monitoring technology to complete the work. At this time, family enterprises will gradually turn to the so-called modern enterprise system. Therefore, it can be said that the kinship among family members plays an important role in reducing the harm caused by opportunism to industrial activities in the primary stage of industrialization. This is also an important reason for farmers to choose family enterprises.

Finally, we have to analyze the concerns of sociologists from an economic perspective.[6] Are Chinese farmers especially inclined to family ownership? Is there a particular distrust toward other families? If this kind of psychology exists, does it have the specific value orientation in the system choice? The concept of the family is of equal importance to the East and the West. The difference is that Western family members pay more attention to emotional ties, while Chinese families intertwine emotional ties and interests.[7] In the field of economic activities, the

------

[6] Sociological studies of relationships and trust provide another way to understand the problem. What is valuable is the sociologist's measurement and investigation of the subject of relationship and trust. Although the results of these surveys are different, they all show one thing in common: the difference between family members' mutual trust and that of outsiders is very significant. In Chinese society, this difference is greater than that in other non-Chinese societies (see Peng, 2000).

[7] Professor Fei Xiaotong' s sociological analysis has provided great insight into the family tendency of Chinese people in his *Native China*. In China, the importance of consanguineous families is incomparable to any other civilization. In a comparative study of the family views of the Han nationality and the Daiwa ethnic group, sociologists found that the former is more concerned about the directness of the kinship between the family members, while the latter is more concerned about the legitimacy or rationality of the family members' role connection. Some have concluded that countries such as Japan have been successful in expanding their corporate systems because of the idea of a fictitious family.

West tends to separate families from businesses, but people in China tend to separate their own family from other families. Chinese people have a strong tendency to internalize the family. Whether it is feelings or interests, family is an irreplaceable carrier. Even if a man goes out to make a living, his income, except for the minimum necessary expenses, will be handed over to the family for unified arrangements; that is a phenomenon that we cannot see in Western societies. The difference between individualism and familism has the significance of institutional evolution. In other words, in China, people will only accept a new institutional arrangement on the premise of strengthening and maintaining the economic and emotional functions of the family. In Western societies like the United States, an institutional arrangement for the benefit of individuals will be more easily accepted, even if it has an impact on the family. This kind of accumulated cultural value orientation is especially obvious in the choice of enterprise system arrangement. The Chinese naturally tend to accept an enterprise system that ensures family functions. This is also the reason why farmers would not hesitate to choose the production organization form of family when they can freely choose the organizational form of non-agricultural industries under the background of the household contract responsibility system, when the "meat grinder" of the big industry did not completely break the farmers' traditional consciousness at the beginning of the reform and opening-up.[8]

We cannot ignore the influence of the natural psychological tendency of a nation on the evolution of the system. The family tendency of

---

[8] We have to admit that the communist economic system, especially the collective labor, broke the bonds of blood families for a long time. However, the concept of family is still not fundamentally destroyed. After the reform and opening-up, household and family concepts are rapidly recovering, and there has been a persistent popularity of restoring the family tree in all parts of the world. The restoration of the concept of kinship among the members of the family, especially the restoration of the concept of family itself, cannot be ignored for the choice of economic organization and the influence of evolution path.

Chinese farmers makes cross-family cooperation more difficult and alert to the opportunistic tendency of other family members. Moreover, if every family does so, the trend of opportunism will be formed, and the internalization of the family is more intense. This is the natural result of repeated non-cooperative games between families.[9]

To sum up, the choice of the family enterprise is due to the industry characteristic that the increase in the scale of production is not obvious, even the trend of diminishing returns of scale is obvious, i.e., unstable market connection, high supervision and detection cost in the production and operation activities, the family internalization psychology of Chinese farmers, and other factors.

4.2 The key to the growth of private enterprises: Family operation

The rise of family industrial enterprises has profound structural, institutional, and cultural reasons. When the family business is growing

---

[9] The trend of internalization of rural families in China is different in different regions. In China, family internalization is combined with a self-sufficient mode of production. Especially in the agricultural cultural circle, the close combination of household, family, and land resources has a more obvious risk aversion characteristic. The family is a cell with complete social functions at the grassroots level, and there is no economic division of labor between them. But in coastal areas, especially in fishing areas, the division of labour, cooperation, and mutual assistance between families is more evident, perhaps because it is the only way to resist the trials of the unpredictable, moody seas. Fishermen, at least not risk-averse, work together to cope with the harsh natural environment. The division of roles on fishing boats will also contribute to the division of labour in daily life. So we can observe a more interesting phenomenon in the Wenzhou and Taizhou coastal areas. The villagers there find it easy to develop the division of work between families. Even when market demand expands further to make the internalization of large enterprises more effective, farmers are still willing to participate in the division of production within the community with family units.

and the constraints of the system and the mainstream ideology are not loose, the form of the family business will be adjusted. After the reform and opening-up, a large number of family industries emerged in Wenzhou, the predecessor of which was the "underground family processing factory". There was no political legitimacy for these processing plants, and it was difficult for them to obtain recognition from superior administrative departments and policies, and even within the region, they had to be cautious. This kind of family business which grew up in the harsh political environment had the legitimacy of open management, but the practical restriction was very obvious. The existence of such constraints makes it impossible for a family workshop to appear as an enterprise entirely independently. Therefore there is strong industrial family internalization motivation, while on the other hand, there is strong anti-family pressure. This pressure has led the family industry to choose a very special form of existence, which is the affiliated operation.

The so-called affiliated operation is a mode of operation for conducting business by families or individuals who did not have independent production and management status. These families or individuals formed an association, which is affiliated with a public enterprise (or government), with legal person qualification so as to conduct business activities. Both parties are required to clarify their rights and obligations through contracts. According to the nature of this relationship, affiliated operation can be divided into the close type and the loose type. The so-called loose-type affiliated operation means that the affiliated enterprise provides a service of "three lendings" to the individuals or families, namely, lending letter of introduction, contract, and bank account but with limited right to use official seal, contract, letter of introduction, and unified invoice with collection of related taxes. Apart from that, no other services are provided and, of course, no financial disputes or liability of the affiliate is entertained. In accordance with a certain proportion of the turnover or the time of their affiliation, the affiliate pays some "management fee" to the affiliated. This kind of affiliation is also called "virtual affiliation". The so-called close type of affiliated operation means that the affiliated enterprise not only provides the services of "three lendings" and "four representations" (for issuing unified invoices, setting up accounts and keeping accounts, collecting state taxes, and paying collective retention) to its affiliate but also provides it with information for production and operation, technical services, even equipment, and raw materials. In addition, all households are subject to unified resource dispatch, unified planning for the establishment of public utilities, unified product inspection, unified administrative leadership, and economic management, and assistance will be offered in resolving economic disputes, and playing a strong role in fund dispatch and external contact economic business. This kind of affiliated operation account management is very similar to the group company mode.

The above two kinds of affiliated enterprises take different paths when they evolve into more advanced enterprise systems in the future. However, whether close or loose, they have common elements listed as follows: First, the affiliated enterprises are public enterprises, some of which are subordinate to government departments with institutional legitimacy and the protection of political power. The affiliates are the family business owners. Second, the basic way of services of the affiliated enterprise is "three lendings" and "four representations", which is not dispensable for all affiliation operations. That is to say, the nature of affiliation is purchase of identity. Although sometimes there are some more considerate services, for farmers to become independent enterprises in the future, seeking the change of identity is more important than capital, technology, and information services. Thus, "three lendings" and "four representations" are the key and core content to the affiliation mode and the rest is derivative service.

It is undeniable that farmers adopted this mode as a rational choice under the constraints of specific politics, culture, and business for a long time and is a very important link in the development of Wenzhou's private enterprises.

The so-called political constraint is the exclusion and discrimination of the family industry which is purely private economy in the system and policy.

Ever since the reform and opening-up, there has been no denying that, over a long period of time, there still has been institutional and policy discrimination on the issue of ownership, and the production and operation of domestic enterprises have been limited in many ways. At this time, the central government has begun to adopt supportive and encouraging policies for township industries. As an important part of socialist collective economy, township collective economy is endowed with political legitimacy and legality. It is an important standard to measure the work performance of leading cadres at all levels whether the township enterprises are active or not and whether the measures taken are effective or not. In 1984, the Central Committee of the Communist Party of China and the State Council forwarded the report of the then Ministry of Agriculture, Animal Husbandry and Fisheries titled On the Establishment of a New Situation of Commune and Brigade Run Enterprise, agreed to change the commune- and brigade-run enterprises to township enterprises, and pointed out that township enterprises were important pillars of agricultural production and an important way for farmers to reach common prosperity. This undoubtedly caused the township enterprises and other rural collective industrial enterprises to be fully affirmed in the nature, function, and status. In the same year, the State Council issued the reports titled Provisions on Sale in Agricultural and Sideline Products by Cooperative Business Organizations and Individuals and the Provisions on Rural Individual Industry and Commerce. These two documents regulated the problems related to the production and operation of individual industry and commerce that appeared in the vast rural areas at that time. In commercial terms, agricultural and sideline products that allowed individual commercial sale were limited to three types of agricultural and sideline products and those that were permitted to go on the market beyond state monopoly and purchase by state quotas. Transporting for sale of agricultural and sideline products was not restricted by administrative divisions or by road routes. For individual industry and commerce, the state allowed them to adopt a flexible and diverse business approach, with one or two helpers and no more than five apprentices. Individual industry and commerce could purchase goods and raw materials from other places with their business licenses or temporary business licenses, adopt a shop name, engrave stamps, open an account, apply for loans, and join the self-employed workers' association of the county (city). At the same time, the management of individual industry and commerce was centralized on the industrial and commercial administration. These regulations played a definite role in promoting the development of rural household enterprises at that time. But because the awareness of the whole society had not fundamentally changed, and farmers had doubts and wait-and-see attitudes toward the stability and true intentions of national policies, as well as the differences between these policy provisions and the drafting style of the relevant documents on the promotion of the development of township enterprises, people tended to have a negative judgment about individual business. In short, although the national policy on the rural individual economy had been loosened in terms of provisions, the actual policy climate and the actions of the lower executive levels did not matched. It was still difficult for the rural household industry to obtain the same rights as township enterprises in production and management. Individual businesses, for example, were often restricted from applying for loans, and if they wanted to scale up production, explicit limits on the number of employees constrained them. This showed that the household industry could not get the same services as formal enterprises. In other words, there was a clear contradiction between the newly developed family industry and government policies and corresponding management requirements.

Especially in areas like Wenzhou, the enthusiasm of farmers to develop industry and commerce was extremely high, with the emergence of 100,000 households of family industrialists. In the face of such a large group of farmers operating in non-agricultural industries, the authorities should have registered them, set up accounts for them, taxed them, drawn collective accumulation, and collected management fees. At that time, there was not enough administrative power to undertake these tasks. Moreover, officials and clerks at grassroots level were still bearing the wait-and-see attitude toward the fate of this economic form, nor could they proactively provide related services. In this case, in order to have a more stable and equitable development environment, the household industry should have sought other forms of operation. It was a natural choice for a rational economic man to make use of the state's emphasis on township collective enterprises and to engage with township collective enterprises. Before the reform and opening-up, the household industry and commerce in Wenzhou had been seeking "political asylum" through affiliated operation. There were precedents to choose the mode of the affiliated operation.

The mode of affiliated operation was a cooperative game mode of township enterprises and family industry caused by government control. The result was a win-win situation both in the short term and in the local area. Although part of collective industrial enterprises had legal status, access to government services priority, and a series of management tools recognized by society, with incentives not endogenous and difficulty in really making a difference in the production and management, many enterprises had only a name. The operators of these enterprises had discovered the possibility of profiting from the form of affiliated operation. They found new growth points in negotiations with peasant households. The relationship between the rights and obligations of the two parties was as follows: Enterprises had to provide services such as letter of introduction, contract letter, and bank account for the affiliate; affiliate operators had to pay management fees to the affiliated enterprises according to a certain proportion of turnover or sales. The legal person enterprise collected a considerable amount of management fees, and the household industrial operator also obtained the magic weapon to break through the system restriction and the "amulet" of legal management through affiliation. In Wenzhou, which had the largest affiliation businesses, affiliation itself was even regarded as a project that could be operated. Some new township enterprises, industrial and trade companies, and supply and marketing companies had to use their own favorable conditions to develop affiliation "business". There were even some dummy companies, which specialized in hanging customers and taking management fees as their main business. The combination of the affiliate and the affiliated enterprise based on benefit formed a new type of industrial organization in the process of rural industrial evolution. A corporate enterprise that takes on multiple affiliates at the same time is similar to a tiny group, a professional market owner that sells a number of stalls, or a foreign trade company that owns many processing companies that do not have the right of conducting foreign trade.

They survived by selling systems and franchises.[10] Such a situation did not gradually disappear until the political restrictions on the household industry were largely canceled. Today, affiliated operation can only be found in a very small number of areas.

The family industry takes the form of affiliation, for which the cultural factors cannot be ignored. For a long time, the value judgment of Chinese society on "public" and "private" was very biased toward the public. Public things are of good quality, and public services are trustworthy; in short, all public things are reliable. The publicity of the superiority of public ownership and the derogation of the private economy after the founding of the People's Republic of China gave people an impression that was difficult to eliminate in the short term: The private sector of the economy is fake and unreliable. At the beginning of the reform and opening-up, because of the chaos of competition order, some individual and private enterprises had quality problems in their products, which even led to serious accidents

---

[10] If we go back to Europe before the industrial revolution, and see how some guilds sold franchises to preserve from imminent demise, we will see how similar the development of history is.

that posed a risk to the safety of consumers' lives and property, and solidified the prejudice to the whole folk economy. In this context, it was much harder to sell the same products in the name of the private enterprise than in the name of the collective enterprise. Because the public ownership enterprises were always subordinate to a certain level of government, their behavior had political guarantee, and there would be no big deviation. For consumers, purchasing products from collective enterprises not only gave them a psychological sense of security but also helped them find a unit of repair or claim as compared to buying products from individual private enterprises in case of product quality problems. There was also a deeper reason for consumers voting against the private sector. Not only was there a lack of a sense of political nobility but there were also those who believed that the purchase of privately produced products helped some people get rich first, which was an intangible loss of interest to oneself.[11] Tolerance of the rich was considered a crime against the poor. Wealth, whether it came from honest labor or extortion, had an inexplicable sense of guilt.

This kind of culture was very disadvantageous to the family industry that fought alone. It made it difficult for individual private enterprises to mobilize resources from the government or from other people as they encountered many obstacles. If this issue was not

---

[11] Professor Eastlin of Yale University put forward a theory of relative welfare, which is used to explain that how individuals feel about welfare depends not only on an increase in absolute self-interest but also on the comparison of the interest of others with the extent of change in their own interests. If there is an increase in income for both A and B, will the happiness of both increase? It depends on which of the two increases in income is greater. If the income of A is increased by 10%, and B's only increases by 5%, then for B, the welfare level is not increased but decreased. It can be seen that envy of wealth was the common cultural characteristic of Eastern and Western societies. But Westerners gradually changed their prejudices against wealth and began to rationally evaluate wealth; in China, which was just at the beginning of the reform and opening-up, the prejudice of most people against wealth and the rich was relatively firm.

resolved, it was hard for the family industry to make a big difference. Affiliation was the best way to exploit people's psychology of worshiping the public and fearing the private and to open up the market. With the protection of the nature of public ownership, selling products was much smoother. Families were willing to pay certain benefits to corporate enterprises. It could be imagined that this kind of family model had a positive effect on the development of the rural family industry in the atmosphere at that time.

The form of affiliation saved a great deal of money for a family workshop. It could be entrusted to the corporate unified management in the financial operation, daily supervision, economic dispute resolution, and other aspects. In this way, farmers devoted to professional management could focus on developing markets and organizing production. This was an effective way to exchange the relative advantage of operation with the relative advantage of management. At that time, most of the operators of Wenzhou household industry only had an education level below junior high school. It is doubtful that people of such a level of literacy were competent for financial and other specialised management, or for dealing with corporate and customer correspondence. But they had their own way of dealing with the problem, which was suitable for business rather than suitable for management; that is, they had a comparative advantage in management. On the contrary, the cadres of the commune- and brigade-run enterprises were mostly well educated and had a basic knowledge of standardized management. Their identity and knowledge structures were not suitable for making a living wandering from place to place. They are willing to work on a regular basis and communicate within and outside the system, so they had a comparative advantage in management. This cooperation between the peasants and the cadres was also in accordance with the principle of efficiency. Cadres' responsibilities to the community also made them more concerned about whether the financial operation of the affiliated enterprises could complete collective retention. In village-run enterprises, village cadres and managers of village-run enterprises were willing to adjust and control the management fees handed in by families through affiliation by considering village-level interests, which was also a win-win game.

Finally, the affiliated operation had the flexibility to adjust the scope of business at any time. Farmers could have more than one affiliated enterprise, or they could change the affiliated enterprise at any time, and the choice of enterprises was close to full competition. In order to compete for affiliates, corporate enterprises launched fierce competition. To win the competition, these companies offered a wide range of services, and charges were also becoming more reasonable. Operators had a considerable degree of freedom in choosing affiliation. It was very important to ensure the flexibility of business scope and means for the operators who were in a situation of sharp change of business environment. This was also a response to the enterprise registration system and rigid management at that time. Without institutional arrangements, some interventions and controls would interfere with or even interrupt the process of rural industrialization.This was by no means alarmist. In the process of rural industrialization in other regions, it could be said that due to the lack of such a buffer mechanism, the industry of peasant households could not easily adapt because of the changing policies. This was the case in other provinces, even in Hangzhou–Jiaxing–Huzhou and Jinhua–Quzhou–Lishui of Zhejiang Province, where the government function had traditionally been weak. One of the important factors in the development of the family industry was that there was no such protection as affiliated enterprises and there was no cushion against policy effects.[12]

Because of the brand-new property right division mode and enterprise management mode of affiliated operation, Wenzhou's folk

---

[12] If the family cannot be cultivated as the leading force in rural industrialization, rural industrialization cannot get on the right track. This situation is also decided by China's national conditions. All regions that have taken detours in the process of industrialization tend to forget this.

economy had a very important development space. At this stage, there were no formal statistics on how many family businesses in Wenzhou took the way of affiliated operation. But the sample survey showed that affiliated operation was important. Jinxiang town in Cangnan county is one of the regions in Wenzhou where affiliated operation was carried out earlier. In 1985, the number of affiliated enterprises in the town had grown to 61, accounting for more than half of the total number of enterprises in the town; the total industrial output value of the affiliated enterprises reached 37.5 million yuan, accounting for 91.5% of the total industrial output value of the whole town. Because of the "golden channel" of affiliated operation, the "four small commodities" (aluminum seal, plastic coupon, plastic certificate, and polyester trademark) produced by the peasant family factory in Jinxiang town rapidly occupied the national market, forming a pattern of "half of the business belonging to Jinxiang". In 1987, this town became Wenzhou City's first market town with an output value exceeding 100 million yuan. According to investigation, among the 16 key enterprises and support enterprises in Jinxiang, most of their predecessors were affiliated to the collective enterprises. Through this form of affiliation, they expanded their business, accumulated funds, and gained experience in production management and marketing. Then, they set up their own organization and sought development at the right time.

Therefore, when we evaluate the historical merits and demerits of affiliated operation, we must pay full attention to its "institutional redemption" function. Through the collapse of the affiliates at that time, some of the constraints against the development of private economy were learned. Other services provided by the affiliated enterprises were not unimportant, but for the rapid growth of the private industrial economic organizations in the future, the "institutional redemption" function was particularly critical. It made private enterprises escape from the query of "capitalism" or "socialism", and develop relatively smoothly under the environment of changeable political orientation. If measured by the standards of institutional redemption, even the much-condemned "virtual affiliation" form had obvious positive effects[13] because it also effectively helped farmers resolve some government regulations that were not conducive to the development of the private industry. When reviewing the development of Wenzhou's private enterprises, it is impossible not to say that affiliation was a key institutional arrangement.

4.3 Cooperation among families: Partnership or joint venture

The shareholding cooperative system is considered to be the third great innovation of Chinese farmers after the household contract responsibility system and township enterprises. Some primary forms or unstable forms of joint-stock cooperative enterprises existed in the rural areas before and after the reform and opening-up. The actual use of the term "joint-stock partnership" was after the mid-1980s.

Ma Jinlong believes that with regard to the idea of joint-stock partnership, Wenzhou was the first to document it and enjoy the "patent". On November 7, 1987, the People's Government of Wenzhou issued W.Z. (1987) No. 79 of the Interim Provisions on Certain Issues of Rural Joint Stock Enterprises. The idea of "joint-stock partnership" in this document was apparently derived from the "joint-stock cooperation" in No.1 Document of the CPC Central Committee in 1985. Until at least 1987, Wenzhou's official document still referred to "joint-stock cooperation" rather than "joint-stock partnership". Since the end of 1987, the term "joint-stock partnership" has been circulated instead of "joint-stock cooperation". Whether Wenzhou or Taizhou is the birthplace of the stock cooperation system is debatable, and Ma Jinlong's opinion is only one part of it. Li Dingfu believes that joint-stock enterprises had begun to show signs as early as the 1980s in Cangnan, Rui'an, Pingyang, Yueqing, Ouhai, and other places.Yueqing City formally registered joint-stock enterprises in 1983. On

---

[13] We think that "virtual affiliation" has a more positive effect on the future system evolution, which reduces the cost that farmers must pay to get rid of the control of production and operation by the community government.

March 8, 1984, the *South Zhejiang Daily* headlines reported that the Ruian Huamin Commune relied on farmers to invest in the stock and that Fengquan Beverage Factory, a private enterprise on the verge of collapse, was saved. In October 1985, for Cangnan County Bridge Pier (South) Brewery, 81 farmers in the town, each with a share of 5000 yuan and a total capital of 405 thousand yuan, formally established a joint-stock cooperative enterprise. Wu Zuzhong, director of the factory, officially became chairman and general manager, thus announcing the birth of the first joint-stock cooperative enterprise in China. It was believed that the traditional rural Taizhou partnership business and "hard stock" practice popular in the 1970s, especially the latter, was the embryonic form of the stock cooperation system. In June 1982, the Wenling County Industrial and Commercial Bureau first broke through the forbidden zone in registration by issuing business license of "joint household enterprise" to 4 enterprises such as Mu Yu handicraft factory; in 1984, Wenling County Industrial and Commercial Bureau officially confirmed four joint enterprises as joint-stock cooperative enterprises in the business registration, and characterized it as a collective (cooperative operation); in October 1986, Huangyan County Party Committee issued document No. 69 *Several Policy Opinions on Joint Stock Enterprises*. According to research, this was the first policy document of the local party committee and the government on the joint venture. Wenzhou and Taizhou were fighting with words over the invention of the joint-stock system, with each thinking they were the inventors of the new enterprise system. Guangdong and Shandong were later involved in the dispute over invention rights, which was later dismissed. Although today it is difficult to determine which region was the first to implement the joint-stock system, one thing is certain. During about 1983–1986, in some economically active areas in Zhejiang, Guangdong, and Shandong, the share cooperation system or an enterprise system similar to the stock cooperation system was innovated. It can be seen that the innovation of a new system was a response to the common demands of some economic development.

In Wenzhou, the rise and evolution of the joint-stock system has gone through three stages. The first stage was about 1980–1986, a stage which could be called the infancy stage of joint-stock cooperation. At this stage, Wenzhou's family industry was booming; on this basis, a variety of associated enterprises, such as joint household enterprises, joint ventures, partnerships, and joint-stock enterprises, emerged through the ties of funds, talents, technology, etc. These enterprises aimed to break through the limitations of the family industry by developing family cooperation. The second stage was about 1987–1992. This is the stage where the joint-stock cooperative enterprise was formally established and regulated, supported, and promoted by the government.

At that stage, Wenzhou Municipal Party Committee and Municipal Government issued W.Z. [1987] No. 79 Provisional Provisions on Some Problems of Rural Joint Stock Enterprises, W.Z. [1988] No. 46 Notice on Some Issues Concerning Private Enterprises and Joint Stock Enterprises, W.Z. [1989] No. 35 Notice on Standardization of Joint Stock Enterprises, S.W. [1990] No. 5 CPC Wenzhou Municipal Committee endorsed the five departments including commission for structural reforms with a series of special documents like Notice on the Report on the Standardization of Some Policies and Provisions of the Joint-Stock Cooperative Enterprise, which stipulated the significance, nature, characteristics, ownership, distribution policy, and preferential policy of the joint-stock cooperative enterprise completely. In particular on December 31, 1992, Wenzhou Municipal Party Committee and Municipal Government issued Provisions on Vigorously Developing Joint Stock Enterprises which provided preferential policies and measures of many aspects for joint-stock cooperative enterprises. In this way, not only were the various original forms of economic cooperation gradually standardized as stock cooperation but the leading position of Wenzhou's joint-stock cooperative enterprises in township enterprises was also consolidated. The third stage was about 1993. At this stage, the joint-stock cooperative enterprise system had been used as a model for the restructuring of the urban collective ownership enterprises and extended to other industries outside the industry. Among these three stages, the most important was the second stage, because at this stage, the government gave affirmation to the action of the system innovation of the stock cooperation system.

Just as the form of affiliated operation cannot be studied without the premise of family economic organization, the research on the nature of stock cooperative enterprises should not ignore the premise of family enterprises. There have been quite a lot of documents on the research of joint-stock cooperative enterprises in China, and there are countless positive comments on the nature and status of joint-stock cooperative enterprises. However, the research on the direction of evolution is relatively lacking, among which the research on the relationship between the stock cooperation system and the household or family is even weaker.

The stock cooperative enterprise is the economic organization form of joint venture and labor. However, joint-stock enterprises in Wenzhou focus more on stock instead of cooperation. In fact, they're disguised as private enterprises. According to observation, the enterprise organization in the Wenzhou stock cooperative system is a factor market first, and then a kind of extended family enterprise. The rise of the joint-stock system, on the one hand, is the natural response to the lagging development of the factor market. On the other hand, it is also a promotion and expansion of the family industrial organization under the constraints of affiliated operation. At the same time, we must also see the anti-system discrimination function of the stock cooperation system. As the family industry moves forward in the form of affiliated operation, contradictions are also accumulating.

4.3.1 The limitation and credit crisis of the affiliated enterprises

The main manifestation of these contradictions is the credit crisis caused by the opportunism management tendency of the two parties. From the point of view of affiliates, the negative externality of management decision exists objectively. The negative externality means that the actual unit of production and management, that is, the home workshop, can have the behavior of harming the reputation of the collective enterprise and obtaining the benefit therefrom, but it does not have to bear the consequences. For example, when the shoes made by the affiliates had quality problems, they didn't need to take responsibility in theory, because the legal person in charge was not him but the company that had been affiliated. Such a responsibility definition mechanism forms a strong motive for counterfeiting and forgery. This can be said to be the cause for the system of a large number of fake commodities in Wenzhou. In fact, the relationship between affiliates and affiliated enterprises in essence has been transformed into a situation where the affiliates obtain the right to arbitrary acts in the name of the enterprises by paying a management fee to the collective enterprises or other public ownership enterprises. A family enterprise that buys this right may seek to make and sell the surplus of counterfeit and inferior goods. As a rational economic person, the manager of the family enterprise always has a strong motive to maximize the positive effect of credit resources of collective enterprises, which can be done by any means. At the same time, in general, several family businesses are affiliated to a collective enterprise, so that every family business will try to predatorily use collective credit resources as much as possible. As a result, the "tragedy of the commons" occurs as described in the classic economic story.

So why would public enterprises allow the predatory use of their credit resources by household industries without stopping them? This is due to the ambiguity of the relationship between the ownership of property and the individual. The collective enterprise is generally carried out by the township government or the village, but it is entrusted to other people to manage it. There are several levels of principal-agent contracts: the contract between the family enterprise and the collective enterprise on the "three lendings" and "four representations", and the contract between the enterprise and the township village. Apart from the certainty and reality of the family enterprise, there are incentive distortions in the other two levels of contract. The legal representative of the collective enterprise is in a contradictory decision-making condition. On the one hand, the more the affiliates, the more the net income. The scale of earnings is obviously increasing. Therefore, from the perspective of income, he will have a big incentive to develop the affiliates. On the other hand, it is completely impossible for these people to carry out comprehensive supervision. A contract that charges a household fee for a fixed turnover makes the interests of the affiliate and the collective enterprise largely consistent at least in the short term. As for the long-term benefits, the expectations of both township leaders and legal representatives are uncertain. The power of distribution of future income is not subject to its own control. This situation will urge the corporate enterprise and its representatives or leaders to seize the immediate income as much as possible, thus causing significant characteristics of short-term behavior.

At that time, the products of collective enterprises had no brand, there was no brand protection, resources were owned by all, and no one would ask to protect the credit resources of corporate enterprises. In the absence of definite subject and motive force to protect the credit resources of the corporation, the "tragedy of the commons" was inevitable. In the end, the domestic market began to resist the products of Wenzhou, and some regions even banned them from entering the local market.[14] This led to an increasingly narrow market for Wenzhou goods. Wenzhou people generally found it difficult to do business. The speed of the turnover of the enterprise slowed down and eventually led to the decline of the income of the corporate enterprise, and the affiliation income moved from a virtuous circle to a vicious circle. In particular, the virtual affiliated enterprise's business reputation became discredited, forming a reverse elimination, and honest family enterprises for fear of the bad reputation of the association withdrew from the company. Their customer base also began to shrink.

Another reason for the crisis was that the government had strengthened the supervision and control over the form of affiliation. The fake and shoddy problems caused by the excessive expansion of the

---

[14] Many stores in places such as Shanghai even declared that they refused Wenzhou goods or that they had no Wenzhou goods to prove their goodwill.

business form of affiliated operation damaged not only the reputation of the enterprise itself, but also the economy of the whole Wenzhou region. The result was that some of the more decent businesses were considering moving their companies out of Wenzhou or moving their operations elsewhere. If this trend had intensified, it would have affected Wenzhou's economic volume and financial returns, and even the commodity reputation of Zhejiang Province as a whole would have been affected, and the market space of Zhejiang products would have been squeezed. The government could not ignore this. Since the mid-1980s, local governments in Wenzhou began to clean up their affiliates, strengthening the supervision and control of the affiliated enterprises. The operating freedom of enterprises was restricted, and the advantages began to reduce gradually.[15]

---

[15] Kong Jingyuan conducted initial analysis over the affiliated operation problems in the article Analysis of Share Cooperation Economy and Its System. He pointed out that although affiliated operation found a way to connect the state, the market, and the scattered individual businesses, it solved the problem of family management in legal form and promoted the development of rural commodity economy. But there were many externalities. In fact, it was difficult for the affiliated township enterprises to supervise the business activities of the operators, to stop the manufacture and sale of fake and inferior products, and to damage the reputation of the legal person enterprises. Some corporate enterprises that accepted affiliates either took unfair means of competition and harmed the interests of the country or imposed harsh claims on affiliates. The minuscule nature of family business transactions resulted in a sharp increase in transaction costs due to the expansion of the size and scope of the market. The inherent "economy" brought about by the high efficiency of household enterprises was offset by the external "uneconomy" of the increase in transaction costs. The increasingly fierce market competition and the contradiction of limited family personal capital hindered the formation of scale economy and the improvement of technical level. Therefore, institutional innovation was urgently needed to reduce externalities, save transaction costs, and promote economic growth (see *Case Study on Institutional Change in China*, vol. 1, p. 230, Shanghai people's Publishing House, 1996).

4.3.2 The substitution of the joint-stock cooperative system for the capital market

We always think that the joint-stock cooperative system is a natural response to the lack of development of the capital market in rural areas. As mentioned earlier, family enterprises not only got a lot of convenience and benefits from affiliation but were also constrained by the mode of operation. In order to extricate from the credit crisis, they needed to seek the survival space again. The enterprises implicated by the affiliation and the enterprises made bigger in the form of the affiliation had strong motivation to seek other development ways. Both were eager to get rid of the market realization problems caused by the poor reputation of affiliated operation and the external interference that was still inevitable in the form of affiliation. Establishing a registered private enterprise was naturally an important way. However, the proportion of sole proprietorship enterprises was not too big at that time because the funds of single households could not meet the requirements of all the funds needed for production and operation. In 1992, there were only 1,232 private enterprises in Wenzhou, and only 5.1% of the number of joint-stock companies. Even with sufficient funds, it was necessary for the family enterprise to choose the sole proprietorship operation, and to consider the existing restrictions of the policy and institutional environment. Family businesses needed to explore new forms of ownership again, as they encountered discrimination in applying for loans, expanding business scopes, and enjoying government services.

It was a good choice to build a new business entity based on partnership or joint-stock. According to Ma (1993), the organization form of share cooperation enterprise was in line with the economic orientation in the decisions by both the government and enterprises, and conformed to the political orientation which was difficult to avoid in the aspect of the government and enterprise decision-making. Indeed, under the dual requirements of developing the economy and insisting on the status of the public ownership as the main body at that time, one may never find a better form of enterprise than the joint-stock cooperative system (Ma, 1993). If we look back at the fact that the construction of China's capital market was seriously lagging behind the need for rural industrialization, it should not be surprising that farmers made the choice of joint-stock. The organized financial sector of the city adopted a policy of capital blockade for rural enterprises, and the rural financial sector only supported the capital demand of the collective enterprises. Pure private enterprises did not have access to capital from the formal financial system. There were only two ways for private enterprises to finance their expansion: One was to resort to private financial markets, such as a variety of "associations" and underground banks; the other was joint-stock. The former had huge political and economic risks. The cost of the private enterprises was also very high. In this way, partnership between family businesses and so-called joint ventures was a logical choice. Therefore, according to our basic judgment, the economic aim for the emergence of the joint-stock cooperative system was to realize the internalization of capital market. Due to the participation of multiple families, joint-stock cooperative enterprises not only enhanced their financial strength but also had the nature of public ownership as they absorbed more partners. Therefore, it was easy to get the identification of grassroots government departments, it was convenient to handle things, and the transaction cost was lower than that of the sole proprietorship enterprise.

4.3.3 The substitution of the joint-stock cooperative system to the human capital market

The growth of joint-stock cooperative enterprise or joint venture is not only the result of the underdeveloped external capital market but also the result of the underdeveloped human capital market. A more important function of this enterprise may be the accumulation of human resources.

The human capital endowment of each family is different. Some families are particularly good at business, but they are not good at organizing industrial activities, and some are the opposite;

some families have extensive and close ties with government departments[16], while some do not have such political resources, but may be very good at organizing raw materials or opening-up foreign markets. The specialization of human resources means the need for cooperation between one another. Cooperation can take the form of market transactions, such as employment of specific types of labour by people with capital, or corporation (integration), such as the acquisition of a company or the establishment of a strategic partnership between enterprises. Exactly what form to choose depends on a number of factors.

According to Williamson (1988), the degree of asset specialization, transaction frequency, and uncertainty are three important factors that must be considered in the study of inter-firm cooperative relationship. The growth of Wenzhou joint-stock cooperative enterprises can be explained by this. The organizational form of joint-stock cooperative enterprises has two situations: prior division of labor and ex post division of labor. The so-called prior division of labor is the division of labor between complementary resources (including human resources). In such cases, households involved in partnerships or association already have different types of dedicated human capital, and there are complementary needs or, through association, greater efficiency of such dedicated human capital. The so-called ex post division of labor is that the enterprises participating in the joint

---

[16] One of the most popular topics in recent social economics (economic sociology) is social capital. The network of social relations or some bonds of interpersonal communication often play the function of capital, which is ignored in traditional economics. The investment model of social capital should be different from the human capital in the general sense, which is difficult to explain in the framework of human capital. So it is necessary to put forward the concept of social capital alone. The connection between farmers and members of government agencies is a kind of social capital, which has a significant positive effect on both the production of the organization and the development of the market.

venture have no obvious professional human capital advantage in advance, and the cooperation between them should be completed through the division of labor assigned by the contract. Cooperation with universal capital will most likely develop into this kind of ex post division of labor.

For example, a joint venture between two farmers producing the same product will have a contract to assign tasks with professional characteristics: who is responsible for financing, who is responsible for marketing, who is responsible for day-to-day management of the employer, and so on. Prior to a partnership or joint venture, participants must complete all their assignments independently.

The joint-stock cooperative enterprise is actually a kind of organization form with different special human capital allocations. No matter whether this kind of professional human capital already existed in advance or gradually formed in the ex post division of labor, this was a kind of human capital allocation market. In Wenzhou, a big difference from Taizhou's joint-stock cooperative system was that Taizhou embodied the dual nature of the joint venture and labor cooperation, while Wenzhou focused mainly on the joint venture and management. This was essentially a partnership.[17] A de facto partnership was known as a joint-stock system. This was related to the political background that at that time, the relevant documents of the government made the joint-stock cooperative system a public ownership enterprise, while the legal status and political status of the partnership were completely uncertain. Of course, some companies were not ruled out from the purely incentive point of view to split the equity to ordinary employees, but they slowly

---

[17] This difference was actually also related to the source of joint-venture formation. In Taizhou, joint-stock cooperative enterprises mainly came from the reform of collective enterprises in urban and rural areas, while in Wenzhou they mainly came from the negotiations between private enterprises and joint household enterprises. The former could avoid the government's deep interference in the decision-making

found that the effect was not obvious. Some private business owners also made their enterprises look more like collective enterprises to split some of the shares to workers. But the government gradually became more relaxed about private and individual companies, which changed the decision of shareholding by employees. As a result, the joint-stock companies that survived in Wenzhou were getting closer to the partnership. Thus, the next stage of the natural development of the sole proprietorship enterprise was the partnership rather than the joint venture. At this point, Wenzhou's situation was basically the same as those of the regions in most developed countries. Moreover, the "joint-stock system" enterprise with joint venture and management had a strong adaptability in Wenzhou.

At present, there is lack of empirical investigation data on the relationship between the choice of prior division of labor and ex post division of labor and the family. We speculate that the more distant the familial relationship, the more likely it is to develop a joint venture or partnership with prior division of labor between two farmers, while those with blood, kinship, or geographical relationships tend to develop an ex post division of labor. Our reasoning is as follows:

The parties with special resources have strong motive of cooperation in interest, opportunism tends to cost higher, the advantage of cooperation is obvious, and it is easy to overcome the limitations of various transaction costs and form a long-term contractual relationship.

---

process of the shareholding structure of the restructured enterprise, while the latter mainly depended on the enterprise's own economic considerations. Therefore, Taizhou's joint-venture enterprises had more government decisions, while Wenzhou had more self-organizing characteristics. Through formal institutional provision by the government to guide the result of the restructuring, it would consider more the basic requirements of distributing shares to the laborer. On the contrary, the equity allocation decided by enterprises was more based on the cost of economic operation.

However, farmers with universal capital lack the motivation of economic association among themselves, and the cooperation between them is mainly due to the existence of super-economic ties. For example, cooperation between two brothers is often not because cooperation is necessary to profit from a complementary point of view, but because a family community principle makes cooperation a natural thing. But in order to make the cooperation meet the economic efficiency requirements, the division of labor between one another should be functional. Division of labor is completed after the event, and this kind of division of labor often stabilizes after many occurrences of trial and error. But no matter what kind of division of labor, one of the main characteristics is being horizontal and at the same level. The brother does not take the other as the object of exploitation or the subordinate of the management, and they basically belong to the horizontal division of labor. This indicates that once there is an opportunity, the kinship between family members will be impacted by the benefits brought by the division of labor, which will gradually disintegrate.[18] Cooperative businesses that span more than two nuclear families on the basis of blood ties can be split into independent businesses. In contrast, the prior division of labour based on the specificity of human capital is much more stable.[19] The reason for this form of stability is that without the influence of blood or kinship, it is easier to reach a purely economic benefit-oriented contract, and it is easy to revise the contract at any time according to changing situations. The partnership between friends is somewhere between a partnership between family members and a

---

[18] In Wenzhou, it is not uncommon for brothers to break up in the entrepreneurial phase of business and business growth. Some close buddies also perform the tragicomedy of helping each other and turning into enemies at various stages of business growth. "Chint" and "Delixi" have become industry rivals. In 1984, their bosses joined forces to set up Yueqing Jiujing Switch Factory and were like brothers.

[19] To consider the mechanism of expanding the cooperative relationship between Wenzhou people's families, the question to ask in "Why is it not a worker who

pure market partnership. Cooperation between different nuclear families in a big family requires an authority beyond them to coordinate. The father or mother of brothers or uncles often plays the role of coordinator. Whether the enterprise is divided or not depends on the ability of the elder as coordinator or the cultural characteristics that determine the intergenerational mode of action. For example, in a society where filial piety is above all else, a person, as long as he is an elder, can coordinate effectively between the people of younger generations, regardless of his actual ability. Therefore, the stability of the family firm ultimately depends on the cultural system on which the coordinator relies. The development of family enterprises depends on the balance between the culture-oriented behavioral motivation and the economy-oriented behavioral motivation.

If the balance is broken, there will be fission in the enterprise, and family businesses will be split into nuclear family businesses. Therefore, we speculate that in regions where the marketization process is relatively fast, the frequency of family enterprise fission as the core family enterprise is higher than that in the region where the marketization process is slow. Fission family businesses will then associate with other families with a more pure interest orientation.[20]

---

employs an entrepreneur, but an entrepreneur who employs a worker" by referring to Zhang Weiying and others. In general, the specificity of human capital and the characteristics of its macroscopic distribution will automatically form a kind of economic rational contract relationship in an economic system with the possibility of self-evolution. The integration of this kind of contractual relationship is a hierarchical enterprise.

[20] Ke Rongzhu and Zhong Hongjun have done an excellent case study on the cooperative relationship between family firms. Their findings from the study of Sichuan Hope Group, the largest private enterprise in the Chinese mainland, are quite typical (see Ke, R. & Zhong, H. The modernization of family business and its driving force//Expert Group on China's Reform and Development Report. *The Experience of Growth: A Case Study of China's Excellent Large Enterprises.* Shanghai: Shanghai Far East Press, 1999).

4.3.4 Expanded family businesses

The joint-stock cooperative system enterprise is the extension of the family business, which in fact is still a kind of family business, because the basis of the establishment and distribution of equity is not the capital needs of the labor process itself, nor the labor needs, but the requirements of the change of governance mode caused by the expansion of the enterprise form after the expansion of the family business. According to statistics, in Wenzhou's joint-stock cooperative system of economic forms, the family business accounted for a considerable proportion. In 1993, family-owned joint-stock enterprises accounted for 88.8% of the private and joint-stock cooperative enterprises. In 1994, according to the statistics of the township enterprises bureau of the city, the total capital of the enterprises was 4.124 billion yuan. Among them, the state owned 7.21 million yuan of shares, accounting for 0.17%; rural collective was 70.02 million yuan, accounting for 1.7%; foreign ownership was 54.19 million yuan, accounting for 1.31%; social legal entities 765 million yuan, accounting for 18.54%; and personal ownership was 3.228 billion yuan, accounting for 78.27%. In the joint-stock cooperative enterprises of the township and village levels, the individual shares were 66. 29%, and the legal person shares were 24.96% (Li, 2000a).

On the premise of the family enterprise, due to the small scale of employees, business owners can realize the comprehensive site management, without any need to use the hierarchical internal management model, and even most business owners often participate in productive labor. But the expansion of the market leads to the refinement of the division of labor, the cooperation between the various processes becomes increasingly important, and the production of enterprises shows signs of vertical integration. The management of bureaucracy becomes increasingly necessary. On top of the productive workers, there is a special management level that varies from person to person. When the number of adult members of a nuclear family does not meet the demands of management, it is inevitable that companies seek partners outside the core family. According to the characteristics of Wenzhou people, seeking managers outside the family actually means expanding the chain of cooperation to other households within the clan. The cooperation between brothers and sisters, in-laws and cousins is the first to be brought into the chain of cooperation, then friends, classmates, etc.

The order in which the chain of cooperation is expanded is similar to that of the "differential order pattern" described by Mr. Fei Xiaotong in his book *Earthbound China.*[21]

The national nature of the situation of expanding the cooperation network of capital and labor according to the "differential order pattern" is inevitable in the case of the joint-stock cooperation system. However, Wenzhou's situation is slightly different from other regions. It is difficult to adopt the planar approach to joint-stock cooperation for family economic cooperation in other regions and it is possible for them to adopt the paternalistic mode of sole proprietorship. In Wenzhou, parents and children can often be seen holding shares in an enterprise, in parallel as shareholders. The relationship of rank or affiliation on blood does not evolve into a subordinate relationship in economy. Here, this kind of super-economic relation based on blood is just a kind of entry direction of economic connection on share.[22]

---

[21] Fei Xiaotong believes that the construction of social relations and their interaction were according to "differential order pattern" operation. Traditional Chinese society constructs a system or network of social relations based on the principle of closeness. The network is "self-centered, cast into the water like a stone. The social relations connected with others are not like the molecules in a group standing on a plane, but rather like the ripples of water, pushing out in a circle, pushing farther and thinner" (see Fei, X. *Earthbound China.* Beijing: Peking University Press, 1998).

[22] As a matter of fact, the relationship between the Wenzhou stock cooperation system and family system was very complicated. The range of resources and

The real joint-stock cooperative system should have the characteristics of both the joint-stock system and the cooperative system, which is the economic organization form of joint venture and labor cooperation. In this form of organization there should be no separation of workers and capitalists. In this sense, the joint-stock cooperative system of Wenzhou is different from the complete joint-stock cooperative system, with focus on stock rather than cooperation. As mentioned above, it is first of all an internalized form of capital market. Compared with the capital market, the complementary cooperation between human capitals has been weakened. As for labor, driving services with capital and joint venture and labor situation is even less common, and the ordinary employees within the enterprise cannot hold shares. This type of enterprise is essentially a partnership, registered only to avoid discrimination. Ma Jinlong, a famous Wenzhou economist, once pointed out, "The joint stock cooperative enterprises in China first became the common organizational form of enterprises in Wenzhou and were the first to use the name of joint stock partnership." However, Wenzhou has never defined a joint-stock cooperative enterprise as an organizational form in which the employee holds shares in the company. Instead, enterprises with "more than two" owners would be included under the name of "joint-stock partnership", which was obviously related to the ideological orientation of that time. When Wenzhou first referred to such enterprises as joint-stock cooperative enterprises, there were a certain number of companies with a total shareholding or even an average shareholding. Later, this part of enterprises was basically eliminated, and the rest of the company was only a form of enterprise called shareholding cooperation with a highly concentrated ownership structure.

Judging from the development of tens of thousands of enterprises in Wenzhou over the past decade, the joint-stock cooperative enterprises

---

elements has been expanded to a very wide extent by Wenzhou people, and the market pricing system could determine the price of the related or non-consanguineous relationship.

in the strict sense of so-called "laborers' labor cooperation and laborers' capital cooperation" have seldom had unsuccessful examples in Wenzhou's industrial and commercial enterprises at that stage (Ma, 1999).

4.3.5 Joint-stock cooperative system: The function of anti-system discrimination

The function of anti-system discrimination of the joint cooperative stock system did not exist in the beginning. In the middle of the 1980s, in China, demutualization was not banned, so those who first adopted this kind of corporate organization took great political risks. The possibility of cooperation in name only could not be ruled out. There have been many repetitions over how to position the political nature of this form. But in the end, both political orientation and economic orientation are beneficial to this new form of enterprise.

Politically, governments at all levels, especially the central government, in a 1985 document called for joint-stock cooperation, which made the Wenzhou municipal party committee and city government more daring.The central government only talked about promoting share-based cooperation, but not the conclusion of share-based cooperation as a new form of public-owned enterprises. Later, public opinion and ideas gradually changed in favor of the political direction of the stock cooperation system, which was indeed a wonderful process of collective choice.

Today, of course, it has a role to play in evading regulation.

As a result of the above characteristics, the joint-stock cooperative enterprise has been a very ideal enterprise system for the areas with strong driving force in the economic development of Wenzhou. Not only did business owners see this but government officials were also interested. On December 31, 1992, the Municipal Party Committee and Municipal Government of Wenzhou promulgated the Decision on the

Development of Joint-Venture Enterprises. The decision put forward a number of policy measures to encourage the development of joint-stock companies as follows: abolition of progressive taxes and a 15% proportional tax; for enterprises with an annual output value of more than 3 million yuan and tax revenue of more than 300,000 yuan, the turnover tax would be reduced and exempted; the first year of tax exemption for new enterprises; in the second and third year, halving of the tax; loans preferential policies; land use to be implemented.[23] Such preferential policies are naturally attractive. The implementation contributed to the rapid expansion of joint-stock cooperative enterprises. As a new type of non-governmental economic organization, the joint-stock cooperative enterprise played an extremely important role in the promotion of rural industrialization due to its special function.

The private enterprises in Wenzhou have developed from the front shop and rear factory type of family production organization to the cooperation between families, which has basically completed the formal transcendence to the family economy. As it develops into the next stage, it still has the trace of family system, but it has opened the door to the formation of the modern enterprise system.

4.4 Introduction of the system of the limited liability company

The joint-stock cooperative system certainly has its own problems. The research of Jin & Ke (1998) shows that the joint-stock cooperative system has a non-standard organizational mechanism of essential elements, which makes available the serious factors hindering cooperation in the joint-stock cooperative enterprise, and the static efficiency of the enterprise is also reduced. The main hindrance factor is the so-called capital combination, also the labor friction

---

[23] *Manual on the Practice of Shareholding Cooperative System* (internal issue), November 1993 by Zhejiang Provincial Reform Commission.

caused by the labor combination, which affects the effectiveness of the incentive compatible mechanism between the labor and the management. Jin & Ke (1998) have analyzed the restrictions on the transfer of provident funds, collective shares, and equity in joint-stock cooperative enterprises as well as the problems brought to cooperation under this system by the aspects of integrated labor and management. The conclusion of this analysis is basically applicable to typical joint-stock cooperative enterprises. However, there is still a certain distance between Wenzhou's joint-stock cooperative system and this typical state. For example, the joint-stock cooperative system in Wenzhou is mostly not a joint venture and labor, but a joint-stock of more than two people. It is rare for common workers to own shares, most of which are distributed among relatives and friends. Wenzhou is a mixture of partnership and joint-stock rather than a joint-stock cooperative system. Because of this, the common factors that hinder the cooperation in the typical joint-stock cooperative enterprises do not necessarily play a role in the joint-stock cooperative enterprises in Wenzhou, which has problems that do not exist in the joint-stock cooperative enterprises of other regions.

Partnership has some limitations in financing scale and developing cooperation between exclusive human capitals. It is suitable for enterprises in labor-intensive industries, and mainly for small enterprises with small economies. Once further development of the enterprise requires a greater expansion in capital and manpower, the infinity of economic responsibility and the limitation of the division of labor within the enterprise will bring strict constraints.

Therefore, in the process of the development of the joint-stock cooperative system, some enterprises with rapid development will first encounter the problem of enterprise system innovation. In this case, limited liability companies will be introduced into these private enterprises.

But in Wenzhou, the limited liability company system or the complete joint-stock cooperative company system is not common. Compared with the private enterprise, the number is small; compared with the stock cooperative enterprise, it is even more insignificant. Even compared with Hangzhou, Ningbo, and other regions, the number of Wenzhou's enterprises with characteristics of the modern enterprise system is still relatively small. At the end of 1999, according to the data of statistical yearbooks, the total number of limited liability companies and joint-stock enterprises in Wenzhou accounted for 0.2% of the total number of enterprises, lower than 0.58% of the Hangzhou area and 0.23% of the Ningbo area, but still higher than those of the rest of the regions of Zhejiang Province. This may be due to the fact that Wenzhou's industrial structure and market structure have not yet put forward the requirement of enterprise modernization. On the contrary, it may be that Wenzhou's familism influence is more far reaching than that of other regions. Even in the name of the enterprise that has already implemented the modern enterprise system, the actual property right structure and the governance structure remain great family features.

Ma (1999) observed and studied several enterprises in Wenzhou that had been reformed according to the modern enterprise system, and found that in most cases, the modernization of Wenzhou enterprise system was still in form. Entrepreneurs have complex inner motives for enterprise restructuring. The so-called modern enterprise system in Wenzhou is mostly a formal need, and most enterprises simply pour the old wine of the private enterprise into the new bottle of the joint-stock enterprise. This kind of enterprise is a family-owned enterprise rather than a stockholding enterprise. The main reason why Wenzhou enterprises have strong family characteristics is that most of them belong to the small-commodity industry, and the economies of scale are not obvious. Therefore, the average size of the enterprise itself is small, the management scope is small, and the management hierarchy is not very necessary; then, due to the short period of enterprise development, founders of the enterprises have not yet reached the age of withdrawing from the ranks of operators. Their personal experience, cultural quality, and management level make them competent for the functions of business management. The life cycle of most enterprises has not yet reached the point where leadership transition has to be addressed; in addition, the law on the protection of private property is not complete enough, and entrepreneurs in Wenzhou will not choose the modern corporate system in essence, so as to prevent themselves from being bound into a passive position.

Zhang (2004) also found that Wenzhou's private enterprise corporate transformation was generally not in place. At present, most of the more than 10,000 limited liability companies and dozens of joint-stock limited companies have transformed from joint-stock cooperative enterprises and even family enterprises and private enterprises. There is no substantial change in the operation mechanism, management mode, or governance structure of these restructured enterprises, but the name of the enterprise is changed to a limited liability company or a joint-stock limited company. It is, to some extent, related to government orientation. After the promulgation of the Company Law in 1994, the Wenzhou Municipal Bureau of Industry and Commerce, in the course of enterprise registration, generally required registration of enterprises to be "joint-stock cooperation" for those whose registered capital was less than 500,000 yuan, while for enterprises with a registered capital of more than 500,000 yuan, it was up to the owner of the business to decide. Business owners generally required registration as a joint-stock limited company. Even at present, Wenzhou is still largely chosen by the enterprise in terms of registration of limited liability companies and joint-stock enterprises. Many business owners don't really know the difference between a corporation and a joint-stock company, but they have changed their names, because the government has encouraged them. As a result, Wenzhou has produced a large number of corporate enterprises in a short period of time. This was not actually confined to

Wenzhou. Corporate enterprises are easily accepted by some owners. Moreover, owners can become general managers and chairman of the company. People can be more dignified in an outlandish way. The image of doing business outside has also changed.

As of 1999, the overall pattern of the evolution of Wenzhou's private enterprises became clear. The total number of industrial enterprises reached 127,980, ranking first among all the regions in Zhejiang Province. Among the prefecture-level cities, a number of enterprises from Wenzhou ranked among the top. In this huge enterprise team, the proportions of state-owned enterprises and collective enterprises were 0.13% and 4%, respectively. The number of joint-stock enterprises reached 16,022, accounting for 12.51%. There were 8,315 private enterprises, accounting for 6.50%. The total number of so-called "other enterprises" was 99,095, accounting for 77.43% of all enterprises. This type of enterprise could not be incorporated into the established enterprise system type, and practically it was still a family enterprise or an individual enterprise.[24] From the above data, it can be seen that after

---

[24] There was no uniform figure on how many enterprises there were in Wenzhou and how many different types of enterprises each accounted for. According to Ma Jinlong's estimate, by 1998, Wenzhou had more than 200,000 individual industrial and commercial households and private enterprises, more than 28,000 joint-stock cooperative enterprises, 16,000 limited liability companies, and dozens of joint-stock limited companies. See Ma, J. Reflections on the system innovation and management innovation of Wenzhou's private enterprises. *Economic Research Data*, 1999(12). This figure was nearly double the number in Zhejiang Statistical Yearbook. According to Zhang Renshou, Wenzhou has more than 200,000 individual enterprises, over 4,000 private enterprises, more than 30,000 joint-stock enterprises, more than 10,000 limited liability companies, and more than 100 enterprise groups established on the basis of private and joint-stock cooperative enterprises. See Zhang, R. Private enterprises need to innovate again. *China's Rural Economy*, 2000(8). We can't say for sure which is more accurate, with the difference of the three analyses being so big. But whatever the absolute number is, the relative difference is small, so it can still be explained.

more than 20 years of reform and development in Wenzhou, private enterprises, including joint-stock cooperative enterprises, individual enterprises, and joint-stock enterprises, account for up to 95% of the total number of enterprises. Among them, the number of joint-stock cooperative enterprises is the highest in the province. The pattern of private enterprises as the dominant position is finally established.

4.5 Problems in development of private enterprises in Wenzhou

Before Coase, Western economics did not have a theory about the growth of the enterprise. An enterprise is simply assumed to be a combination of a set of production functions. Schumpeter pioneered a theory explaining the relationship between entrepreneurial innovation and enterprise growth, which is not a study of the nature and function of the firm itself. It was not until 1936 when Coase published his "Nature of the Enterprise" that the economics without business theory changed. Since then, theories about the nature and origin of enterprises have emerged endlessly.[25] These should be the original theories of enlightenment. However, it is not appropriate to use these theories to explain the growth of enterprises in Wenzhou. Because these theories are relatively abstract with in-depth research, there are many intermediary factors between them. The growth of Wenzhou enterprises is inseparable from the theory established by Coase *et al.*, but we should also pay attention to the roles of various intermediary factors. For example, in neoclassical economics, enterprises are not only equivalent to abstract production functions but also independent of any realistic institutional environment and cultural conditions. Such a pure form of

---

[25] In addition to the famous argument that "enterprise is a substitute for the market" proposed by Coase, the theories about the origin and evolution of the enterprise also include the view put forward by Archian and Demsez, "Enterprises are for the purpose of supervision of cooperative labor", and Zhang Wuchang's viewpoint that "enterprises are a combination of contracts".

enterprise certainly does not exist in reality. In reality, the enterprise is always the product of multiple factors, so some factors behind the enterprise should be further investigated. From the development of Wenzhou's private enterprises, we find that we need to think further from the following aspects.

4.5.1 Family and business growth

The relationship between the private enterprise in Wenzhou and the family or the household is a topic that lacks research but is very meaningful. The problem has been covered in our description above, but it is still at a very superficial level. The relationship between the family system and the enterprise has aroused deep concern in sociology and historiography in recent years. People's understanding of the advantages and disadvantages of the family enterprise is very different. Some people criticize the family system, holding that it does more harm than good. Some argue that the role of the family business cannot be simply asserted, and it has a considerable positive effect (Chu, 2000). Economics is slow to respond to this.[26] But overall, the family business is more negative than positive. The argument is that family businesses are hampering accumulation and innovation, both of which are the source of modern economic growth. Therefore, it is asserted that the trend of family ownership will seriously affect the healthy growth of China's private economy if not contained and the negative impact on China's entire economic and social development will follow.

---

[26] The exception is research of Chen Ling, Li Xinchun, and others. See Chen, L. Information features, transaction costs and family organizations. *Economic Research*, 1998(7). Li, X. Family system and business organization in China. *Chinese Social Sciences Quarterly*, 1998(3). In addition, a research group on Sino-German cooperation has published a series of case studies on the relationship between rural communities and families and economic activities in China. Wang Xun also conducts a preliminary study on the interaction between family and economic organization in his book *Cultural Tradition and Economic Organization*.

Among the negatives, economists in Beijing seem to have the strongest voices.[27] We also find that the same person's assessment of a family business seems inconsistent. For example, Li Dingfu, on one occasion, enthusiastically eulogized the family enterprise, believing that it created the miracle of Wenzhou's economy. "The family business is not a poem, not a painting, but it has created a picturesque artistic conception and miracle in Wenzhou" (Li, 2000c). He analyzed in detail the advantages of family enterprises, such as the primitive accumulation of capital, hard work, harmony, unity of goals, unification of the two powers, and so on. On another occasion, however, Li Dingfu severely criticized familism. "Practice has proved that family-style management has formed a strong closeness, produced exclusiveness, and artificially blocked the integration with staff and talented people. At the same time, because of the restriction of kinship and friendship, the enterprise behavior cannot be standardized, and the management relationship is difficult to be straightened out" (Li, 2000c). In fact, one can actually appreciate his true tendencies from these two seemingly contradictory comments.

Li Dingfu's affirmation of Wenzhou's family enterprises was well grounded, and he even applied a philosophical proposition to describe the position of family enterprises in Wenzhou's economy — "Everything that exists is reasonable". His criticism of family management was clearly framed. It was understood that most local economists and officials in Wenzhou were not opposed to the phenomenon of family-owned enterprises, and they were opposed to the fact that the joint-

---

[27] For example, Li Yining, a famous economist, pointed out the limitations of the family management system in five aspects: personal decision-making, hereditary power, appointing persons by favoritism, closed property rights, and vague management objectives. These five limitations are for all family businesses, but this generalized view does not necessarily stand the test. In addition, as early as 1992, accusations were made about the performance of familism in business operations. See Fan, J. Family doctrine in microstructure in China. *Academic Journal*, 1992(1). But this kind of criticism remains a proposition lacking empirical argument.

stock system was indeed a family system. In other words, on the issue of establishing a modern enterprise system, "they sell horse meat as beefsteak ", such as family system management in joint-stock cooperative enterprises.

We feel that the serious differences in the relationship between the family and the firm in the view of China's theorists stem from the fact that the following aspects cannot be analyzed in a differentiated way: The first aspect is the family control of the enterprise, and the second one is the family management. The former is mainly about the ownership of property rights, while the latter is the problem about the governance structure. Family enterprises and family management should not be confused, and not everything related with family should be denied. In fact, there are four kinds of relationships between family enterprises and family management: The first is the family enterprise that implements family management; the second is the family enterprise that implements non-family management; the third is the non-family enterprise that implements family management; and the fourth is the non-family enterprise that implements non-family management. The four kinds are examined separately: In the first case, the management right of a family-owned enterprise is allocated in accordance with the operational mechanism of the family system, which is beyond reproach at all times and all over the world, and this case in fact has proved to be efficient. In the second case, the combination of the family property right structure and the non-family management power allocation mechanism has been adopted by quite a number of large family enterprises today, and the results are generally good, such as the famous Ford Motor Company and Hilton Hotel. In the fourth case, the combination of public companies and open management power allocation mechanism is regarded as the basic characteristic of the modern enterprise system in developed countries, and there should not be too much doubt about this situation. So the whole question is to focus on the third case, the family management of the public company. This is strictly not a family business problem.

The existing research on the relationship between families and enterprises in sociology and economic literature is mostly from the perspective of family enterprises. The study of rationality and efficiency of family enterprises is mainly based on comparative statics. Research on the relationship between family and business growth is generally lacking. From the perspective of the growth mechanism of Wenzhou's private enterprises, there is great tension between the family organization and the economic organization. The family can not only accommodate primary forms of industrial activities such as the handicraft workshop and the manual workhouse but also be compatible with machine production and a more detailed specialization system based on this.

As for the relationship between the family and the business scale, it is not that the family can only be compatible with small-scale production as some scholars have claimed. Once the enterprise becomes bigger, family management and operation are difficult to adapt or even cause a hindrance. In fact, some sizeable, multi-billion dollar companies are still effectively controlled and managed by families. Some companies seem to have adopted the modern enterprise system, but in fact they are "new bottles with old wine", and actual decision-making remains firmly in the hands of family members. Zhang Renshou also pointed out, "About the innovation of Wenzhou's private enterprise system, people tend to break the family system." But it is worth reflecting on the fact that since the implementation of the second entrepreneurship in Wenzhou in 1993, the family characteristics of Wenzhou's private enterprises have not only changed greatly in general but are also particularly obvious in some strong and sizable enterprises. Blood ties and family control are clearly visible in many of Wenzhou's so-called private companies, such as Chint, Delixi, Tianzheng, Xinhua, Wenzhou Pacific, Wenzhou Hi-tech Meter, Wenzhou Heming, Wenzhou Precision Machinery, and Wenzhou Guangyin (Zhang, 2004). Economists in Beijing were once worried about the erosion of the family system due to Chinese companies. If the concern is for the public company's family-based management, there may be some truth, but if it is directed at the family business, we think it is too far away from the nature of the problem. Whether we should curb the development of family-owned enterprises or curb the family management of public companies is a question that needs rethinking. In foreign countries, attitudes toward family businesses may not be as feared as in China.[28]

In addition, the following distinctions need to be made when evaluating family-owned enterprises. The problems of family enterprises should be distinguished from the problems that occur in family enterprises. At present, people who make assertions on the advantages and disadvantages of family enterprises unconsciously regard all problems that occur in family enterprises as the problems of family enterprises. This is in line neither with the logic of the study nor with the facts. For example, some people equate decision-making mistakes in family-owned enterprises with the failure of family-closed decision-making, and everyone knows that decision-making mistakes are unavoidable problems for any enterprise. If all family firms are prone to misjudgement, how to explain the fact that family enterprises have more impressive performance than those of non-family enterprises?

Some people confuse the property right structure of the family enterprise with the internal governance structure of the enterprise, asserting that any family enterprise will have the problem of employment. In fact, the family enterprise is not of the governance

---

[28] Galsik writes on page 3 of the book *Prosperity of Family Business*, "Even the most conservative estimates suggest that between 65% and 80% of the world's companies are owned or operated by families. It is estimated that 40% of the world's top 500 are owned or operated by families. Family businesses account for half of America's GDP and half of its workforce. In Europe, home companies dominate small and medium-sized companies and make up the majority of larger companies in some countries. In Asia, ... Of all the economically developed countries except China, family enterprises dominate. In Latin America, large companies established and controlled by families dominate most industries."

structure; on the contrary, it is of the ownership structure. The family-controlled enterprise does not mean that the family members monopolize the management power. On the contrary, there are too many examples of family enterprises going beyond the boundaries of the family to select specialized managers. There is no basis for asserting that family enterprises are bound to practice cronyism.[29] Family-owned enterprises are carrying out a new round of institutional innovation and management innovation, which is not the result of government compulsion or scholars' teaching, but a natural product of enterprises' own evolution (Ma, 1999). This innovation shows that the family enterprise has the function of self-adjustment.

The research on the relationship between family and enterprise can be carried out from many angles, from the perspectives of the particularity of Chinese culture, the historical evolution of industrialization, economics, etc. The conclusions are naturally different.

At present, there are many analyses of advantages and disadvantages of family-owned enterprises. But for economic research, it is necessary to answer why so many private enterprises choose the ownership structure and management mode of the family system. It can be discussed from the following three perspectives: The first is the accumulation motivation of Chinese people, especially Chinese farmers; the second is the credit status determined by the national character of China and the transaction costs resulting from it; and the third is the special coordination problem arising from Chinese culture. The first angle explains why the expansion of family-owned businesses has a strong momentum; the second angle explains why family-run enterprises are

---

[29] At present, there are few conclusions about the criticism of family-owned enterprises, mostly taken for granted. For example, some famous economists in Beijing discuss the private economy far from the facts of Wenzhou. See Healthy and rapid development of private economy. *Macroeconomic Research*, 2000(6).

efficient. The third angle explains the special type of human capital of family enterprises. Although there has been some discussion on these three aspects, it is obvious that it is not enough, especially the analysis of family enterprises by using the new economic analysis method. Perhaps the growth of private enterprises in Wenzhou just provides a good case.[30]

4.5.2 Market and enterprise growth

Enterprises and markets always grow together. There is no business without market. The market plays an extremely important role in a self-evolving enterprise growth mode. This effect is manifested as the expansion of the market size to the enterprise as a supplier, thus providing market space for the growth of enterprises and also as the order of market competition to promote the growth of enterprises. The analysis of the relationship between the enterprise and the market can also be carried out from two aspects: One is the relationship between commodity market and enterprise growth; the other is the relationship between factor market and enterprise growth.

From the perspective of the commodity market, the synchronism between Wenzhou's market development and enterprise growth is reflected at the three stages of enterprise growth. At the first stage, the main forms of enterprises were family workshops and home-based workhouses. At that stage, most of the market types were the market activities of merchants; that is, the supply and marketing personnel went out to seek the product market. At its peak, Wenzhou had more than 1 million supply and marketing forces active across the country, sending information of product demand from every corner of China and selling products from local companies elsewhere. At the second stage, enterprises began to transform into the joint-stock cooperative system, and the market was dominated by various types

---

[30] In fact, in other areas of Zhejiang, there are many successful family enterprises; Wanxiang Group and Jinyi Group are typical.

of the professional markets, that is, the market activity of the type of tradesman was the main type. During this period (around the mid-1980s), the professional market in Wenzhou was booming. In 1985, Wenzhou had 415 professional markets of varying sizes, including 10 with an annual turnover of more than 80 million yuan. The market turnover of the year was 10,060 million yuan, accounting for 57.28% of the retail sales of social commodities. At the third stage, after some enterprises started to develop into the shareholding system, the relationship between the enterprise and the market underwent some qualitative changes as the scale of enterprises became continuously expanded. The internalized marketing system began to appear and gradually replaced the functions that were previously played by the supply and marketing personnel and the professional market. Private enterprise groups such as Chint, Delixi, Tianzheng, and "BonWay" have internalized marketing functions through mergers and reorganizations, and the companies have established specialty stores and other marketing networks. The relationship between enterprises and suppliers of raw materials and consumers is gradually incorporated into the framework of strategic cooperation. These three stages are not absolute, especially at the third stage, but the path of this evolution should be clear. Today in Wenzhou, there exists a connection between enterprises and the market containing multiple mechanisms, the activities of the supply and marketing personnel, the professional market, and the company's own marketing network. But the function of the professional market is much weaker than it was in the mid-1980s to the mid-1990s. The trading patterns of professional markets are also changing dramatically. If compared with Yiwu's professional market development mode, the network trend of Wenzhou market is more obvious. Does this mean that Wenzhou's market-oriented process is ahead of Yiwu and the academic community has different opinions? From the perspective of the global trend of market economy development, Wenzhou's change seems to be more in tune with this trend.

In terms of the factor market, the relationship between market development and enterprise growth in Wenzhou is much more complicated. In the first place, after the reform and opening-up, the state immediately opened up the private factor market, especially the capital market. Then Wenzhou's enterprises might not have passed a generalized joint-stock system. The previous analysis has also proved that the joint-stock cooperative system is essentially a substitution for the capital market and labor market, which is the product of the growth of the factor market lagging behind the production expansion requirements of the enterprise. So far, Wenzhou's enterprises have been plagued by the lack of development of private capital markets. In order to break through the government regulation of the capital market, Wenzhou's enterprises have tried many times and still have no results. Today, Wenzhou's joint-stock enterprises and private capital markets are closely related to one another, becoming a symbiotic organism that is interlaced with growth. Wenzhou's private companies are small in size. The so-called big companies such as Chint and Delixi are nothing more than a loose conglomeration of small private enterprises. This kind of enterprise is similar to a department store that contracts to operate the booths, not the actual integration of the production organization. The average size of Wenzhou's enterprises is small, mainly due to the poor financing channels. Government-run banks are too selective and too restrictive to lend to private companies to meet the changing needs of their capital. The private financing mechanism is difficult to grow freely by breaking through the government regulation and the result is that the capital that enterprises need to expand cannot get the ideal supply. If the problem is not solved in a timely manner, Wenzhou's enterprises will not be able to get rid of the "light, small, intensive and add" situation in the process of growing up.

There are strict government controls in the element market, especially in the private financial market. However, in the process of the growth of Wenzhou's enterprises, the phenomenon of pan-marketization is still very common. That is to say, the resources that the Wenzhou people can deal with are extremely extensive. Wenzhou's private enterprises are highly tradable in terms of both internal economic resources and external social network resources and political resources. There is basically no problem that can't be solved by trading tracks. This moral identification of trading behavior supports the expansion of market order.[31]

Intuitively, in Wenzhou, economic resources are not simply endowed with property rights by the government. Instead, the market is more like a means of defining property rights. Unlike the government's definition of property rights, the market is approaching the real economic value of a property through repeated transactions. Such a definition is more likely to prevent the distortion of property prices than the top-down mandatory definition of government. The constant definition of the market can make some of the public property boundaries clear in a definition of property rights.

Therefore, the distributive efforts that are often unavoidable in a defined pattern are transformed into productive efforts, and the degree of distortion of corporate behavior is less than that in other places. Because of the government's definition of property rights, some of the value of property rights is often placed in the "public domain",[32] resulting in economic subjects taking the rent-seeking behavior to seek this unallocated income. The property right pricing of the enterprise through the market transaction can basically decompose the valuable property rights that can be recognized and discovered at present. Therefore, the possibility of rent-seeking in such transactions is minimal. It is

---

[31] It may be very meaningful to compare the behavior of enterprises in Wenzhou and South Jiangsu Province in choosing the transaction items.

[32] The definition of property rights through free trade between individuals also creates undefined public domain problems. But this kind of public domain is not dependent on any one subject, and can be obtained by establishing competitive activities on innovation. So private transactions do not generate rent-seeking.

impossible for enterprises to seek the best interests through distributive efforts, and innovation becomes the only way for enterprises to grow. This is an important reason why Wenzhou's enterprise innovation ability is strong and innovative behavior is extremely active.

From the perspective of Wenzhou's private enterprises and market relations, we can arrive at some conclusions that are consistent with economic liberalism. Du Runsheng has stressed that Wenzhou's economic model is a spontaneous order (Du, 2000), which is the most profound understanding of Wenzhou model by domestic scholars. If we look at the relationship between British firms and markets before and after the industrial revolution through Paul Mantoux's works, we will find that history is strikingly similar.

The role of the specialized commodity market in the growth of Wenzhou's private enterprises cannot be ignored, but we should pay more attention to the functions of various markets built around the transaction of factors. However, because the free factor market, especially the free money market, has been underground for a long time, it is difficult to see its true features, which brings considerable difficulties to the research. The current research on this issue is only the tip of the iceberg.[33]

4.5.3 Growth of governments and enterprises

Many people think that one of the basic characteristics of Wenzhou's economic mode is inaction. A simplistic understanding of this argument is dangerous. This book proves that the government's role in the growth of private enterprises is not optional; instead, the government's interference must have a limit. In fact, Wenzhou's local

---

[33] Shi Jinchuan, Zhang Jun, and others have conducted a preliminary study of Wenzhou's private financing. See Zhang Jun's *Informal Financial Sector in Rural China after Reform*: Wenzhou Case and Shi Jinchuan's research on private finance in Taizhou.

government has played a protective and coordinating role in the growth of enterprises. Its role is mainly manifested in the following aspects:

First, resolving the adverse impact of external environmental pressure on the growth of enterprises.

As we all know, concerning whether the nature of Wenzhou model is the "social" or the "capital", there were a lot of fierce debates throughout the country. The most controversial issue was the nature of private enterprises; that was, whether such a high proportion of private enterprises would threaten the socialist economy. The central government also sent investigation teams to Wenzhou, where local leaders were under enormous political pressure. In the face of such political pressure, the attitude of the local party committees and governments was of vital significance to the growth of Wenzhou's enterprises.

It should be said that in the past 20 years, except for a few periods, the main leaders of Wenzhou have been concerned about, supportive of, and even fostering the development of private enterprises. As early as July 22, 1980, the Wenzhou Municipal Administration for Industry and Commerce drafted the Report on the Comprehensive Rectification, Registration and Certification of Individual Industrial and Commercial Households. This report recognized the flexibility, variety, wide distribution, and convenience of individual businesses, which have not only played a complementary role in commodity circulation and services for people's lives but also enabled some people to find jobs and solve life problems. At the same time, it pointed out some problems in the operation process of individual industrial and commercial households, changed the principle of examination and approval of application for registration of individual industrial and commercial enterprises, allowed the registration of some mom-and-pop stores, father-and-son stores, brother stores, and sister stores, allowed a master with technical expertise to bring one or two apprentices, and so on. These measures should have been very loose in China at the time. The Wenzhou revolutionary committee forwarded the document on August 11 of that year and further affirmed the positive role of individual businesses in the forwarding notice and believed, "This city has always had the tradition of individual industrial and commercial operation. If guided correctly, made the best use of, developed appropriately, it will be able to have positive effects." The notice also required the authorities to further emancipate the mind and do a good job. In order to overcome the farmers' doubts about the central policy, the Wenzhou municipal party committee conducted a wide survey of rural professional households and key users in 1982. The "two households" congress of the city was held, and ten specific policies to support the development of "two households" were formulated and redressed as "eight kings". Especially from December 16 to 19, a meeting of specialized rural households and key households was held with more than 1,200 participants in the city. City leaders awarded and commended 171 delegates. Yuan Fanglie, the then newly appointed secretary of the municipal party committee, announced at the meeting that the key households, whether contracting professional households or self-employed ones, were of a socialist nature. The "two households" made their fortunes by diligence, and were fully in line with the party's policies. Their creative work was encouraged and supported by the party and the government, and their legitimate business and legitimate rights and interests were protected by national laws. At the meeting, Secretary Yuan also announced the 10 policy measures adopted by the municipal party committee and the municipal government to support the development of "two households", namely, five permits and five supports.

The five permits were as follows: permit "two households" to contract or not to contract farmland; permit "two households" to either individually or jointly contract undeveloped or collectively undeveloped barren hills, beaches, and water; permit "two households" to have several apprentices and helpers after approval; in addition to grain and timber, other agricultural and sideline products to be free in terms of production and marketing directly after the completion of the national purchase and distribution of purchasing tasks; and permit individual traders and itinerant purchase and sale specialists to carry out long-distance transportation under the national plan's guidance and the unified management of the administrative departments of industry and commerce. The five supports were the development of "two households" in the aspects of the seedlings, feed, and other materials as well as financial and technical guidance, information service, and product promotion. The state would mainly support the settlement of seedlings, processing, storage and transportation facilities and funds of commodities, while establishing irrigation, plant protection, seedling, feed, veterinarian, transportation, processing, technology, information, and other professional services to solve the problems that cannot be solved by "two households" in the production process. The meeting caused a strong reaction.

Since then, Wenzhou Municipal Party Committee and Municipal Government issued the Report on Wenzhou Rural Development Commodity Economy Situation (S.W. [1985] No. 45), Report on the Establishment of the Wenzhou Experimental Area (S.W. [1986] No. 98), The Provisional Regulations on the Management of Affiliate Operation in Wenzhou City (W.Z. [1987] No. 54), and Decision on Encouraging Further Development of Individuals and the Private Sector (S.W. [1992] No. 4) successively. These documents put forward the positive policy measures for individual private economy development. In particular, S.W. [1986] No. 98 document proposed to reform and develop diversified ownership structures to create a harmonious and equal competitive environment for all kinds of enterprises. In this document, it is proposed to develop the individual and private economy, the joint-stock economy, and the private economy, and give a free hand to farmer entrepreneurs and operators. To be specific the following measures were proposed: first, to recognize and affirm their status; second, to allow their employees to operate without the restriction of the number of employees; third, to recognize the legal status of the operators; fourth, to protect the legitimate rights and interests of the private economy, to embody the principle of "who invests, who owns, who benefits", and not to make even adjustments; fifth, to adopt the policy of encouraging long-term investment, and guide individual and private enterprises to invest most of their income in expanding reproduction, and so on. Such a policy is also very progressive today, from which we can see the determination of Wenzhou Municipal Party Committee and Municipal Government to develop non-public enterprises. In 1987, the interim provisions on the management of affiliated operation were issued. It stipulated the form of the new enterprise organization, made clear the rights and obligations of the two parties, and provided the policy basis for the operation. All these policies and government actions played a great role in promoting the development of Wenzhou's private enterprises. There is a big gap between policy efforts of the other regions of Zhejiang and Wenzhou.

As a commentary published in the *People's Daily* on July 8, 1986 pointed out, Wenzhou Municipal Party Committee and Municipal Government adopted the attitude of "respecting the reality instead of the superior and theories" when implementing the policy. The documents prepared by the superiors could be executed in a creative way according to local conditions.

Second, rectifying the economic order.

The consolidation of the trading order was essentially a collective action, often beyond the reach of private enterprises alone. The work called for government intervention. In the 1980s, the inferior low-voltage electrical appliances in Liushi of Yueqing, false advertising in Yongjia, counterfeit trademarks produced and sold in Cangnan, "daily shoe" and "weekly shoe" of Lucheng leather shoes, counterfeit inferior valves in Ouhai, and management and sales of inferior machines in Pingyang were circulated in the whole country, which had serious consequences and bad influence. The low-voltage electrical appliances of Yueqing even caused a series of casualties. For a while, the credibility of Wenzhou goods was in crisis all over the country. Wenzhou goods became a synonym for fake and inferior commodities, resulting in a hit to legitimate businesses and legitimate activities of private enterprises. The negative influences of counterfeiting enterprises could destroy the entire Wenzhou civil economic system. In response, authorities in Wenzhou took action.

As early as September 10, 1983, Wenzhou people's government approved the notice of the municipal administration for industry and commerce, titled Opinions on the Implementation of the Spirit of the Meeting of the State Administration of Industry and Commerce to Investigate and Deal with Counterfeit Trademark Fraud Cases ASAP, taking resolute measures against Cangnan's counterfeit trademarks, Ruian's counterfeit medicine, Yongjia's counterfeit watches, and so on. On June 21, 1990, Wenzhou Municipal Party Committee and Municipal Government issued a report on the fake and inferior low-voltage electrical appliances, titled Opinions on Resolutely Implementing the Notification on Investigating and Dealing with the Production and Sale of Uncertified and Inferior Products in Yueqing county by the General Office of the State Council, while putting forward the slogan of "establishing a city of quality and building up famous brands". In May 1994, Wenzhou Municipal Party Committee and Municipal Government issued the Decision on Strengthening the Management of Product Quality and Improving the Level of Economic Development of Wenzhou and initiated "establishing a city of quality system engineering", stating that it would take 3 years to make the quality of the main products in Wenzhou reach the advanced level in the province, 5 years to reach the domestic advanced level, and 8 years to reach or approach the international level. In October 1994, Wenzhou Municipal Government issued the Implementation Measures of Wenzhou City on Quality Establishment, which was China's first quality municipal local regulation. After more than 5 years of hard work, a wide range of "fake, counterfeit, cheat" disappeared, and the quality of products in Wenzhou increased rapidly. In particular, the original leather shoes and other products began to take the path of branding, some of which were already created; in 1995, the quality sampling rate of industrial products in the city's key assessment reached 90.12%, and the percentage of pass of export products was 98.8%, which exceeded the average level of Zhejiang Province.

Third, improving the joint-stock cooperation system.

The joint-stock cooperative system was supported and regulated by the government at the beginning. From 1987 to 1994, the documents issued by Wenzhou on the development of joint-stock cooperative economy were as follows: November 7, 1987, W.Z. [1987] No. 79 document Wenzhou Municipal Government's Temporary Provisions on Some Problems of Rural Joint Stock Enterprises; Autumn 25, 1988, W.Z. [1988] No. 46 Wenzhou Municipal Government's Notice on Some Issues Concerning Private Enterprises and Joint Stock Enterprises; November 20, 1989. W.Z. [1989] No. 35 document Wenzhou Municipal Government's Notice on Standardization of Joint Stock Enterprises; June 5, 1990, S.W. [1990] No. 5 document, Notice on the Report on the Standardization of Some Policies and Provisions of the Joint Stock Cooperative Enterprise; December 31, 1992, S.W. [1992] No. 7 document Wenzhou Municipal Government's Provisions on Vigorously Developing Joint Stock Enterprises; November 29, 1993, Wenzhou Municipal Government's Pilot Measures of Wenzhou City on the Reorganization of Collective Enterprises in Cities and Towns with Share Cooperation System; and so on. An important policy measure was introduced almost every year. After the 15th National Congress of the Communist Party, on December 10, 1997, Wenzhou Municipal Party Committee and the Municipal Government jointly issued Some Opinions on Further Supporting and Guiding the Development of Share Cooperation Economy. From these documents, it can be seen that the Wenzhou Municipal Party Committee and Wenzhou Municipal Government attached importance to the new economic form of joint-stock cooperation system.

In addition, the local government of Wenzhou made great efforts to stimulate public goods supply to meet the demand for public goods.

To sum up, in all the policy initiatives taken by the local government, the most important points for the growth of Wenzhou's private enterprises were the policy measures to support the rural "two households" at the beginning of the reform and opening-up the policy of affiliated operation in the mid-1980s, and a series of policy measures implemented to support private enterprises for more than 20 years throughout the reform and opening-up process. These policy measures were either ahead of the rest of the country, or more intensified than elsewhere, reflecting the Wenzhou government's determination, courage, and ability to emancipate the mind and actively promote the system innovation since the reform and opening-up. Few in the rest of the country have been able to take such a big step, even in special regions with strong political backing.

Why the local government of Wenzhou had such an attitude toward private enterprises is a problem that needs to be studied deeply. The governments of Wenzhou at all levels basically followed the market rule in dealing with the relationship with enterprises. When choosing to enter or exit, the government does not blindly follow the instructions of the superior or the instruction of the theory, but pays close attention to the reflection of the enterprise.

The government intervenes in whatever business requires the government to do; whatever the enterprise can do well, the government exits. The government does not deal with enterprises in a regulated way, but guides decision by the independent choice of private enterprises. In this sense, the government of Wenzhou was like a political enterprise. It operated in the face of the market and adjusted its decisions according to the changes in social needs. Many of the institutional innovations introduced by the people were supported or protected by the government, which is also related to this market-oriented attitude.[34] Therefore, we can assert that

---

[34] In the analysis of the counterfeit in Wenzhou, we found that the government's cleanup and rectification of low-voltage electrical appliances in Liuzhou greatly

in Wenzhou, the market mechanism not only regulated enterprises but also regulated the government. This market-regulated government was very beneficial to the prosperity of the induced institutional innovation of private enterprises. But whether the market-oriented government was in line with the government's philosophy is worth discussing.

It is interesting to note that the main leaders of Wenzhou's Municipal Party Committee, when came to office, were mostly averse to the economic and political phenomena in Wenzhou, and more or less wanted to curb them. But over time, ideas changed, and the most conservative officials became "liberated". In a sense, officials would be assimilated by Wenzhou's political and economic culture for some time, and would come to the Wenzhou side to deal with the intervention from above.

The relationship between officials and entrepreneurs in Wenzhou was fairly close. Some scholars[35] who have visited Wenzhou have created a worry: Does the union of political power and private property rights form a new community of interests? Will the emergence of such a community worsen the competitive order? We are short of firsthand information and we will not make arbitrary comments. But news from Wenzhou suggests that such fears are by no means unfounded. This community of interests has not only appeared but has also been

---

affected the market structure of the low-voltage appliance industry. As the predecessor of Chint, Yueqing Qiujing Switch Factory that had first obtained the production license of electrical products issued by the state department of mechanical and electrical engineering was able to pass the strict inspection. A lot of the companies that actually had the quality of the product were not so different from these companies but the companies that didn't have the licenses were hit hard by the counterfeit activity and the surviving enterprises were less than 1/5 of the original. This kind of control objectively provided a very favorable development opportunity for the development of private enterprises protected by the government.

[35] He has visited Wenzhou many times. In a long talk with the authors of this book, Zhou paid great attention to and worried about the trend of the collusion between government and businessmen of Wenzhou.

quite common. The higher the positive appraisal of Wenzhou model, the stronger the community. Private entrepreneurs not only seek the possibility of establishing special relationships with government officials through general commercial activities but also actively participate in political and quasi-political "public welfare" activities. Zhou Xinghong's research regarding Wenzhou power and money trading showed that the phenomenon of collusion between government and businessmen was quite serious, specifically the following points:

(1) It was very common for government departments to generate revenue based on their authority. The regulation of scarce resources, especially land, created a huge "rent". In addition, there were a variety of management charges, and the practice of management to money led to a serious phenomenon of arbitrary charges. The city's billing fees reached $3 billion yuan a year, the same as taxes. (2) The rent-setting and the rent-seeking phenomena of civil servants were very common, especially among the land management personnel and tax personnel. (3) There was power participation and power interference competition. Obviously, the result of the government's participation in market resource allocation was to disrupt the competition order, to spread the unfair competition, and finally to eliminate the private enterprises that were honest and legitimate. Because of the high economic value of political power, the political participation of entrepreneurs was extremely inflated. One survey found that Wenzhou's bosses had the best hope for their children. The top priority was not in business, but in government. The political enthusiasm of private entrepreneurs showed that the government in the combination of government and enterprise was still dominant. It was good that market relations regulated government behavior. But because of the government's natural monopoly, it was in a dominant position throughout the negotiations with entrepreneurs. As long as the political power was controlled, the economic benefits would be assured. It was no wonder then that Wenzhou's entrepreneurs had no real government positions, and they had to do everything they could to get into the

legislature, the CPPCC, or the federation of industry and commerce. When it was unlikely for their generation to be officials, they had high hopes for the next generation.

This kind of strong political orientation of Wenzhou market economy was a serious hindrance to the construction of fair competition market order in the Wenzhou area. Many entrepreneurs lost their confidence and had to move their businesses elsewhere. In recent years, the number of the overall external migration of Wenzhou enterprises has risen significantly. In 1988, there were only 93 enterprises that relocated outside Wenzhou, which rose to 135 in 1999 and 73 in the first five months of 2000, breaking through 200 in a whole year. Some large private enterprises such as Delixi, Chint, and Tianzheng have moved their headquarters to Shanghai, Ningbo, Hangzhou, or other places. The phenomenon of emigration of the whole industry in Wenzhou occurred. For example, more than 50 household enterprises in the production of woolen sweater in Changqiao and Baotian of Ruian, zipper companies in Longwan, the standard parts industry in Qiaotou of Yongjia, and the air compressor parts industry of Longwan moved out of Wenzhou. This trend that should be taken seriously. Whether this trend indicates that the development environment of the private enterprises in Wenzhou is going downhill is still to be verified. But continued and regular corporate migration must mean that the regional comparison entrepreneurial environment is deteriorating. This environment is definitely not a hard environment but a soft environment because the hard environment of Wenzhou is much better than before.

There is no reason why entrepreneurs want to stay in Wenzhou when the hard environment is bad, and leave Wenzhou when the hard environment is better.

On the one hand, it is the external migration of enterprises; on the other hand, there are few enterprises introduced. It is difficult for foreign enterprises to gain a foothold in Wenzhou, and the key is that they are not able to adapt to the social and political environment of Wenzhou. The stability and particularity of social network in Wenzhou play an exclusive function. This is starting to converge with the situation in the Pearl River Delta region. In the network of social relations, foreign enterprises are often not allowed to enter, or the cost is too high to be compensated. So Wenzhou's performance in attracting investment is very bad.

The collusion between public power and private property around market mechanism was the first to appear in Wenzhou, which should have aroused great vigilance. The spontaneous role of the free competition market mechanism is by no means unconditional. How the government plays a role in the legal framework of procedural justice is a crucial issue for the development of market economy. Wenzhou's system of inducing system change is the system pattern that achieves the modern market economy or will be locked in the trap of colluding and closing the competition. The key is the effectiveness of the law in administrative power control. As scholars, we'll soon find out.

4.6 Research conclusions and enlightenment

The above survey on the growth of Wenzhou's private enterprises can be summed up as follows:

First, private enterprises are growing in a particular cultural tradition. Even in the era of strict planned economy, Wenzhou's private economy has never been completely curbed, but turned into black market prosperity.

Second, the path of private enterprise growth in Wenzhou embodies a very obvious balance mechanism, that is, the balance between family culture and official political culture, as well as the balance between private internal incentive and dominant public orientation ideology. Whether it is to choose affiliation, the creative form of enterprise organization, or to invent the joint-stock cooperative system, which is an automatic and balanced form of private enterprise organization, it embodies the ability of system innovation of Wenzhou people and the ability to seek balance and maintain tension under all kinds of strict constraints.

Third, affiliated operation and the joint-stock cooperative system are the most important institutional innovations to promote the growth of Wenzhou enterprises. Looking at the growth and evolution of Wenzhou's private enterprises, we can find an important regularity. That is, both entrepreneurs and officials in Wenzhou always take the political dimension and economic dimension into account when promoting institutional innovation.

The choice of enterprise organization system should conform to the economic standard and the political standard; whether it is the affiliated operation form or the joint-stock cooperation system, it embodies the unification of political standard and economic standard. The wisdom of Wenzhounese is vividly demonstrated in the unification of political standards and economic standards.

The enterprise form of Wenzhou is very diverse; it is not easy to divide several types accurately. It's like the color spectrum: The transition from one color to another is continuous, and there is no distinct boundary. There are a large number of intermediate forms between the joint-stock cooperative system, the shareholding system, and the limited liability system. Whether these intermediate forms will be classified into a few standard enterprise systems in the future is unclear. But this rich form of organization provides rich organizational resources. It can be said that the private enterprises in Wenzhou are still in the process of rapid development and restructuring. As long as the external market environment or the market capacity is large enough, the income of scale expansion is greater than the cost paid by the system rent-seeking, and the innovation behavior of the enterprise is unrestrained and emergent. Most of these innovations are transient local behavior. But as long as one or two of these survive, its demonstration effect is immeasurable.

However, we must also see that Wenzhou's private enterprises go from the family industry to the affiliated operation, the joint-stock system, and finally some enterprises take the path of the corporation system, which is squeezed and solidified by government, market, and family. The central government's restrictions on employees and the clampdown on private capital markets have made the region's companies not entirely move along the path of classical growth. This kind of regulation from government is in constant disintegration, but as long as it exists, the environment of enterprise growth will further shape the existing form of the enterprise. We should admit that the evolution of Wenzhou's private enterprises is based on the economic subject's judgment on relative price system and its changes. The influence of cultural factors on enterprises should not be overestimated. For Wenzhou's private entrepreneurs, some political or cultural appeal is rooted in the judgment of relative prices. So avoiding the relative price distortion is the main guarantee to ensure the healthy growth of private enterprises along the efficient path. Instead of maintaining and enforcing controls, the government should deregulate, including controls on private capital markets (see Tables 4.2–4.7).

Table 4.2.   The numbers of various types of enterprises in various regions of Zhejiang Province in 1999.

Names of cities and counties	Total number of industrial enterprises	State-owned economy	Collective economy	Joint-stock enterprises	Joint ventures	Limited liability companies	Company limited by shares	Private enterprises	Other enterprises	Hong Kong-Macao-Taiwan invested enterprises	Foreign-invested enterprises
Hangzhou	68,275	457	5,625	852	126	336	57	16,015	44,085	381	341
Ningbo	81,132	199	10,811	2,088	268	140	47	14,671	51,892	607	409
Wenzhou	127,980	168	3,835	16,022	4	233	28	8,315	99,095	199	81
Jiaxing	91,832	132	3,987	1,139	52	136	20	5,308	80,620	214	224
Huzhou	61,218	153	2,846	351	29	69	11	5,373	52,307	49	30
Shaoxing	75,775	143	5,591	665	839	48	20	13,605	54,618	144	102
Jinhua	60,874	118	1,453	824	434	26	26	16,388	41,517	61	27
Quzhou	26,852	73	4,445	135	4	25	10	2,653	19,451	43	13
Zhoushan	5,046	35	530	149	14	28	1	1,271	2,986	22	10
Taizhou	87,564	159	1,565	10,427	156	83	31	9,851	65,085	129	78
Lishui	19,884	118	659	122	65	11	11	3,564	15,304	3	27

Table 4.3.   Development of Wenzhou's commodity market.

Year	Number of commodity markets	Number of professional markets	Annual turnover (100 million)	The volume of commodities in the commodity market accounted for the retail sales of social goods in that year
1979	117			
1981	251			
1984	393	79	6.95	41.87
1985	417	135	10.6	50.26
1986	472	267	13.19	51.54
1987	486		17.97	60.6
1988	504		29.44	68.5
1990	519	293	27.89	63.9
1991	454	241	34.36	70
1992	480	310	43.9	74
1993	505	354	74.05	80
1994	513	363	137.82	75
1995	523	214	248.3	77
1996	528	245	353.19	81
1997	505	210	397.59	78
1998	533	202	407.23	78

Table 4.4.   Individual industrial and commercial households in Wenzhou.

Year	Number of households	Number of people engaged	Registered capital (10,000 yuan)	Business value (10,000 yuan)	Industrial output value (10,000 yuan)	Tax (10,000 yuan)
1980	1,984	1,584	39	1		
1981	13,231	14,587	295	38		
1982	20,363	23,838	437	7,252	204	33
1983	39,698	45,228	2,331	19,979	642	1,223
1984	100,286	117,192	4,846	7,912	2,310	
1985	130,407	156,726	11,595	85,700	22,228	4,365
1986	138,384	169,473	15,592	89,325	17,866	5,804
1987	145,224	180,342	19,655	139,891	28,787	6,352
1988	146,622	183,752	28,514	195,916	46,064	9,233
1989	141,725	179,681	37,714	218,714	68,598	12,119
1990	156,652	197,396	42,344	220,070	86,555	15,783
1991	153,582	195,579	44,457	258,780	101,294	20,308
1992	154,044	202,723	60,987	318,514	104,946	23,035
1993	202,000	289,000	109,000	424,000	203,082	30,217
1994	214,697	312,892	150,785	1,090,631	388,512	43,125
1995	223,276	337,894	210,112	2,179,848	381,111	50,228
1996	214,328	331,368	208,005	3,215,214	761,581	56,220
1997	197,785	313,960	201,517	3,661,871	840,136	77,500
1998	203,440	333,859	250,472	3,814,732	964,548	

Table 4.5. Situations of Wenzhou's private enterprises.

Year	Number of households	Number of employees	Registered capital (10,000 Yuan)	Business turnover ($10,000)	Industrial output value (10,000 yuan)	Tax (10,000 yuan)
1988	350	4,377	3,289	/	/	/
1989	1,045	11,453	9,358	5,332	8,383	64
1990	1,210	9,182	8,561	8,210	14,923	346
1991	1,137	11,441	9,340	7,668	17,592	1,031
1992	1,232	12,194	12,598	8,783	21,804	982
1993	2,380	24,300	65,400	28,900	48,418	33,000
1994	2,977	31,463	105,804	122,294	122,168	44,700
1995	3,989	40,227	184,254	151,168	277,192	54,300
1996	5,328	52,287	283,633	211,444	353,603	60,230
1997	5,616	54,658	352,145	423,877	493,721	/
1998	6,590	64,677	452,185	463,228	576,941	/

Table 4.6. Ownership structure of Wenzhou industrial economy and its changes (1980–1998).

Year	1980	1985	1990	1995	1996	1998
Industrial output structure	100	100	100	100	100	100
(1) Township and above industries.	86.7	77	69	38	34.5	30.7
State-owned economy	32.7	18.2	16.5	6.6	4.6	3.9
Collective economy	53.9	58.1	50.8	25.7	22.5	22.2
Rural	12.2	15.7	19.2	15.2	12.3	12.1

Subdistrict	2.8	7.7	9.8	3.4	2.5	2.7
Other economic types	0.1	0.7	1.7	5.6	7.4	4.6
Three kinds of investment enterprise			0.7	3.3	2.7	3.3
(2) Township enterprises and those below.	13.3	23	31	62	65.5	69.3
Village enterprise	9.4	10.8	9.2	4.7	5.7	7.9
Town cooperative enterprise		0.9	2.8	5	13.8	6.1
Rural cooperative enterprise	3.5	5.5	10.7	19.7	15.6	20.9
Individual enterprises in cities and towns	0.4	0.9	3	11.3	11.7	14
Rural individual enterprises		4.9	5.3	19.2	18.7	19.5

Table 4.7.   Structure of total retail sales of consumer goods in Wenzhou %.

Year	1980	1985	1990	1995	1996	1998
Total retail structure	100	100	100	100	100	100
State-owned business	37.2	28.1	21.9	9.7	8.1	5.9
Collective business	57.3	38.1	21.9	7.7	8.4	11.3
Individual business	2.1	25.1	40.1	55.1	63	65.2

Chapter **5**

From a Family Workshop to a Modern Enterprise: A Case Study of Chint Group

5.1 Introduction

Family workshops widely existed in pre-industrial society, but they had been regarded as heretical for more than 20 years before China's reform and opening-up. After the reform and opening-up, small family workshops were allowed to operate and develop rapidly. In the coastal areas, family workshops have even become one of the important forces of local economic development, which contributes to the economic recovery of people even more than state-owned and collective enterprises. Among them, Wenzhou model is famous for developing family private economy earlier. In Wenzhou, the cultivated land per capita is only 0.43 acres. However, it produced nearly 400 billion yuan of gross domestic product (GDP) in 1998 (see Table 5.1), more than 5,400 yuan per capita, where the industry accounted for 60%, the tertiary industry accounted for 32%, and the agriculture accounted for only 8%. A vast majority of Wenzhou's industries are private enterprises, with state-owned enterprises accounting for only 1,000 of the total industrial enterprises and less than 4% of the total output value. Most forerunners of Wenzhou's private enterprises evolved from "front shop, rear factory" and with the average output value of more than 10 million yuan only and their overall size much smaller than their influence in the country. The reason is that the association between enterprises in Wenzhou is often difficult, and assets of many enterprises are separated for various reasons after a little development. People attribute it to the Wenzhou people's "individual-based" consciousness and lack of spirit of cooperation, so "division after prolonged cooperation" has become the judgment for family enterprises and the partnership between the friends in Wenzhou.

Table 5.1. Economic Profile of Yueqing and the whole Wenzhou.

Regions		Total	State-owned companies	Collective companies	Joint-stock cooperative companies	Joint operation companies	Limited liability companies	Companies limited by shares	Private companies	Companies funded by foreign countries and Hong Kong and Taiwan of China	Other companies
Number of industrial companies	The whole Wenzhou	127,980	168	3,835	16,022	4	233	28	8,315	280	99,095
	Yueqing	15,114	21	47	3,425	1	28	—	519	33	11,040
Value of gross output	The whole Wenzhou	13,845,968	530,608	167,597	462,160	12,671	632,986	12,464	10,166	52,205	4,703,282
	Yueqing	2,393,797	64,681	22,565	103,733	1,740	125,902	1	10,536	54,736	981,743

Chapter 5   From a Family Workshop to
a Modern Enterprise: A Case Study of Chint Group

With the intensification of competition, enterprises are demanding increasing economic benefits, and the contradiction between the market risks faced by family workshops or small private enterprises and their own business models is becoming increasingly prominent. Therefore, it is necessary to break through some difficulties and obstacles in the process of growing from the family workshop to the modern enterprise. So people explore the way to realize the capital combination and management and organization innovation from small to large by means of joint venture, joint-stock cooperation, stock system, and so on. In this process, people also encountered difficulties like definition of property rights, the distribution of control rights, income division, and other thorny problems; many enterprises born out of small workshops failed or split on their way to success not because of the market, but because of internal reasons. Surprisingly, however, in just a few years at the beginning of the 1990s, in a small town in Yueqing (see Table 5.1 for economic indicators of Yueqing), larger private enterprises such as Chint Group and Delixi Group emerged, which was rare in Wenzhou. This small town called Liushi was not the county town of Yueqing City. It was more than 40 kilometers from Wenzhou, with a total population of nearly 90,000 and an area of only 26,711 mu of cultivated land, but the per capita industrial and agricultural output value exceeded 70,000 yuan. The proportion of township industrial output value was far greater than agricultural output value. It was a more developed rural town. It had a good reputation for producing low-voltage electrical appliances.[1] At the end of the 1980s, the town had more than 2,300 low-voltage electrical enterprises and more than 9,000 family workshops. In the 1990s, after consolidation, there were still 1,200 low-voltage electrical enterprises and more than 2,000 family workshops. In this

---

[1] The production history of low-voltage electrical appliances in Liushi can be traced back to the first low-voltage electrical appliance fittings factory "Mingdong Process Electrical Appliance Repair Factory", which was set up in 1972. As the market demand was strong, by 1975, the plant had 11 workshops with more than 100 workers, and that year it realized an income of 350,000 yuan. But as a result, the departments concerned were disturbed, and soon the plant was forced to be closed down.

12 square kilometer area, there were more than 1,000 low-voltage electrical equipment factories, with an average of nearly 100 plants per square kilometer, and their output and production value accounted for more than 30% of the national low-voltage appliance market.

Chint Group came into being under such a background. Here, through a more successful corporate story, we want to provide a case study of how small workshops can be merged and how to avoid deadly conflicts in the process. We will discuss the process and related problems of modern enterprise reconstruction.

Furthermore, this is not only a matter of an individual enterprise's growth but also alliance of a small family workshop or a group of small workshops without the support of capital markets and the consciousness of capital operation norms of modern market economy. This process involving various factors, especially family management, enterprise property right, management control right, and so on intertwined together, has extremely complex bargaining and very intelligent organization innovation. This story, from family workshops to modern enterprises, may have reference significance for all private enterprises facing the dilemma of family management or the confusion of ownership and control and for enterprises and entrepreneurs who try to gain economies of scale and improve their competitiveness quickly in an environment that lacks both capital and the basic norms and conditions for modern capital operations.

5.2 Development overview of Chint Group

Chint Group is a native enterprise developed in Liushi. It was founded in July 1984, at that time Nan Cunhui and his school fellow Hu established the Yueqing Qiujing Switch Factory,[2] which was a typical small family workshop with only 5 employees, an annual sales income of less than 10,000 yuan, and total assets of only 50,000 yuan. From 1984 to 1988,

---

[2] Nan Cunhui is the eldest son of the family. At the age of 12, his father was ill in bed, and when he was 16, he became a cobbler. Later, he had a short experience with his friend in the business of renting a counter for electrical appliances.

Qiujing Switch Factory and other small family workshops in Liushi experienced the initial period of rapid development. It was in this rapid expansion process of scale and output that there were many problems in the quality of low-voltage electrical appliances in Liushi: The quality of products was poor, with fake and shoddy products prevailing. When a lot of people hadn't realized the importance of the quality or were not very aware of the importance of quality and reputation, Nan Cunhui was one of the first batches to obtain 3 licenses for electrical products production issued by National Ministry of Machinery and Electricity through great effort in 1988. This farsighted decision won an important pass for the future development of the enterprise. At that time, the quality of all electrical products was not very high. Even though Yueqing Qiujing Switch Factory obtained the production license, it didn't mean that the quality of its products was much higher than its counterparts in the market. However, due to the quality problems of electrical products, in 1989, the relevant departments of the country rectified and cracked down on the counterfeit and shoddy products of Liushi together with the local government. At that time, there was a disagreement between the state authorities and the local government on whether to completely ban the production of electrical appliances. Finally, the companies that had been licensed like Yueqing Qiujing Switch Factory were retained and given the policy's permission and encouragement.

Many other small businesses, which hadn't obtained a license for production, had suffered a big setback, and less than a fifth of them survived. Yueqing Qiujing Switch Factory took advantage of this great opportunity to make great progress. In a year, it made a profit of about 100,000 yuan for the "Yueqiu Brand" products. In 1990, its profit increased more than 10 times. In 1991, it increased more than 10 times. Sales in 1991 were more than 20 times what they were in 1988. In 1990, due to different opinions on the development of enterprises, the Nan brothers and Hu brothers, who founded the Qiujing Switch Factory, split into two. Nan Cunhui named his own enterprise "Chint". In September 1991, Nan Cunhui and his relatives in the United States jointly established the Sino-American joint-venture Chint Electric Co., Ltd., utilized the preferential policies of the joint venture, introduced technology and equipment, and opened up the international market. By 1993, sales were 48 times higher than in 1991, and exports reached $2 million. After 1993, Chint began to absorb and combine other small factories, enterprises, and workshops. The first group of nearly 10 enterprises were converted into core branches, and they set up a group company. This initiative continued to evolve in the years to come. In 1994, Wenzhou Chint Group, which had 53 member enterprises, was established. At the same time, Chint has established its own sales center by independent legalization of its sales functions. In October 1995, it was registered as the first non-regional enterprise group in the low-voltage electrical industry in the State Administration of Industry and Commerce. In 1996, Chint reformed the original branch again and in the beginning of 1997, it adjusted the internal structure of the enterprise. As a result of continuous absorption and combination of small businesses, Chint's scale expanded rapidly. So far, Chint has become a large modern enterprise that produces low-voltage electrical appliances, automotive electronics, communication equipment, complete sets of equipment, and other products. It has 12 branches, 16 chip enterprises, more than 800 collaborative enterprises, more than 5,000 employees, with an annual sales income of 1.6 billion yuan, and total assets of 400 million yuan (Chint output and assets as shown in Figure 5.1). In 1999, according to the survey results of the All-China Federation of Industry and Commerce, Chint ranked the 8th among the top 100 private enterprises.

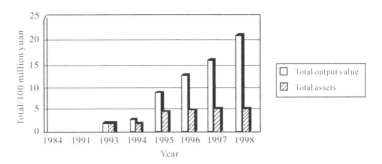

Figure 5.1. Total output value and total assets of Chint.

In this short period of more than 10 years, Chint's growth from a small family workshop to a large modern enterprise was undoubtedly a difficult process. In addition to the market opportunities in a certain period of time, the more important reason may be that Chint has absorbed and combined many other small enterprises at the right time, so that its size and strength could develop rapidly. But we know that when the market economy was not standard, the operation of the capital market was still without a set of effective rules, and merger and association with rural small businesses with rich family business characteristics were very difficult, let alone to break through the original management system and achieve management innovation.

This series of questions as to how to deal with the issues, and the actual performance, will be our main concern and these problems will be described and analyzed below.

5.3 Growth of Chint: Association and absorption of small enterprises

The most important feature of Chint Group's growth process is its continuous association and absorption of small enterprises and small workshops, and continuously promoting the optimization of governance structure in this process.

5.3.1 The road of association and merger in the growth of Chint

After the separation of the Nan brothers and Hu brothers, the main founders of the Qiujing Switch Factory in 1990, Chint was established. Its association and merger dates back to September 1991, when Nan Cunhui and his brother-in-law in USA associated an enterprise in Pudong, Shanghai, and managed to weather the credibility crisis of Wenzhou products by building their brands. Two years later, in 1993 the Nan brothers founded the Sino-foreign Joint-Venture Chint Co., Ltd. (the US side accounted for 50% of the shares), used the preferential policies of the joint venture to introduce advanced equipment and technology, expanded the overseas market, and improved the visibility.

In early 1992, Chint expanded at low costs. By the end of 1994, it had absorbed more than 390 enterprises and formed more than 20 branches. Chint changed these enterprises into the joint-stock cooperative system, and invested 51% to 85% of the tangible assets and intangible assets of Chint, where brand investment accounted for 10%–20%. However, as a large number of small enterprises joined through low-cost mergers and acquisitions, they didn't have much change in the management and were independent legal persons, and the Group had very weak control over them in the aspects of capital, production, and sales.

In order to solve these problems caused by the rapid expansion, in 1996, Chint carried out a shareholding transformation of the enterprises. This transformation mainly involved the shareholding transformation of the original 48 branches and hundreds of member enterprises, for the purpose of implementation of "big group, small accounting". Different companies were transformed according to different products, and the number of independent legal entities was reduced as much as possible. The transformation adopted the following principles:

(1) The proportion of the equity was assessed, the sales revenue index was 30% of the weight of the share, and the profitability was 70% of the weight.

(2) The weight was adjusted according to the market capacity. Products with high market share, such as circuit breakers, were multiplied by 1.3 times the initial weight, while the sunset product was multiplied by 0.7 times of initial weight. Products between the two were no longer changed of share proportion, which was determined by (1).

(3) First, the shares were quantified to the individual, then the legal person shares were included.

(4) The real estate of the entire core of the group was not included in shares.

(5) The above principles were discussed and decided by the shareholders' meeting.

According to this principle, for example, if the sales revenue of a certain enterprise accounts for 5% of the whole enterprise, and the profitability is 10% of the whole enterprise, its equity ratio should be $5\% \times 30\%: 10\% \times 70\% = 8.5\%$; if it is a product with a high market share, then the equity ratio should be $8.5\% \times 1.3 = 11.05\%$. These measures were not very popular at the beginning, and many companies were reluctant to join. However, the return on assets of the associated enterprises increased rapidly in the short term, it increased by 60% to 70%, and the whole production cost was reduced; in the severe market competition of that time, more than 100 companies that did not associate together went bankrupt within a year, so many small businesses soon joined in. In this way, the method of stock assessment was quickly passed. From 1994 to 1996, Chint developed into a multi-tiered group company. At the beginning of 1997, the Group reorganized the nine subsidiaries and holding companies that produced circuit breakers, the core product, and established Zhejiang Chint Electrics Co., Ltd. (as shown in Figure 5.2).

After restructuring twice, there were only 6 core companies in the group and 21 other companies were transformed into 6 branches and 2 limited companies. Most of the member companies were corporations, more than 70% of them owned by the group. In addition, there were also some joint ventures. In this way, the number of independent legal persons was reduced to a great extent, and many small enterprises transformed to small shareholders of the group company from the former independent legal persons, and the group company achieved remarkable efficiency in resource sharing and management integration. Chint transformed the enterprise into a parent company and established a three-level management system, and the control of the parent company and the power of the core level were strengthened. The group was divided into three levels, namely, the investment center, the profit center, and the cost center.

(1) Close-type management over the joint-venture subsidiary company was realized through management contract.

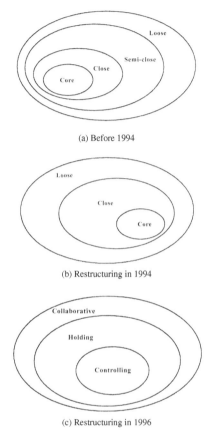

(a) Before 1994

(b) Restructuring in 1994

(c) Restructuring in 1996

Figure 5.2. The merger and consolidation process of Chint Group.

Notes: The core level consisted of 18 joint ventures, the controlling level had 20 joint-venture subsidiaries (the group accounted for over 51%), the holding level had 10 joint ventures, and the collaborative level had more than 800 subsidiaries. Shares could only be transferred and could not be sold.

(2) Control over the controlling subsidiary was realized by appointing equity representatives to the shareholders' meeting and the board of directors of the subsidiary by investors.

(3) Limited management was realized over the joint-stock company by exercising shareholders' rights and assessing the return on investment.

Specifically, the relationship between the parent company and subsidiaries could be summarized as follows.

(1) The group company took control through capital (including intangible assets) to obtain the equity gains of its subsidiaries and exercise the rights and powers of the asset owners through the board of directors of the parent company; subsidiaries provided profits and dividends to the parent company.

(2) The real estate of the parent company was not included in the stock. The shareholder representative was appointed within the group company according to the defined amount of assets occupied.

(3) The finance and sales of the whole company were consolidated.

(4) Each branch had an independent board of directors, a board of shareholders, and a board of supervisors, and had greater autonomy in personnel and small investment.

(5) For internal and external financing, the external investment was controlled by the group, and the subsidiaries' loans were based on the principle of "whoever uses and benefits pays the loan", "top loan-down appropriation", and "unified loan repayment".

(6) The power of approval of the financing project lay with the parent company. The group established the repayment scheme for the long-term debt caused by the implementation of major investment projects by the subsidiaries.

The real estate of the parent company was not included in the stock. The shareholder representative was appointed within the group company according to the defined amount of assets occupied.

Since the implementation of this reform scheme, the efficiency of the enterprise has been greatly improved, the large number of managers has been streamlined, and the control of the subsidiary companies has also entered a standardized operation state. Shortly after, the company continued to transform. The parent company set up the "Five Committees and One Office", namely, the Human Resources Committee, the Marketing Committee, the Scientific and Technological Development Committee, the Finance Committee, the Enterprise Planning Committee, and the Group Office, which are responsible for the management of the whole group as administrative departments of the group, and the transactional work of the whole group is independent. Furthermore, Chint is now preparing to transform the original management system into a division management system, dividing the whole group into nine divisions according to its products. The production function of the whole group is completely accomplished by the divisions. The management department of the core company is merged with the Head Office. The group is only responsible for the management and investment operation, and no longer has direct control over any company.

This system is a great challenge to the traditional management system, which has always depended on the development of industry and gained control. This is especially true when people do not necessarily have confidence in and are not familiar with this completely detached form of control, or are not familiar with the way in which it is operated. The current organizational structure of the group can be seen in Figure 5.3.

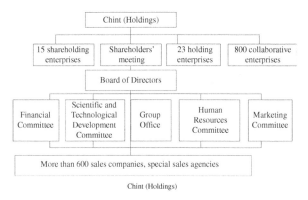

Figure 5.3. Organizational chart of Chint Group.

5.3.2 A review and theoretical analysis of the merger and capital operation experience of Chint

Looking at Chint's merger and capital operation experience, we try to find a better explanation for this kind of large-scale horizontal merger between small enterprises. This horizontal merger is quite different from the horizontal merger based on market monopoly or the merger based on market access discussed in the classical literature.

(1) The initial absorption and merger of Chint was not the horizontal integration of enterprises in the strict sense. It may be more similar to a kind of organizational arrangement of the club system. First of all, in the 1990s, the joint crackdown by the state ministries and the credit problems caused by proliferation of fake and shoddy goods turned local production of low-voltage electrical appliances in the area into a passive situation. Chint was not affected but supported by taking a step forward to obtain the national production license. The value of Chint's brand was highlighted. Many small businesses had the benefit of relying on Chint to produce products, mainly as follows: (1) obtaining the production license, accessing the umbrella, and making the profit by the Chint brand; (2) borrowing Chint's relatively stable marketing network and benefiting from the credibility of its products. From the actual situation, Chint at that time did not have the ability to merge many small enterprises and transform them, let alone control them.

In this case, it is not so much that Chint merged these enterprises, but that these small businesses became members of the Chint brand club. Chint was only charging for the club's products, enjoying the right to profit from and manage the brand, and had little intervention capacity in the operation and management of those small businesses. This situation turned around gradually after the great success of the Sino-foreign joint venture in 1993, so it was only in 1994 that the meaningful merger and acquisition action began. At that time, Chint had the initial strength to integrate some small enterprises with relatively close ties. Through the competitiveness of its more powerful core products, Chint attracted some enterprises that relied more on the Chint brand and transformed the same. At the same time, it also opened the Chint brand club to many small enterprises and workshops, which made its peripheral enterprises grow rapidly in momentum and scale, although this didn't have a lot of substantive control.

(2) In the vertical relationship of Chint, the legalization of marketing function was more than vertical merger. After the initial success of club merger and association, especially after the joint venture and partnership brought great benefits to Chint, Chint began to integrate the club-type loose system on the one hand, and carried on limited vertical merger on the other hand. Its efforts in the construction of marketing network were much greater than the backward merger, which was the best strategy to improve the bargaining position of Chint in the merger, because for those small enterprises facing fierce competition, the sales network was decisive. Recognizing this, as long as they were provided with adequate distribution network sharing, the power of control over them was naturally strengthened, so backward mergers were clearly not important. At the same time, the gains from bargaining power were likely to be greater than the economies of scale through internal integration. Therefore, as long as the quality was good, and the advantages of the enterprise's technological resources were not obvious, the integration of Chint from the outside to the inside might be a better choice. This situation changed when the sales network construction in the market became saturated. The efforts of Chint to establish outlets across the country were sufficient to illustrate the significance and effectiveness of this strategy.

(3) It was necessary to follow certain paths for the club-style and the loose enterprise to evolve into a compact enterprise. The path of the Chint merger and acquisition process was actually composed of two complementary clues. First, as an independent production function, the product operation was constantly strengthened, which not only enhanced the value of the brand but also raised the threshold of the club, thus enhancing its bargaining position. At the same time, it made substantial merger and association possible and the innovation

Figure 5.4. Chint's Brand Club and its materialization in the association process.

on production and management in this field had been continuously integrated into the innovation of the club system.

This continuous process will eventually integrate the production enterprise of the Chint entity and the virtual Chint brand club (see Figure 5.4). All aspects of the process must be taken seriously, or the result will be very different. If there is a well-known brand but not a strong enough production entity, the merger will eventually become an organization that charges brand rent. Similarly, had not the brand club attracted a large number of members when the enterprise was on a relatively small scale, Chint would never have developed so fast, and its brand and popularity would have increased more slowly than today.

This is our basic summary of the path of association and merger of Chint, which is also the reason for the rapid expansion of Chint. Next, we will discuss the change of equity of Chint Group, which will help us understand the change of property right and decision right of Chint Group as a private enterprise in the process of its development

5.4 Change of property rights and decision-making control of Chint Group

5.4.1 Changes in equity

The analysis of the property right and stock right change of Chint could be traced back to the stage of Nan Cunhui and Hu brothers' partnership to open Yueqing Qiujing Switch Factory. In 1984, Nan Cunhui and his classmates (later Hu brothers) agreed that the equity of each party was 50%, and the risk of investment interests and decision rights was equal.

At that time, because they were also worried about the interference of their families, the two sides agreed that the families would not participate in the operation. They agreed that if relatives and friends wanted to enter the company, they might receive salary and funds but not shares. If not, one could only divide within 50% of one's own shares, not the other party's shares. But less than half a year later, the younger brother of Nan's partner came to work in Yueqing Qiujing Switch Factory and Hu asked to offer additional shares to his brother besides the 50% of his shares. Nan agreed to transfer 10 shares to Hu's brother on the condition that the new relatives had no decision-making power. In this way, the shares were gradually increased to more than 100 shares, with relatives joining one after another, and the shares of both sides were diluted by the participation of relatives and friends on average. Until the separation, there were about 130 shares, and Nan Cunhui accounted for more than 30%, the Hus accounted for over 40%, and 3 relatives and friends accounted for more than 10% with only, 3% to 5% remaining. But the newcomers basically had no decision-making power.

This factory-like joint-stock partnership (or partnership) system lasted until 1990. As a result, there were some differences in management. Because although Nan was mainly responsible for enterprise management, Hu was mainly responsible for the establishment of the external marketing network, and the capabilities of both sides were complementary. After years of cooperation, the two sides had reduced their ability to complement each other, and the demarcation line in decision-making began to blur and diverge, resulting in separation. In Chint, which was founded after the separation, Nan Cunhui accounted for 45% of shares and his relatives accounted for the rest. His brother accounted for 15%, his nephew 15%, and his brother-in-law 10%.

It later added 120 shares, and Nan Cunhui's own stake fell to 36%. The joint venture was initiated in 1991 and the board of directors was established. In the joint venture, Nan's USA relatives and Nan himself accounted for 50% shares. When the group was formed in 1994, the property rights were actually not clear. Each subsidiary was an independent legal entity with its own shareholders' meeting and board of directors. After 2 years of adjustment, by 1996, the situation began to substantially change, many independent legal persons became branch companies without legal person status, and some small businesses simply became small-scale production units, no longer belonging to individuals or families. In addition, two joint-stock limited companies and specialized division of labor were established, and four limited liability companies and one Sino-US joint venture were established. The equity of the core level did not change after forming the group. The core level had more than 10 shareholders, who accounted for less than 20% of the total equity. Seven of them formed the board of directors, which accounted for 100% of shares of the core level of the board of directors. The holding level was controlled by the group to 65%–75% (of which the group only accounted for 50% of the Sino-US joint venture). The group had about 100–200 shareholders, 10% of whom accounted for 35% of the total equities of the group.[3]

5.4.2 Changes in the decision-making mechanism

The decision-making system of the group underwent four stages: The first stage was the centralized manager responsibility system management, which was very simple. At the second stage, the board of directors was set up and the post of general manager was established. At this time, the project and matrix management were adopted, the bar was crossed, and Nan's brother and other relatives began to participate in the business decision-making. The third stage was the establishment of the M-type group operation mode, and the core layer occupied 70%

---

[3] Inside holding accounted for only 10%. There were dark shares subject to quotas (minimum of 10,000 shares).

of the output value. At that time, one of the principles was that for its member companies, it would hold a controlling stake if possible; otherwise, it would take a stake. At the fourth stage, starting in 1996, the control authority of holding mode was strengthened, the investment center was set up, and the parent company system was adopted, but it was not yet perfect. The current implementation of control has been basically stratified, subject to the decentralized decision-making of the chairman and the president. But most of the board members were relatives of Nan, the chairman of the board. His brother was the president, and as for the other four vice presidents, one of them was his brother-in-law, and the other three were major shareholders. The one-person one-vote system was adopted by the board of directors and the board of shareholders to make decision. The board of supervisors would be supervised by the supervisory board of the parent company. The board of supervisors would have 6–7 members of the audit team, directly responsible to the chairman of the board of supervisors, which is one of the most important means to strengthen control. For the subsidiaries, the chairman of the board was originally a member of the board of directors of the core layer, with a veto power, but later that power was centralized and returned to the chairman of the parent company directly. The group mainly influenced the decision-making by the representatives of the directors, while the scope of the board of directors and supervisory board members of the middle tier was more extensive.

In the next step of the reform, the group will further improve the control and manner of shareholding. The manager's shareholding plan will be implemented in three batches.

(1) The first batch of shareholding objects usually consists of specially invited personnel of the group company or the sales center (people with senior title or senior of the company). They can invest 100,000 to 300,000 yuan after working for more than one year and others can invest 50,000 to 200,000 yuan after working for more than 2 years; for college graduates, they can invest after working for over 3 years while

the technical secondary school and high school graduates can invest after working for over 5 years. If these people are underfunded, they can apply for a loan and deduct from the bonus and dividends. However, they are required to keep the dividends of the first 3 years in the company without interest, which will be paid 50% in the fourth and fifth year. In addition to those with special provisions, the principal of the shares of the company of those under 65 years of age or less than 15 years' service in the company shall be transferred to the company only and they still bear the risk.

(2) The second batch of shareholding objects consists of the managers of each sales company.

(3) For the third batch, the company will consider going public and the employees have the preemptive right to subscribe the shares.

But these are only plans, and there is no employee stock ownership. If the first plan is implemented, it will dilute the control of minority shareholders. In the whole process of the equity change, it is said that few equity transfers occur.

Obviously, from the whole equity structure and decision-making mechanism of Chint, its family governance characteristics are very obvious. Nan's brothers and relatives have absolute control over their core businesses, although their control over their subordinate companies may not be quite in place. Although we can't generally judge the merit of the family business system, which doesn't necessarily have low efficiency, we must understand clearly the characteristics of family business as a kind of governance by blood relationship where the key lies in whether it can continue to guarantee that the most capable people are chosen constantly and obtain decision-making power. Another very important aspect is whether there is sufficient capacity to deal with and resolve this disagreement without separating the assets when there is internal disagreement. Many family businesses do not have both. We have discussed this issue in detail in other cases. For Chint, its leaders are now in the prime of their lives. The chairman is 36 years old and the president is around 30. Moreover, the authority of the enterprise, the authority of the ethical family, and the authority of the equity have an asymmetrical collocation. In this case, it is always possible to deal with the differences.

5.5 Marketing, R&D, and personnel management of Chint Group

5.5.1 Chint marketing strategy and network construction

Almost like all other private small businesses in Wenzhou, Chint at the beginning of its establishment depended entirely on the supply and marketing forces of Liushi throughout the country for product marketing. Over time, some dealers began to establish themselves around the country, buying products from some manufacturers in Liushi and then selling them. Of course, the trading relationship was a short-term one and not fixed. In order to take advantage of the resources, Chint established a stronger marketing network and began to build their own special distribution outlets in major cities in the country from the early 1990s. At the time, there was no agreement on whether this was feasible or not, and Nan made the decision by prevailing over all dissenting views. Massive substantive action began in 1994, when Chint gave a series of preferential treatments with respect to capital operation and supported the distribution party in the form of interest-free loans in order to attract dealers. On the basis of the credit investigation, supplemented by the family guarantee, it was decided that the group would invest some of the advance funds, which would be gradually deducted when the dealers went into normal operation. In that year, the group lent out millions of dollars.

Later, it was changed into the loan deducted according to the purchase amount of the previous year with discount. The new company would be deducted with a low discount and would be later discounted as per the sales volume. Later, it was changed again: At the provincial, county and local levels, the new company would be discounted at different levels based on the total amount at the end of the year targeting the one-time purchased amount. For the established company, the discount would be given on the target completed in the previous year; for distributors who needed funds to expand the scale, the discount was calculated on the basis of interest; and for the key sales companies with large sales volumes, the premium discount was applied to the excess part, and subsidies were paid in the advertisement according to the prescribed level. Chint argued that the reason for binding interest expenses, sales expenses and venture capital in the general period of money collecting together and benefiting dealers would produce the internal support for agent distribution. It could also enable the enterprise to concentrate energy, financial resources, and material investment on new product development, forming a virtuous circle.

(1) Management of marketing outlets

The management of such a large number of outlets was also an important part of marketing strategy, which required a global perspective. Chint proposed and implemented the marketing strategy of "key breakthrough, peripheral extension, rolling development, national expansion, unified policy and whole promotion".[4] In 1994, the group established the marketing center and established the marketing department under it. First, on the basis of credit and market research, it set up agency sales companies in Beijing, Dalian, and some other major cities, which were authorized to use the "Chint" brand. It developed business rapidly and achieved greater success. This attracted other Wenzhou supply and marketing forces across the country, and they asked to be dealers. Then, Chint expanded the development department into a development center and divided the national market into six areas for management. In a few years, the marketing network of Chint developed rapidly, with a year-on-year growth rate of 484% in 1995, 94.08% in 1996, and 33.33% in 1997. The year-on-year growth rate of

---

[4] In 1995, there were repeated outlets, and the internal consumption caused by multiple outlets was relatively large with more disorderly price, which was later corrected.

marketing revenues was 216% in 1995, 409% in 1996, and 145.44% in 1997 (see Table 5.2).

By the end of July 1998, Chint Group had established 210 sales companies and 268 special distribution agencies in China. Its network covered more than 200 large- and medium-sized cities and prefecture-level cities.

Among them, there were more than 30 key companies with large sales volume, accounting for 10% of the total number of outlets, but the purchase amount to the total purchase amount was 50%. Chint had franchise and price buyout distribution systems. The former sold the Chint brand in accordance with the agreement, and the latter bought out the Chint products for sale. Later, it further developed in a variety of ways, such as distribution members, shares, and agency joint ventures (see Table 5.3).

Due to the strong strength, Chint gradually began to implement some new measures in the consolidation and improvement of the network. Each year, it would eliminate a batch of distribution outlets with a purchase value less than 200,000 yuan, and special distribution outlets with purchase value between 200,000 and 500,000 yuan. It would

Table 5.2. Growth of marketing outlets of Chint.

Year	1995	1996	1997
Year-on-year growth rate (%)	484	94.08	33.33
Marketing revenue growth year-on-year (%)	216	409	145.44
Output value (%)	100	100	33.33

Table 5.3. Various forms of distribution system.

Form	Distribution	Member	Shares	Agency	Joint venture
Proportion or (number)	80%	(5 places) N series products	2 companies	10%	1 company (Beijing)

reward good dealers according to 1%–2% of the purchase amount and grant awards of honor to those having distributed for over 5 years. The entire group spent millions of dollars each year on rewards, which accounted for about 0.5% or 0.3% to 2% of the annual purchases. In addition, in order to strengthen the long-term relationship,[5] Chint also made special investment in human capital for marketing staff, organized training, and helped with the customer management, and the distribution agreement was also renewed from the original every one to two or three years.

In addition, it is worth mentioning that in the international market, Chint obtained market access though quality certification. Currently, it has had five branches in the United States, Singapore, Greece, Iran, and other countries and its foreign trade exports have reached $15 million a year.

Further measures will be aimed at the vertical integration of some dealers, or the integration of distribution outlets. It will adopt the method of the shareholding system, such as the internalization of the investment of intangible assets or the capital investment, which involves the interests of many parties, and has not yet been fully implemented.

(2) Advertising and public relations, and counterfeiting

While establishing the domestic sales network, Chint also invested more in advertising and public relations to improve the products' popularity and brand value. These investments were generally carried out by the head office, with an annual advertising investment of more

---

[5] When choosing wholesalers, Chint paid special attention to the "fellow-townsman" relationship, and specifically divided them into "fellow-townsman wholesalers" and "non-fellow-townsman wholesalers". It emphasized emotional investment on the former to unite them and endeavor to promote the formation of the "fellow-townsman marketing network", while it laid stress on service quality, price advantage, product image promotion, and so on for the latter.

than 10 million yuan, and a portion of the advertising expenses were shared with the franchisors.

The proportion of apportionment should be less than 1% of the total purchase amount and less than 50% of the advertising fee. In other words, if the purchase amount of the franchiser was 10 million yuan and the advertising cost was 250,000 yuan, the group will only pay 1%, namely, 100,000 yuan; if the franchised dealer spent 150,000 yuan on advertisement, the group should bear 50% of the advertisement, namely, 75,000 yuan. The system encouraged dealers to focus on the role of advertising. Altogether, the annual advertising cost of the whole group was about 20 million to 30 million yuan.

In terms of public relations, like many well-known private enterprises, Chint established a good public image through donations to honorable causes, hope projects, and poverty alleviation. The company donated 200,000 yuan for a "Sight Restoring Project", more than 5 million yuan to the poor rural towns for the construction of "Chint Teaching Building", etc. It was selected by the Organizing Committee of the First Chinese Good Works of Public Welfare to be one of the 100 exhibitors for China's first exhibition of outstanding achievements in public welfare undertakings.

In addition, it is worth mentioning that, in order to maintain its own brand, Chint also had to crack down on fake products.

5.5.2 Product development and technology investment
(1) Quality management

In the early stage of development, the technical content of the product of Chint was not high. When it obtained production license from the National Ministry of Machinery and Electricity, in fact, it didn't mean that its product quality was much better than similar products on the market. However, with the development of enterprises, Chint had a higher requirement for quality. In December 1994, it was the first to pass the ISO 9001 quality system certification in the national low-voltage electrical appliance industry, and it has received two reevaluations. In 1996, the quality management system was improved according to the requirements of ISO 9004 quality system. At the same time, Chint products successively obtained international CB security certification, Finnish FI certification, Belgium CEBEC certification, Dutch KEMA, USA FMRC, and UL certification. This was certainly not the same as the company's massive investment in quality testing. Since 1993, the group has invested more than 5 million yuan to establish a product testing and testing stations, and then invested more than 300,000 yuan in 1997 to introduce advanced foreign physical and chemical testing equipment and instruments. In 1996, an instrument company controlled by the group had invested more than 3 million yuan to update all testing equipment. At present, the Quality Assurance Department of the group has more than 300 professional and technical personnel, including more than 10 senior engineers. The 38 member companies of the group have established the Technical Department and Quality Inspection Department, equipped with the section chiefs, team leaders, and corresponding personnel. The company has also implemented the green, yellow, and red card quality control system, to check the quality of products of the enterprises wishing to join the group.

For all enterprises that asked to join the group, they had to pass the certification according to the regulations and be given a green card; for enterprises that had problems, the yellow card would be given for improvement within deadline. For those who failed to meet the requirements, the red card would be given, and the membership would be canceled.

(2) Technical innovation input

In 1996, Chint established the technology development center. In addition, 16 regulations related to the development of science and technology were formulated, and detailed provisions on scientific research input, personnel treatment, and management system were made. Annual investment in scientific research accounted for more than 3% of sales. There were more than 40 R&D personnel, among whom there were 8–9 senior engineers. More than 100 series of products have been developed.

The treatment of science and technology developers has been superior. The salary of the assistant engineer to the engineer level is 20,000–50,000 yuan, and the salary of the senior technician is higher. For product development designers, the company's incentive is to use 1%–3% of sales as a bonus for developers, decreasing by 50% annually. The award has now reached more than 100,000 yuan. The group will also consider making technology workers permanent shareholders to make them millionaires. So far, although there is no patent of invention, more than 30 products have obtained utility and appearance patents and it is developing high technical content, which is expected to be put into production soon.

As for the project and its feasibility, it is decided by the company's technology development committee and coordinated with the marketing department.[6] The group company is prepared to implement the three-level management system in the future: (1) the R&D center of the group will focus on research and development decisions; (2) the business department will be responsible for specific development work; (3) the branch will be responsible for the development of short-term and fast products, and the testing of core products. As far as the enterprise is concerned, the R&D capability is not very strong with few 35–55-year-old technical people. Many technical people are retired technicians, so the introduction and cultivation of talents need to be strengthened.

In the aspect of R&D project management, the company implements the form of the research group and signs the contract. The funds shall be managed by the financial and economic commission and shall be

---

[6] The research and development department has asked the marketing department to provide advice on product development in September every year, but the effect is not significant at the moment.

implemented according to the expense-based system, which shall be deducted from the bonus in case of failure to meet the deadline.

5.5.3 Human resources management

(1) Management system

The human resources management of Chint may be a weak link, which is related to the development process and characteristics of Chint. Because the company has been very weak in the personnel right control of the member companies, the personnel of each branch are independent. The company does not participate in the personnel appointment and removal of the branch, and the monthly meeting of personnel directors is actually a matter of procedure. At present, the human resource department of the head office actually only has the responsibility of the headquarters personnel.

(2) Salary system

The salary system of Chint is divided into three kinds: piecework salary, hourly wage, and annual salary system. For most front-line workers, the salary of piecework is implemented, and for the basic service personnel where piecework salary is not easy to implement, hourly wage is implemented and for the senior and some intermediate managers and technical personnel, the annual salary system is implemented. The salary is divided into 4 grades and 30 levels, and the wage differential is large (see Table 5.4).

Table 5.4. Wage and wage differential.

Level	Worker		Deputy manager	Manager	Vice general manager	General manager	Vice president	President (chairman)
Absolute (10,000 yuan)	1–1.5	1–1.5	2–4	3–5	5–7	9–11	11–13	14–16
Median differential	100	100	240	133	140	167	120	125

(3) Staff composition, recruitment, and training

The company has more than 5,000 employees. About 70% of them are women, and more than 600 people are educated in with junior college degree or above, and the number is expected to increase to 1,000. Among them, there are 500 university graduates, more than 10 master degree graduates, and about 1,500 high school graduates, with more than 300 secondary school graduates (see Table 5.5).

The employee has a two-month probation period, and enjoys a salary during the probation period of one who will be officially employed after passing the examination after the probation period. There are interview procedures at the time of employment. The interview is co-chaired by the company's human resources committee and department heads, and different procedures are utilized according to different personnel. But senior staff members are largely not responsible for the company's human resources committee, which is directly assessed by the board. After employment, it will be assessed every six months. (It was originally evaluated once a year).

With regard to staff training, the company has special education funds, and the faculty comprises external and internal staff. So far, 178 professional training sessions have been conducted and 8,000 person times have participated in the training. If the training assessment is qualified, the training cost is borne by the company; otherwise, the

Table 5.5. Education structure of employees.

Type	Below high school	High school	Technical secondary school	Junior college	Undergraduate	Above graduate
Number (person)	2,100	1,500	300	500	500	10
proportion	42	30	6	10	10	0.2

training expenses are borne by the individual. For senior managers, training is also linked to performance appraisal to motivate employees to invest in human capital.

In addition, in order to motivate the operators, the company also provides them with housing (three rooms and one sitting room), but the ownership right belongs to the company. There are not many managers, only about 10 people a year.

5.6 Existing problems and development trends of Chint Group

From the previous analysis, we can see that there are several basic reasons for the success of Chint: (1) It took one step forward to receive the production license and had the superior consciousness in the aspect of the market access; (2) it took advantage of the credit crisis of similar enterprises, seized the opportunity to absorb club members boldly, quickly expanded strength, and gained substantial profits; (3) it carefully and in a timely manner reformed club members to create the core competitiveness of enterprises; (4) it took the first step to set up the marketing network and preemptively occupy the market; and (5) it adhered to improving competitiveness while developing club members at the same time, creating a foundation for constantly raising the club threshold and for the substantive significance of integration. But we should also notice immaturity and problems of Chint in many ways as a young company. These problems may be associated with Chint's own development characteristics and successful experiences, so we should have a clear understanding of them. There are the following specific points.

5.6.1 The conflict between the rapid expansion of membership and the limited resources of the club

Chint has made great progress through the rapid expansion of club membership, but this expansion is limited. Due to the limited resources of the club, excessive expansion may bring down the value of the club; moreover, members of the club are required to enjoy certain network resources, especially the marketing network, but the construction ability of the network must depend on the development and coordination ability of the whole Chint Group. If the size of the membership exceeds the normal absorption range of Chint, there is a possibility of indigestion. The study of its history shows that horizontal mergers and acquisitions were not a common and viable long-term strategy in the United States at the end of the last century.

Chandler (1977) pointed out that the companies that started to become larger through mergers were able to maintain profits simply because they followed the vertical integration strategy after the mergers. The differences between the initial merger of Chint and the horizontal merger in the history of Western enterprises lie in the fact that the latter often formed cartels in order to seek price and control and restrict competition in the market, while Chint basically did not make this its main purpose. This shows that Chint should be more careful in recruiting members; especially when it does not have any basic conditions for association, it should not blindly pursue a large size and scale.

At the same time, in order to better provide club resources and integrate the club, Chint should consider the integrated operation of marketing network. This is related to the future competitiveness of Chint, and the opportunity of network integration should not be lost because of internal integration. Measures such as mergers and acquisitions and fixed contract can be taken, and it needs to be aware of the problem of market downturn due to a division of interests conflict with the sellers in the choice of marketing network internalization and independence.

5.6.2 Coordination between integration and conflict of interest

Chint integration has not been a big problem so far due to severe competition in the market and the unique bargaining position and reasonable equity evaluation scheme of Chint. But we also see that through mergers, we are united outwardly but divided at heart. This is not surprising in the early days of all cartels or clubs, but in the long run it can lead to a decline in corporate cohesion. So a company with too many independent legal persons may not be very efficient, especially if they exist solely because of problems of property and control rights, not because of technical needs. Chint needs to make a trade-off between frequent bargaining between shareholders due to accelerating consolidation and potentially reducing the overall competitiveness of the company. Judging from the current measures, Chint is under pressure from minority shareholders, and radical reform measures may be difficult to implement. Chint has turned several of its subsidiaries into branches, and it is worth considering whether it is appropriate to turn a core company into a transactional organization.

5.6.3 Organizational structure design, functional division, and leadership turnover at the middle and senior levels

Chint wants to establish the three-level management system of divisional system, but the divisional system has its specific application scope. Generally speaking, a divisional system is to make better use of enterprise resources, but it brings dual management problems at the same time. The principle of division is to distinguish different series of business units according to the needs of process and resource sharing. Some sectors generate profits, while others do not create profits directly. As the business unit of the profit center, there is a lot of competitive institutional arrangement in coordination with other departments. It is not that more incentive and competition is better; excessive incentive and competition may lead to internal consumption.

For example, it may not be a good idea to turn the scientific research department into a business unit of the profit center; at the same time, Chint is still in chaos in the billing of settlement and resource sharing between various business divisions. It is more difficult to monitor the finance of the financial department of the head office through the division of the subsidiary; in addition, it also faces the unification and decentralization of marketing, financial, and technical resource contributions between the regional business divisions and the professional product divisions. At present, there is no consensus on these aspects.

In addition, it is important to note that the age structure of the head levels of the enterprise also has some problems. Originally as a private enterprise, due to various reasons, it was inclined to hire some retired department cadres. However, during further development, the age of the leaders should be considered, especially in the future when the competition is increasingly fierce and concepts are updated very quickly.

5.6.4 Development of staff quality and internal labor market

Chint staff's overall cultural level is low, which is not coordinated with the industry characteristics. It has to be improved gradually through the reeducation of the staff and the corresponding provisions in the recruitment of new employees. At the same time, in order to better establish an effective and strong organization, there must be a relatively developed internal labor market, especially if the external labor market is not developed. At present, the internal labor market of Chint is not enough, which may be related to the weak control of the personnel power of subsidiaries. If consolidation is to be strengthened, an important approach is to incentivize new talent and reoptimize the allocation of existing human resources through jobs offered in the internal labor market. This needs to exclude resistance from some small shareholders, but the group may be able to achieve its objectives by buying control of these small shareholders and by compensating for the loss of control.

5.6.5 Product positioning and diversification

At present, there is still a gap between the products of Chint and the high-tech products in general, and some of its products mainly remain in the imitation stage. Despite some scientific research, the product is still labor intensive. We can see that its scientific research strength is still relatively weak, and the new product development ability is insufficient. There should be a clear product positioning in the future, whether it is in the high-tech field or in the general applied science and technology field. One should do according to one's abilities and not try to keep up with the Joneses.

5.7 Relationships between private enterprises and the growth of private enterprises

The association of private enterprises has been regarded as a difficult thing. Indeed, not only is the association between the private enterprises very difficult but, if it is associated, a few partners in a joint venture also tend to split up after a slight improvement in business, due to conflicts of interest, competition for control, and divergent management ideas. Separation after long-term cooperation has almost become a judgment of private enterprises. So it is meaningful to discuss how private enterprises can associate. Chint was originally separated, but later it was associated with a series of enterprises, and it has successfully embarked on the road of modern corporate governance, which is worthy of study. At the same time, the growth model of enterprises like Chint is not unique in Wenzhou. Delixi Group, which separated from Yueqing Qiujing Switch Factory, also basically took the road of association between enterprises like Chint. At present, the strength of Delixi Group is comparable to Chint's. Apart from these two, Liushi also has some other influential enterprises in the area such as Ten Gen. They are either more integrated or less structured, but they seem to be more likely to be associated. This is a valuable experience. How should we evaluate these experiences? Here are some ideas from the experience of case studies.

5.7.1 The basic judgment about the difficulty of the merger of private enterprises

Many people think that the difficulties of merging private enterprises are determined by the special cultural background, but in fact, we should not overstate the role of culture. Western companies grew slowly after decades of free competition development and they also encountered many difficulties when beginning to merge. Finally, thanks to the support of financial and capital market, merger and acquisition became a broad wave. At present, China's basic property right system is not yet perfect, and the road to merger and acquisition between private enterprises is certainly more difficult, which is not surprising.

5.7.2 About separation after long-term cooperation of the family business and the private enterprises

Family businesses can be divided into four types according to the business owners or their entrepreneurs: (1) parents' entrepreneurship, family participation, and leadership core with ethics and management; (2) joint venture of brothers, without ethical leadership, their respective positions being almost equal; (3) father and son start a business together, have ethical leadership core, but do not necessarily have the leadership core of management; and (4) family-owned enterprises, friends and relatives start their business together, but their leadership mechanism is similar to that of family businesses.

The family power structures of these kinds of family enterprises, the structures of corporate power, and the relationships between them are different. They also face different problems in the modernization of their property rights and governance structures. We need to pay attention to the laws of various enterprises in the process of change and analyze their causes. We can assume the following: (1) In each period of business operation, there is an optimal governance structure corresponding to it, and there should be operators who can best adapt to the operating environment at that time; (2) the actual situation tends to deviate from this optimal state, and the degrees of deviation of different enterprises are different, so their performance is very different; and (3) with the change of market competition pressure, survival — the elimination mechanism — will choose the most effective operator and operating mechanism, namely, the best corporate power structure. It may conflict with the power structure of the family, which may lead to the split of private enterprises. It is pointless to generalize about whether it is good or not. The important question may be whether there is a mechanism for them to be able to separate effectively. Several factors may affect the separation performance of private enterprises — people's patience, humility, ability, and information.

5.7.3 About the association between private enterprises

Vertical merger of enterprises often happens due to asset specificity and the need to improve product competitiveness. But the purpose of horizontal mergers is often to monopolize and occupy or secure the market (we can also view this horizontal integration as a special vertical integration). It is often a common skill to bypass barriers when there are entry barriers or controls. At this point, Enterprise A, which is trying to enter the market, achieves its goal through Enterprise B, which is already free of barriers. Of course, the average fixed cost is reduced, and the management of economies of scale is also a reason for merger and acquisition. When we look at the association experience of Liushi low-voltage electric appliance enterprises in the early 1990s, it is not hard to see that the reason for their horizontal association is not monopoly or market domination, nor is the scale economy factor a reason for their main consideration. Here, mainly Enterprise A which intends to enter the market is merged and acquired by Enterprise B with barrier pass. A and B actually form a "brand" club. First, it is to circumvent government regulation; second, it is used to avoid people's reputation crisis. As a result, the products of the companies providing the brands have sufficient advantages and can continue. So other businesses have a certain dependency on the club. The dominant enterprise can obtain the bargaining power of the merger, and integrate it continuously. Many small businesses in Wenzhou merge in this way. For small businesses with weak initial strength, it is an attractive growth path.

The risk, of course, is that without quality control and timely integration, it could drag itself down. The success of Chint is that it guarantees both.

Chapter 6

Development of Wenzhou Centralized Industrial Wholesale Markets

In the era of social division of labor, "economy begins with the threshold of exchange value" (Braudel, 1993), and the market is the core of the whole economic system and the most important part of the economic process. There is no doubt that in the course of the great economic and social changes in Wenzhou since China's reform and opening-up, the wholesale market of centralized industrial products has played the most active role in this historical drama.[1] This is because the wholesale market of centralized industrial products is an indispensable point for Wenzhou to break through the barriers of the planned economic system and move toward market economy, and it is also an important driving force for Wenzhou's marketization. It is the inter-regional trade developed from the fringe and gap of the planned economy and it is the source of motive force for the initiation of private industrialization; it is the most important carrier of "path dependence effect" in the process of marketization of Wenzhou's history and regional culture. It is the main way of spreading and transplanting Wenzhou model and commercial culture. Therefore, the wholesale market of industrial products is an ideal window for the analysis and interpretation of Wenzhou model.

6.1 Centralized industrial wholesale markets and market-oriented reform

We define the centralized industrial wholesale market as the place which focuses on spot wholesale with centralized trading of a certain type of industrial product or some kinds of industrial products

---

[1] In China, most people call the centralized industrial wholesale market a professional market.

that are highly complementary and mutually substituted. It is a large-scale centralized shopkeeper-oriented market system arrangement. The centralized industrial wholesale market has five characteristics: (1) The centralized industrial wholesale market is a place where a commodity is traded centrally or where one category of commodities is traded mainly while operating a small number of other commodities. Thus, the centralized industrial wholesale market is a typical tangible market.

There are two ways to define whether the commodity in the market is the same kind of commodity. One idea is to regard a commodity with a certain degree of interdependence or complementarity as a "similar commodity" (Chen, 1996). However, the substitution coefficient and complementary coefficient of the lowest limit have not been measured quantitatively. The second idea is based on the classification of the catalog of commodities issued by the official statistics department, and it is advocated that the same commodity of the secondary catalog and below shall be regarded as a similar commodity (Luo, 1996). It mainly focuses on wholesale, concurrently operating retail. The number of sellers must reach a certain scale. It focuses on spot transactions, supplemented by forward contract transactions. Daily trading or weekly trading days are significantly longer than closure days. The first characteristic distinguishes it from integrated markets, supermarkets, and department stores. The second characteristic distinguishes it from the food market and the retail store; the third characteristic distinguishes it from the specialty store; the fourth characteristic distinguishes it from the commodity futures exchange; and the fifth characteristic distinguishes it from the rural periodic market (also known as intermittent market). Of course, in many cases, it is difficult to subdivide all kinds of markets strictly.

In the process of modern economic growth triggered by the great changes of industrial revolution and institutional structure, the development of Wenzhou's centralized industrial wholesale market plays a leading role in Wenzhou's economic and social development.

6.1.1 The centralized industrial wholesale market breaks through the barrier of the planned economy in Wenzhou and is the breeding ground for market economy

In the era of planned economy, the circulation of commodities was mainly controlled by the national commercial network. People participated in the wholesale and retail of industrial products as individual businessmen, which was treated as "speculation". However, Wenzhou, located on the fringes of the planned economy, the "street market" belonging to the underground economy, began to appear in Yongjia and other places before the 3rd Plenary Session of the 11th CPC Central Committee. To escape from the government's street market supervision, these "black markets" were mostly located in small towns and remote islands in the mountains. For these "street markets", the government adopted the policy of "banning, blocking and dispelling". But it turned out that there was no way to ban, block, or dispel it. Instead of being outlawed, these markets developed into the centralized industrial wholesale market with a certain scale after the 3rd Plenary Session of the 11th CPC Central Committee. Why did this happen? In our opinion, although "work contracted to households" and "fix farm output quotas for each household" and the household contract responsibility system caused the transformation of the production system within the agricultural sector, the role of this reform in stimulating Wenzhou farmers to transfer to non-agricultural industries couldn't be underestimated.

After calculating the actual income of Wenzhou farmers, we can find that the actual income of the peasants in the 1970s was lower than that in 1957, and that in 1957 was lower than that in 1952. This indicates that farmers who engaged in production activities under the system of people's communes and production teams not only had very low absolute values of the actual income but their marginal returns also tended to be zero or even negative. This was not only related to rural population growth and the law of diminishing marginal income of land but also caused by institutional factors. Under the traditional system, farmers had to rely on system breakthrough and institutional innovation to get rid of difficulties.

In the process of induced institutional change in rural China, the institutional change of the agricultural sector was first recognized by the government. The government organized and promoted the popularization of the household contract responsibility system in rural areas nationwide. Due to the influence of the law of rural population growth and the decline of marginal income of land, the potential of productivity growth brought about by the reform of agricultural production system was limited. With the popularization of the household contract responsibility system, the marginal income generated by the agricultural production system reform decreased and tended toward zero. When the level of agricultural production technology could not break through continuously in the short term, the only option for farmers was to shift to non-agricultural industries to increase profit opportunities and space. The productivity growth caused by the reform of the agricultural production system greatly increased the agricultural surplus labor force, which to a certain extent further strengthened the farmers' impulse to get rid of land bondage. It is also worth mentioning that under the traditional system, political risk was a powerful restraining force for farmers wanting to engage in institutional change and innovation. The impact of change of agricultural production systems on farmers' spontaneity in fact reduced the expected value of the political risk of farmers engaged in non-agricultural industries, thereby enhancing the farmers' spontaneous courage and confidence for institutional change and innovation. Therefore, by the end of the 1970s, with the implementation of the household contract responsibility system, the Wenzhou region, with a strong institutional innovation potential impulse, was the first to launch a major change involving agriculture, industry, and the circulation field.

The "street market" in Wenzhou came to being and survived under such a complicated system background, which contained the inevitability of the centralized industrial wholesale market.

By 1985, there were 2,847 markets in Wenzhou, followed by the top ten professional markets and professional production bases in China.

It was this batch of centralized industrial wholesale markets which made it possible for Wenzhou's private enterprises to obtain raw materials and wholesale goods outside the state-owned circulation channels controlled by the government. Therefore, the centralized industrial wholesale market was not only the main driving force of Wenzhou's industrialization but also the most important breeding ground for the market economy.

6.1.2 The centralized industrial wholesale market is the "special market" in Wenzhou's economic system transformation period

The centralized industrial wholesale market offers a relaxed and secure market trading environment that is different from the outside. This is because the centralized wholesale market has a more important role in increasing the local fiscal revenue and employment, and promoting development of the tertiary industry and "one township, one product" and the "one village, one product" specialized industrial agglomeration area. Local governments, driven by their own interests, are interested in creating a "special market zone". Inside the centralized industrial wholesale market, discriminatory distinctions are eliminated against non-local commodities and operators and tax rates reduced significantly, directly or indirectly, in the form of an inclusive tax system. In the area of social security, the security of market activities is provided by focusing on protection. In the aspect of market supervision and administrative law enforcement, there is more tolerance for selling counterfeit and inferior commodities and other illegal acts, and even intentionally protecting the same. In terms of the credit guarantee, government and market intermediary organizations act as mediators of the trilateral governance structure, providing credit guarantee for market trading activities not based on geopolitical relations and kinship. Under the existing social development background and in the institutional environment, local governments cannot create a more fair, more free, and safer system environment for the trading activities of the whole social market. However, local governments, driven by their own interests, tend to artificially create a system gap in the local area of the wholesale market.

The local government's policy orientation and the formation of direct participation in the market have accelerated the development of the wholesale market. The formation and the development of the centralized industrial wholesale market play a significant role in increasing the fiscal revenue of local governments, starting and accelerating regional industrialization and economic development.

6.1.3 The rapid growth of centralized industrial wholesale market has greatly promoted the marketization process in Wenzhou

The centralized industrial wholesale market is a kind of completely competitive market. In the internal market, there are a large number of buyers and sellers with great transaction amounts. It is very difficult for any individual household to manipulate the market through its own pricing behaviors and sales, and the competition between the buyers and sellers is sufficient.

Not only that, driven by their own interests, the local governments will attract non-local businessmen and goods to the local centralized industrial wholesale market in order to expand the scale of the local market business scope and radiation. To this end, local governments have generally implemented non-discriminatory policies within the market for local and non-local goods, local businessmen and non-local businessmen. In the process of China's reform, local protectionism has disappeared under the specific circumstances of the centralized industrial wholesale market. In a sense, at the beginning of the reform, the centralized industrial wholesale market was the most market-oriented form of market organization. Therefore, in the early stage of the reform and opening-up, a local wholesale market for industrial products was developed. The larger the proportion of the turnover of the centralized industrial wholesale market in the whole society, the higher the degree of marketization. In the 1980s and the beginning of the 1990s, Wenzhou was the most developed region with a centralized industrial wholesale market in China, and its turnover ranked first in Zhejiang Province, known as the "big market province".

The contribution of the centralized industrial wholesale market to the marketization of Wenzhou's economy is not only directly reflected in the growth of its own trading scale but also in the drive of a large number of market players who make one's own management decisions and take full responsibility for one's own profits and losses. The growth of township enterprises and family enterprises provides a broad market for the formation of factors outside the system. The distribution network of the centralized industrial wholesale market is mainly controlled by a plan compared with that of state-run cooperation commercial sales network. Due to the obvious functional substitution relationship between the two sales networks, the comparative efficiency advantages of the centralized industrial wholesale market determined by the low transaction cost and flexible mechanism have put great pressure on the national commercial sector. Therefore, the rapid rise of the industrial wholesale market has broken the situation that state-run cooperation business monopolizes the wholesale industry, and the competition between the two has greatly sped up the marketization process of the mechanically rigid state-run cooperation commerce.

6.2 Centralized industrial wholesale markets and the industrialization process

6.2.1 The centralized industrial wholesale market provides a shared sales network with low transaction costs

In real economic life, in the process of entering the field of human consumption from the field of production, the products have to go through a number of marketing organizations or individuals, who together form a channel to make the goods flow freely. More precisely, the sales network refers to the channel formed by the middlemen connected in the process of the transfer of certain goods or services from the producers to the consumers and in the process of transfer of commodity ownership.

As a shared distribution network, the centralized industrial wholesale market is a place where the wholesale trade is dominant and focuses on a certain type of commodity or a number of commodities that are highly complementary and interchangeable. It is a centralized trading shopkeeper market system. This tangible market is a huge commodity circulation network. It is not only the center of distribution of commodities but also the center of information agglomeration. There are a lot of shops and trade fairs outside as the end of the network spread to urban and rural areas. The enterprises that sell products through the centralized industrial wholesale market can share the marketing scale economic advantages formed by the huge flow of specialized market goods, information, and logistics and large scale of radiation. Therefore, for thousands of small-scale enterprises, the centralized industrial wholesale market is a kind of low transaction cost-shared sales network. The reason for the small- and medium-sized enterprises being unable to establish their own sales network with the centralized industrial wholesale market as the sales channel is obviously not accidental factors, because from the perspective of the development course of Western specialized markets, it is the same. In fact, through further investigation, it is not difficult to find the benefits of centralized trading.

(1) It saves the cost of searching for information.

There is no doubt about the fact that through centralized trading it is obviously easier to obtain useful information at low cost than decentralized transactions. A simple comparison was made by Sheng assuming that all parties in a group lived along a circle, and one of them had to walk around at least once to get complete information, with a circumference radius of $2nR$ (R is the radius). If there was a centrally traded market at the center of the circle, he completed a transaction with a

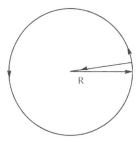

Figure 6.1. A centrally traded market.

walking distance of $2R$ (see Figure 6.1). A frugal walk distance was 68% ($=1-2R/2nR$). It is clear that many of the initial markets largely developed driven by this cost-saving search for information.

(2) It restrains opportunism tendency and improves trading efficiency.

In the absence of the introduction of advanced transaction methods (such as standardized transactions, letter of credit transactions, network transactions, etc.), the traditional transaction of "cash on delivery" of cash to physical goods is utilized. The seller has more information advantages. Therefore, the seller will take advantage of this to produce opportunism. In the absence of other credible measures for credit protection, the buyer is most likely to counter passively by canceling the transaction. Obviously, the seller is not able to form a credit mortgage because the seller is mobile under the itinerant trader system. So it is difficult to complete a deal unless it is of small value.

However, the shopkeeper system is different. Because the information of a fixed place of sale is actually a kind of mortgage, it can reduce the cost of return and compensate for the demand, so it can effectively restrain the opportunistic behavior of the seller. Therefore, the buyer definitely prefers the shopkeeper to the itinerant trader. For the seller, only small and small-value trading can be completed under the itinerant trader system, and an effective credit and information screening mechanism cannot be provided to enable the buyer to select a reliable seller. Therefore, in consideration of the expansion of the transaction scale and the continuous transaction, the seller must also choose the form of the shopkeeper business to obtain the buyer's trust. Therefore, it is a Nash equilibrium to choose the shopkeeper business transaction system.

(3) It is a platform for trading for highly fragmented needs and small-scale production.

A common phenomenon is that centralized markets prevail in countries and regions where social division of labor and socialized mass production lag behind. Setting up one's own sales network and purchasing organization is possible when the modern production and technology are developed. When demand and production supply are still scattered and on a small scale, independent buying and marketing networks are certainly not economical. Centralized transaction provides such transitional support that even fairly fragmented and small deals can be successfully completed. As a result, when individuals scattered and bound small-scale supply and demand together, they would form a sizable group of transactions. In this group, the general supply can find the demand, and the general demand can also find the supply. The cost of the meeting of the supply and demand is greatly reduced, and the probability of completing the transaction is greatly increased.

(4) It is convenient for government market supervision.

If we pay a little attention to history and reality, we will find a universal fact that no matter how most of the markets were originally developed, finally, it is always the government that sets or sets up a fixed place to trade. In fact, it would be profitable for the government to use administrative power to fix and centralize decentralized transactions. These interests include the convenience of government fee collection and the control of trading order. In his great book, *Civilization and Capitalism 15th–18th Century,* the famous French economic historian, Fernand Braudel, discussed the rise of Western professional markets on the eve of the industrial revolution and believed that the government's purposeful construction of trading venues had undoubtedly contributed greatly to the rise of these markets. But the government's original motives are often not so simple. The control of the transaction and convenient tax collection are more likely to be the original starting points. Decentralized trading is the easiest way to foster liberalization and undermine the power of government control. Therefore, in the early stage of the growth of the centralized industrial wholesale market, the local government sets up a number of fixed places for traders to focus transactions on while at the same time it tends to suppress the scattered transactions.

In the history of the Wenzhou market, the impetus by the government has been quite remarkable. In the early stage of the reform and opening-up, Wenzhou formed a large street market. The local government initially tried to suppress the circulation of goods outside the system by means like chasing and blocking, but with little effect. Finally, the local government guided it in the light of its general trend. Its policy orientation for the centralized industrial wholesale markets has experienced the process from prohibition to default to encouragement. Since the mid-1980s, most of the centralized industrial wholesale markets have been initiated or led by the government and relevant functional departments. This clearly has a motive for seeking profits, but it is important to facilitate the government's aim for more effective supervision of the market.

6.2.2 The centralized industrial wholesale market has promoted the regional division of labor and internal division of labor in Wenzhou industry

Adam Smith put forward in his *The Wealth of Nations* long ago the proposition that the division of labor is limited by the scope of the market, which is called the Smith Theorem. Later, the economist Young further proved that the degree of division of labor determines the scope of the market, namely, the Young Theorem. Superficially, there seems to be a logical circular argument, but in fact the inherent meaning of the "Smith-Young Theorem" indicates that the deepening of division of labor and the expansion of market boundary are mutually reinforcing processes. The division of labor is not only restricted by the existing market scope but also promotes the expansion of the market scope. The rise of the centralized industrial wholesale market in Wenzhou provides excellent realistic materials for the above theory.

(1) The centralized industrial wholesale market and inter-regional division of labor.

The centralized industrial wholesale market promotes the inter-regional division of labor in the form of the so-called "characteristic industrial agglomeration area", which is commonly known as the "block economy". "Block economy" is a prominent feature in the process of rural industrialization in Wenzhou, and the phenomenon of "one village, one product, one township and one product" is very common. It is inseparable from the expansion of commodity circulation in the professional market. In theory, the centralized trading place is actually a typical public product, and it is a public product with a strong positive externality. The acquisition of this external revenue is sufficient to attract the participation of a large number of operators. In the process of rural industrialization in Wenzhou, the reason why "front stall and rear factory" with small-scale production and marketing integration can exist efficiently is that it depends on the existence of a professional market with a large scale of centralized trading. Without the professional market, it is not economical for a single enterprise to sell what it produces. However, the existence of the centralized industrial wholesale market not only makes the self-selling method exist but also reinforces the "block". Because there is an obvious scale effect on sales (circulation), the more people who run a business, the better the market will flourish.

Therefore, the concentration of the specialized industry in a space with the centralized industrial wholesale market as the core is naturally formed and continuously strengthened.

From a macro point of view, the centralized industrial wholesale market plays an important role in fully exploiting regional comparative advantages. In the absence of the centralized industrial wholesale market, it is difficult to support the logistics required by a region for the so-called "indirect production". More specifically, the existence of a centralized industrial wholesale market makes it easier for a region to sell its distinctive products, reducing the cost of trading. In this situation, it is helpful for a region to give full play to its comparative advantages and make specialized production. Wenzhou's practice fully proves this point. The rise of the centralized industrial wholesale market has led to the vigorous growth of local industries.

(2) The centralized industrial wholesale market and regional division of labor.

While enhancing the formation of "block economy" between the regions, the centralized industrial wholesale market also promotes the formation and deepening of division of labor within the region. For the regional production system, the primary role of the centralized industrial wholesale market is to promote the expansion of the product market, that is, the expansion of product sales, and then the expansion of the scale of production. But the problem is far from simple. There are different ways to expand the scale of production. It can be the horizontal expansion of the scale or the deepening of vertical division of labor of all enterprises. The centralized industrial wholesale market has significantly promoted the deepening of the vertical division of labor. The reasons are as follows: First of all, the accumulation of human capital in specialized production should make it easy for horizontal expansion, because the accumulation of specialized human capital is vertical. It is very easy to produce a certain product in the household handicraft industry to a skilled or superb level, but it is quite difficult to cross the variety, and the horizontal expansion also involves management problems, which is simply not acceptable to the general rural household industry. Therefore, the need for expansion of the result is to make the household industry more specialized with more detailed division of labor. Second, the centralized industrial wholesale market also provides a platform for more detailed division of labor with lower transaction costs. The division of labor leads to the increase of production efficiency but also increases the transaction cost. The equilibrium point of division of labor must be the increase of marginal transaction cost offsetting the increase of marginal productivity. However, the centralized industrial wholesale market has greatly reduced the transaction cost of intermediate products, thus greatly improving the degree of division of labor. For example, in the production and processing of the regenerated cloth of Cangnan, Wenzhou has an extremely detailed division of labor (as shown in Figure 6.2) (Ke, 1998), where the maintenance of the production is dependent on the organization and distribution of a series of intermediate products in the market of acrylic fabric.

Third, the centralized industrial wholesale market has effectively replaced the sales function of many enterprises, so that these small-scale enterprises can exist efficiently. According to Coase's understanding, the substitution of enterprises to the market is due to the existence of transaction costs. However, the reverse substitution of the centralized industrial wholesale market to enterprises precisely shows the reduction of transaction costs in the market. Because of the low transaction cost in the market, it is economical to refine the division of labor. Enterprises do not have to pay a high cost for purchasing upstream products and selling the products produced. Thus, they can produce more specialized intermediate products to achieve a higher efficiency and scale.

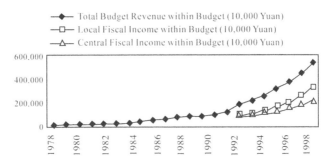

Figure 6.2.   Process of labor division of Cangnan Cotton Yarn.

6.3 Centralized industrial wholesale markets and changes of social structures in Wenzhou

The so-called social structure refers to the composition or distribution of various social relations, including interpersonal relations, clan relations, organizational relations, class relations, economic relations, political relations, and community relations. Social structural change or transformation is referred to as the so-called the "third hand" or "another invisible hand" beyond market regulation (intangible "invisible hand") and state intervention (tangible "visible hand") (Yuan, 1998).

The transition of social structures is a gradual process. When the continuous change of social structures is sufficient to make one social state transform to another, a comprehensive and holistic transformation of social structures takes place. From the sociologist's point of view, the changes or transformation of social structures should at least be reflected in the aspects of economic development and economic structure (including industrial structures, division of labor structure, population structures, and system structures), the level of modernization, the social value system and its realization ways, governance means of social economic order, etc.

In other words, what people need to pay attention to is the following: Is economic development balanced or unbalanced? Is it sustainable or predatory? Under what economic system is the allocation of resources and social products realized? How does agricultural civilization change to industrial civilization and rural society to urban society? How can society change from closed to open, from single to diverse? How do the social groups divide and break through the social network that is tied by blood or geography, and reweave the new social network that is bound by karma?

In the process of social structure change and transformation in Wenzhou, the centralized industrial wholesale market undoubtedly plays a very active role. It plays a huge role in promoting the transformation of the rural and urban areas of Wenzhou into the commodity economy and then the socialist market economy from the product economy characterized by self-sufficiency or planned supply, the transformation from the agricultural society and the rural society to the industrial society and the urban society, the transformation from the closed, semi-closed society to the open society, from the homogeneous and single society to the heterogeneous and diverse society, and the transformation from the ethical society, which is bound by blood and land, to the legal society, which is bound by karma and contract. We can analyze it in five aspects.

(1) The centralized industrial wholesale market of the industrial wholesale market promotes the circulation of commodities and provides the conditions for the establishment and improvement of the market economic system.

After the rural household contract responsibility system made the farmers become independent commodity producers, and after opening of rural centralized trading, the rural economy and farmers' living consumption gradually broke the closed state of self-sufficiency. After the centralized industrial wholesale market came into being, farmers were more free from the production and consumption mode of "buy for use" and "buy for sale", and started to "buy for sale", which was mainly producing for society and not for their own consumption. This fundamentally broke the self-sufficiency of production and consumption patterns. In the cities, the centralized wholesale markets also changed the way of supplies, introducing the competition mechanism in the field of circulation to promote the establishment of a series of systems that conformed to the laws of market economy. To some extent, in Wenzhou, the early emergence and development of a number of centralized industrial wholesale markets on the basis of primary markets in the countryside or city street markets provided a good market foundation for smooth and quick establishment of a market economic system framework.

(2) The development of the centralized industrial wholesale market has accelerated the pace of industrialization and urbanization in the countryside.

Before the emergence of the centralized industrial wholesale market, the rural primary market, the urban farmers' market, and also the street market, to a certain extent, promoted society to increase the possibility of resource allocation and acquisition, especially having accumulated capitals for the development of township enterprises and private economy. However, it is undeniable that the trading scope of the primary market is narrow, the level of organizational standard is low, and it is difficult to directly promote industrialization and urbanization in the countryside.

After the emergence and development of the centralized industrial wholesale market, the scale of the transaction expanded and the scope expanded beyond agricultural and sideline products. It was based on the light industrial products necessary for people's daily life. As a result, it broke out of the local rural community, and began to radiate to the surrounding areas and to the whole country, which led to the development of the surrounding areas. The centralized industrial wholesale market broke the boundary between traditional agriculture and industry, blurred industrial boundaries, and increased the proportion of secondary and tertiary industries in rural areas, promoted the transfer of agricultural labor force to industry, reduced the difference between rural and urban income, and promoted the process of rural industrialization. With the process of industrialization, rural urbanization or urbanization increased day by day.

(3) The centralized industrial wholesale market promotes social openness and increases the radius of communication.

The characteristics of the centralized industrial wholesale market are different from those of the traditional intermittent market: The main subject is not a necessity for life but for the purpose of profit. It is "buy for sale". Therefore, it is not restricted by rural areas, agricultural products, sideline products, etc. It operates those that can make money and extends transaction relation to areas where it can make money. It has broken the limitation of system, industry, and class. Operators take part in the market and competition in the form of organization, use modern means of transport and communication, strengthen the function of radiation, and extend and enrich the denotation and connotation of the trading network. This greatly expands people's trading radius and improves the openness of the whole society. Wenzhou's centralized industrial wholesale market began to expand toward other cities and provinces since the mid-1980s. Commodity distribution centers like "Wenzhou village", "Wenzhou street", and areas with relatively centralized Wenzhou businessmen appeared.

(4) The centralized industrial wholesale market promotes the social differentiation between urban and rural areas and increases the heterogeneity of society.

The development of the centralized industrial wholesale market has freed more rural labor from agricultural work, and transferred them to the second and tertiary industries and also turned some workers or unemployed people in cities and towns into business operators. This has greatly changed industrial structures of rural and urban areas, and employment structures. Economic status or identity is no longer the only measure of social stratification. Occupation has gradually become an important basis for the formation of a new social group structure. In a professional market, it does not matter whether the operator is a farmer or a laid-off worker, a cadre on leave or a person released from prison. What matters is what goods he manages and to what extent he has a shared sales network. In short, in the market, everybody's profession is businessman. It forms the benefit distribution relation by the commercial law. In this kind of relation development, some people became professional and specialized in business, forming a new social stratum.

(5) The centralized industrial wholesale market has introduced a new regulation mechanism to traditional rural society — the mechanism of interest — thus breaking the past situation of regulating social relations only by blood and geography.

As we have said above, the centralized industrial wholesale market is different from the rural primary market in that the operators are not engaged in business activities only for their own needs, but for profit. The organization of the market is also better. The main subject of the market is not only an individual farmer but also an organizational entity comprising different operators. In this way, the purpose of organization is to shorten information searching time, reduce transaction cost, and gain more benefits. The "blood" of life for maintaining an organization can only be of interest. Kinship and rural relationships, at best, can only be a priority at the beginning of a network organization. After accessing the network, the main role is still interest. That is to say, the mechanism of interest regulation transcends the relationship between blood and geography. This fundamentally broke through the traditional patriarchal clan, small peasant economy, and geographical constraints. The legal person organizations based on the business edge are more and more obviously replaced by family, clan, and local patriarchal and administrative organizations to realize the benefit adjustment function of the allocation of resources. In Wenzhou, during the reform of the so-called "Ten Specialized Markets", including Yongjia Qiaotou Button Market, Yueqing Liushi Low-Voltage Electrical Apparatus Market, Ruian Mayu Glasses Market, and Pingyang Shuitou Leather Market at the beginning of the reform and opening-up, the connected production industries adopted single-family production. However, the household industry technology was not high, and the testing means were backward, so it was difficult to meet the requirements of the wholesale market for the concentrated trade industrial products, especially the specialized market with relatively high technology content, such as the low-voltage electrical apparatus market in Liushi. Therefore, around 1984, the "economic union" partnership organization appeared. This organization was mostly bonded by blood and affection. There was no standard contract with characteristics of the "family economy", but it hired a certain amount of labor force to carry out business activities through the capital, technology, and business cooperation, featuring equal shares, risk sharing, and benefit sharing (Zhao & Zhu, 2000). Economic associations are beneficial to expand scale, increase varieties, and meet the requirements of the market for product upgrading. After 1987, the joint-stock cooperative enterprise in the form of economic union development emerged from the general township enterprises and became a relatively independent form of enterprise organization. At the beginning of the 1990s, it was popularized in Zhejiang Province and even the whole country. This kind of organization highlighted the significance of "share" in the organization, and the mechanism of resource allocation and interest regulation had been established on the basis of legal person to a greater extent.

6.4 Development prospect of centralized industrial wholesale markets

In recent years, the rapid development of the centralized industrial wholesale market in Wenzhou has slowed down greatly, mainly because the annual turnover growth rate of commodities has been decreasing year by year. There are even many "shell markets" or "semi-shell markets". The proportion of the total sales volume in the local market has dropped from 70% to 40%, and the proportion of transactions in the intangible market has been greatly increased. Many large companies have withdrawn from specialized markets to build their own sales networks. Wenzhou's rank of total trade volume dropped from No. 1 in the 1980s to No. 7 in Zhejiang Province. The enterprise sales network has become the main product sales channels in developed areas. In 1996, for example, the annual sales of Zhengtai Low Voltage Electrical Group was 1.24 billion yuan, compared with 156 million yuan for Liushi China Electric City. To a certain extent, these phenomena reflect the decline of the function and status of the wholesale market of centralized trade industrial products. The main reasons are as follows:

Chapter 6 Development of
Wenzhou Centralized Industrial Wholesale Markets

(1) The weakening of the function of the centralized industrial wholesale is the concrete manifestation that the stage characteristics of China's economic development have begun to change greatly. Since the early 1990s, the industrialization of the country has entered the leading stage of heavy chemical industry, and the economic development strategy in the coastal developed areas has gradually shifted from quantity expansion primarily to give priority to structural adjustment and optimization. Under this new developmental background, the centralized industrial wholesale market has weakened the driving force of Wenzhou's economic growth. This is because, since the reform and opening-up, Wenzhou has taken advantage of the regional business culture and business talents to greatly develop the individual private economy and the professional market, achieved the development of the traditional economic sectors (mainly those based on traditional technology and marketing means), and gradually formed the economic structure of "light and small" and the institutional structure with remarkable characteristics of classical market economy (it was mainly manifested in the large number of enterprises, but with a generally small scale, as there were no organization, sufficient market competition, and higher degree of economic freedom that were suitable for large production), which was adapted to the initial stage of industrialization. The process of industrialization in Wenzhou had been promoted by the long-term development of the "ten professional markets of rural industrialization". As a result, the total volume of traditional economic sectors was relatively large and the modern economic sectors (mainly the economic sectors based on modern production technology and marketing methods) were insufficient. This had become the most significant structural contradiction in Wenzhou's economic growth, and had seriously affected the development of Wenzhou's economy. In the early 1990s, the local government put forward the slogan of "second entrepreneurship", and accelerated the structural upgrading as the main task of Wenzhou's economic development.

In the structural transformation times of the economic development, for the centralized industrial wholesale market as a market system that fits the traditional sectors of the economy, its function and strategic status in Wenzhou's economic development were bound to fall.

(2) The weakening of the function of the centralized industrial wholesale market is the concrete manifestation of the deepening of the system reform. As the reform moves forward, the framework of the market economic system will be gradually established, and the institutional gap between the internal and external systems of the centralized industrial wholesale market will gradually disappear. For example, the institutional barriers to the entry of rural enterprises into the commercial circulation network have been largely eliminated. The formation of the unified market and regional integration are gradually breaking down the regional barriers of commodity circulation. The implementation of the unified tax rate will make the preferential tax policies in the centralized industrial wholesale market lose legal basis. More importantly, the overall positioning of the economic system reform in the country is as a modern market economic system, and the centralized industrial wholesale market is a traditional market system that fits the classical form of market economy. With modern enterprises becoming the most important micro foundations of national economy, traffic, communication, methods of settlement, information transmission channels, and other technical factors affecting the market transaction have experienced a substantive change, and the function of the traditional market system will tend to be weakened.

(3) The weakening of the function of the centralized industrial wholesale market is the inevitable result of industrial organization transformation. Industrial organization refers to the competition and cooperation between enterprises in an industry. The basic characteristics of industrial organizations that are suitable for modern mass production and modern market economy are as follows: The

small- and medium-sized enterprises in the industry are connected into an organism directly or indirectly through large enterprises, forming a variety of divisions of labor and collaboration networks at the core of large enterprises. The market competition among independent enterprises in the industry is partially replaced by the organized divisions of labor and cooperation between enterprises. Dominant large enterprises undertake the function of adjustment and organization of the competitive and cooperative relationship between enterprises, and the market competition pattern shifts from the mainly dispersed market competition between enterprises to the market competition between the dominant large enterprises. Therefore, with the continuous development of the economy, not only will the expansion of enterprises lead to an increasing number of enterprises leaving the centralized industrial wholesale market to establish the exclusive sales network but the development of the integrated division of labor will also make a large number of small enterprises become the cooperative enterprises of large enterprises. The sales channels will shift from the centralized industrial wholesale market to the sales network of large enterprises, as shown in Figure 6.3.

Curve I, curve II, and curve III, respectively, represent the sales cost curve of the unit product of the "itinerant trader" direct personnel

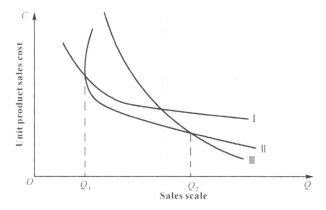

Figure 6.3. Sales network of large enterprises.

promotion, shared sales network, and exclusive sales network. When the size of the enterprise is in the $(0, Q1)$ interval, due to the small scale of production and sales scale, whether through buying the centralized wholesale market stalls for obtaining shared sales network or setting up exclusive sales network, the cost of sharing of the unit product is too high to be economical. Therefore, it is the most economical for enterprises to choose "itinerant trader" direct personnel promotion.

When the enterprise scale is in the $(Q1, Q2)$ interval, as the scale of the business expands, if companies continue to adopt "itinerant trader" personnel promotion, it will lead to higher sales costs due to the need to hire more salespeople. Since the enterprise is not large enough, establishing the exclusive sales network by enterprises is difficult to compense completely, and it is possible to meet the necessary capital barriers. Therefore, for enterprises of this range, the centralized industrial wholesale market is a kind of sales network with lower unit product sales expense and necessary capital quantity. When the enterprise scale is larger than $Q2$, the cost of establishing the exclusive sales network is relatively easy to compense by the scale economy of marketing due to large scale. As a result of stronger enterprise financial strength, it is more easy to overcome barriers to acquire the necessary capital amount. Thus, it has the advantage of economies of scale in marketing. Most larger companies choose to set up exclusive sales networks. In the late 1970s and the early 1980s, such "market zones" were difficult to form in a city with planned economy and a relatively developed network of commercial circulation. This to a certain extent can explain why the centralized industrial wholesale market in the 15th and 16th centuries took place in the city, while at the beginning of the reform, China's centralized industrial wholesale markets took place in the rural areas.

From the point of view of system demand and supply, the development of the centralized industrial wholesale market has experienced four stages: In the first stage, the demand for the centralized industrial wholesale market is obviously stronger than that in the supply of the system. The main bottleneck restricting the development of the centralized industrial wholesale market is the shortage of system supply.

In the second stage, the supply capacity of the centralized industrial wholesale market system is suitable for the demand of the society. In the third stage, the system demand of the centralized industrial wholesale market is weakened, and the supply capacity of the centralized industrial wholesale market in the traditional centralized industrial wholesale market is excessive. However, due to the insufficiency of functional innovation in the centralized industrial wholesale market, the centralized industrial wholesale market system supply is unable to create a new market of this kind — a system demand of a modern centralized industrial wholesale market that fits modern commerce. In the fourth stage, with the adjustment of the centralized industrial wholesale market system and the reorganization and function innovation of the same market, the quantity of the traditional centralized industrial wholesale market will be reduced to the level corresponding to the traditional economic sector, and the supply capacity of the modern centralized industrial wholesale market will also adapt to the development of modern economic sectors. At present, the centralized industrial wholesale market is in the process of transition from the second stage to the third stage. The system demand for the traditional centralized industrial wholesale market is weakening, and the development prospect of the centralized industrial wholesale market will mainly depend on its function innovation abilities. System supply factors have become the main contradiction restricting the development of the centralized industrial wholesale market. There are two main reasons why the functional innovation of the centralized industrial wholesale market is seriously deficient. The first reason is that the theoretical research is lagging behind. Till now, most scholars in the theoretical circle have realized that the function and position of the traditional professional market in the economic system will tend to weaken. However, there is a lack of strong theoretical argument for the future development direction and the operation mode of the centralized industrial wholesale market, especially the ultra-large market. In addition, the theoretical circle does not attach importance to the "tradition" of the centralized industrial wholesale market, which leads to serious shortage of the theoretical innovation subject of the centralized industrial wholesale market system. The second reason is that the centralized industrial wholesale market lacks modern management personnel, leading to serious shortage of system innovation subject in the practical aspect.

At present, the theoretical circle, government departments and market organizers generally believe that the development of the centralized industrial wholesale market is in the adjustment stage. With the improvement of the macroeconomic situation, the centralized industrial wholesale market achieves a certain scale. The centralized industrial wholesale market will bottom out, and enter a new development climax. We think the reason why these optimists come to this conclusion is mainly the lack of analysis of the long-term factors which can decide the future basic trend of the centralized industrial wholesale market from the dynamic and historical perspectives, which is the foundation of gradually weakening existence and development of the centralized industrial wholesale market. This blind optimism may lead to more investment mistakes in practice. At present, many places still blindly build a variety of "malls" and "squares", and undertake large-scale investment attraction.

Such phenomena are common in many other provinces and cities. Therefore, there is an urgent need for objective analysis over the development prospect of the centralized industrial wholesale market.

The centralized industrial wholesale market is developed under special development backgrounds and system backgrounds. With the change of such a development background and system background, the development conditions of the centralized industrial wholesale market also change greatly. At present, the function weakening dilemma in the development of the centralized industrial wholesale market is not caused by accidental factors, nor is it mainly caused by the failure of policy operation. In a sense, this is determined by the long-term and in-depth factors affecting the future direction of the centralized industrial wholesale market. It is the manifestation of periodical shift in economic development and reform progress, and is the symbol of evolution from the traditional market system to the modern market system.

Of course, the function weakening of the traditional centralized industrial wholesale market is a long-term development trend. However, this does not mean that in the short and medium terms, the centralized industrial wholesale market will absolutely shrink or even disappear. Even in the long run, the mission of the traditional centralized industrial wholesale market will not end. Moreover, in the short and medium terms, the centralized industrial wholesale market still has some vitality in China, which is decided by the fact that the country has a vast territory, a low level of urbanization, a large and dispersed rural population, a large number of low-income people, and other factors conducive to giving play to the traditional centralized industrial wholesale market in the short and medium terms. Moreover, with the deepening of functional innovation in the centralized industrial wholesale market, the market itself will evolve continuously. The centralized industrial wholesale market, which is compatible with the modern economy, will continue to develop. The centralized industrial wholesale market will not only be important at present but will also play an important role in China's economic development in the future.

Chapter 7

Evolution of the Leather Shoes Industry in Wenzhou

7.1 Introduction

In a market of information asymmetry, it is an important guarantee for normal operation of the market that the informed doesn't deceive the uninformed by its information superiority. Especially when there are institutional market obstacles, correction of information asymmetry in market transactions deserves suspicion. It is generally acknowledged that if there are institutional market obstacles, to break one's promise in business is unavoidable because of imperfect laws and regulations and the stage of capital accumulation. Though we cannot deny effects of these factors on impeding or facilitating market credit, it seems that they cannot offer more information about the loss of market credit and the internal mechanism of development. What we need to discuss is how institutional market obstacles lead to general credit loss of enterprises and how market development drives credit behavior of market subjects. According to experience, distortion of enterprise behavior is associated with a specific market system and structure and does not necessarily depend on scale and technology of enterprises and internal quality of operators. Profit-seeking behavior of enterprises promotes market competition. Market credit is closely related to changes of a market system and the structure, and enterprise behavior is only the optimal choice in a specific institutional structure. Therefore, the problem of market credit in essence is an institutional problem. However, the existing theory often explains the loss of market credit caused by deficiency of a market system from the perspective of external standard only. In other words, the theory attributes the loss of market credit to imperfect regulations of market competition (namely, "lack of a legal basis") and insufficient supervision and punishment of violators in market competition (people who break their promise) by administrative departments (namely, "slack law enforcement"). Furthermore, formation of market credit is attributed to sound rule of law and improvement of administrative quality. Similarly, people always attribute changes of market credit to the government.

However, we attempt to study the loss and reconstruction of market credit. The intuitionistic logic given in this book is that market segmentation under a planned system results in poor circulation of market information. Market subjects who received the property right reform first deceived the uninformed because of extension of the segmentation in a market-oriented reform leading to information difference between the two parties. As a result, a market of substandard goods is formed by the mechanism of adverse selection. When these market subjects gradually expand the market, they also gradually reduce information negentropy of the market to promote market mergence and information circulation. In this process, mutual signal transmission of both sides of transactions leads to gradual segregation of a market, where substandard products are gradually separated from certified products. As a result, dishonest behavior of selling seconds at best-quality prices disappears in the market and market credit is established. Of course, perfection of rules of market transactions and the mechanism of market supervision play an extremely important role in this process. It seems that the establishment of market credit in essence reflects an evolutionary mechanism in a market, which is what we need to explore. The industry of leather shoes in Wenzhou changed from manufacture and selling of fake commodities to creation and protection of brands and is a good example for us to carry out relevant research.

7.2 Development and changes of the leather shoes industry in Wenzhou

Wenzhou's shoemaking industry dates back to the Southern Song Dynasty.[1] During the Ming Dynasty, Wenzhou shoes were famous as articles of tribute.[2] Before the founding of the PRC, Wenzhou's shoemaking industry was an important part of Wenzhou's industry and commerce. After the founding of the PRC, Wenzhou's shoemaking industry developed slightly mainly because several state-owned shoe factories were founded through transformation of industry and commerce. By 1957, the output of leather shoes had reached 163,000 pairs in the urban district of Wenzhou and Wenzhou became an important place of production of leather shoes. In 1978, there were more than 10 state-owned and collective factories of leather shoes in the urban district with an annual output of 496,800 pairs. Thus, it can be seen that a complete shoemaking system had been established in the urban district of Wenzhou with a strong atmosphere of shoemaking before the reform and opening-up. Before the reform and opening-up, many Wenzhou people moved away and mended and polished shoes for a living.

Since the reform and opening-up, many farmers in the suburbs and some off-duty workers started to set up domestic shoemaking workshops. Originally, the production and selling pattern of these domestic shoemaking workshops was simple. An enterprise founded by off-duty workers was

---

[1] In "Number One Scholar Zhang Xie", a classical local opera of Wenzhou in Zhejiang Province, compiled by the Jiushan Book Club during the Southern Song Dynasty, a song named "Leather Shoe Zhao" is regarded as the earliest record about the origin of Wenzhou's shoemaking industry by historians.

[2] According to relevant historical records, in the 1890s, there were 13 tanneries with a capital of 288 million yuan and 128 employees in Yongjia. By 1932, there were 26 tanneries with a capital of 461 million yuan and the total value of export was 320,000 yuan. According to "Records of credit investigation of taxes of firms in Yongjia" in 1931, "there are nearly thirty tanning factories and seventy shoe factories" in Yongjia.

often attached to a unit (a state-owned or collective enterprise). If products of the enterprise belonged to the same industry as the unit, they were sold via channels of national controlled procurement and distribution, that is, operations of enterprises run by individuals but attached to public institutions. If products of the enterprise didn't belong to the same industry as the unit, these products were sold via road markets and acquaintances who went out and engaged in trade, as did products of enterprises run by farmers. It's worth noting that in the initial stage of the national reform, products produced by informal enterprises outside the planned system generally could not be sold via channels of national controlled procurement and distribution. Fortunately, the long-term business tradition of Wenzhou contributed to solving this problem. Many Wenzhou people who were spread out throughout the country formed a huge marketing network and survived in the planned economic system. In the mid-1980s, Wenzhou's industry of leather shoes boomed. In 1983, the output of leather shoes of Wenzhou was 239,000 pairs and its value of industrial output was 4.545 million yuan, accounting for 2.52% of the gross value of industrial output of Wenzhou, where a large number of small domestic shoemaking workshops were not included. In 1986, the value of industrial output of the industry of leather shoes reached 129.13 million yuan and the annual output of leather shoes was 9.29 million pairs. In 1988, it rocketed to 10.43 million pairs with an output value of 172.46 million yuan, accounting for 3.4% of the gross value of industrial output of Wenzhou (see Figure 7.1).

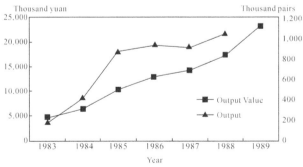

Figure 7.1. Development of Wenzhou's shoemaking industry in the initial stage of the reform and opening-up.

With the rapid development of Wenzhou's shoemaking industry, quality problems became increasingly severe. In 1985, a consumer from Nanjing wrote a letter to *Economic Daily* and said that a heel fell off from one of her new high-heeled shoes made in Wenzhou after she wore them for only one day. After taking a close look, she found that heels were connected to shoes with paste and the so-called genuine leather was just synthetic leather. All of a sudden, various nicknames, such as one-day shoes, morning-and-night shoes, and week shoes, were invented to describe the inferior leather shoes, spearheading attacks at Wenzhou's industry of leather shoes. In 1986, a newspaper office found by means of statistics that Wenzhou shoes received most complaints from consumers in ten major cities in China. What's more, in the border trade between China and Russia in the late 1980s, a great quantity of inferior leather shoes from Wenzhou were sold to the Soviet Union. As a result, lots of slogans like "Combat Wenzhou fakes" and "Evict Wenzhou people from Russia" appeared in the streets of Russia. In the summer of 1987, the event reached its climax when Hangzhou Administration for Industry and Commerce, a main sales (wholesale) area of Wenzhou's leather shoes, seized more than 5,000 pairs of inferior leather shoes (which were mainly made in Wenzhou) and these shoes were burned at Wulin Square on August 8. Suddenly, major media reported it and Wenzhou was indignantly denounced by the entire market. In April 1988, a counter of Wenzhou, leather shoes at a department store in Nanjing was destroyed by consumers who bought inferior leather shoes. Similar scenes of burning of Wenzhou's leather shoes occurred in Nanjing, Changsha, Harbin, and Zhuzhou successively. Consequently, various cities in China forbade selling Wenzhou's leather shoes. Departments of commercial distribution prohibited sales of Wenzhou's shoemaking industry products by official order in Shanghai, Nanjing, Wuhan, Dalian, Changchun, and Shijiazhuang. As a result, many stores put up the slogans "This store doesn't sell Wenzhou goods" and "No Wenzhou goods" at their gates to demonstrate the quality of their products.

The burning of Wenzhou's leather shoes deeply influenced consumers' understanding of the quality of Wenzhou's leather shoes (actually all Wenzhou goods). At that time, media and general consumers got used to regarding Wenzhou goods as inferior. In September 1990, a Xinhua dispatch reported that a commerce minister bought a pair of leather shoes during investigation in Hubei, but the heel dropped off the next day. A few days later, in the meeting of directors of commerce bureaus of 11 cities, this minister flew into a rage and instructed the departments concerned to investigate inferior goods strictly. Although this pair of shoes was unrelated to Wenzhou according to a later investigation, the local government started to pay attention to the quality of Wenzhou's leather shoes.

However, the situation was not improved effectively. Soon after the burning of Wenzhou's leather shoes at Wulin Square, Hangzhou, the Zhejiang provincial government specially issued documents and asked the departments concerned to "track down forged and fake commodities by following clues and treat both principal and secondary aspects of the problem and remove origin and sources of forged and fake commodities".[3] Afterward, the Wenzhou government and departments of industry and commerce and quality inspection also issued related policies to deal with forged and fake commodities. In Lucheng District where production of leather shoes was clustered, the departments concerned conducted an influential one-week quality course for households of individual businesses and nearly 400 people took the course.[4] However, the problem was not completely solved. Wenzhou's leather shoes were just sold in the market in another form. As Wenzhou's leather shoes were boycotted by the whole country, some leather shoe

---

[3] Zhejiang Provincial Government's Notification on Resolute Investigation and Treatment of Forged and Fake Commodities (ZZ [1987] No. 68), 1987-11-19. *Zhejiang Gazette*, 1987(2): 22–24.

[4] *Wenzhou Daily*, 1987-10-01(1).

factories associated themselves with state-owned and collective shoemaking enterprises in Shanghai and other cities. In other words, they paid these state-owned and collective enterprises for usage of their brands and addresses. At first, associated operations were standard and these state-owned and collective enterprises often assigned personnel to inspect quality of goods and guide and supervise manufacturing techniques. However, shortly afterward, a large number of shoemaking enterprises followed this example. As a result, lots of Wenzhou shoes "disappeared" and were replaced by "Shanghai shoes". What's more, in the late 1980s and the early 1990s, in order to write literary works about Wenzhou's shoemaking industry, several writers searched every corner of Wenzhou for a pair of shoes made in Wenzhou, but failed (Hu, 1994a). Excessive joint operations led again to uncontrollable quality. As most shoemaking enterprises of Wenzhou were attached to small shoemaking enterprises in Shanghai's suburbs, which did not have strong abilities of technology and business guidance, joint operations had to pay to use other brands. Even worse, many Wenzhou enterprises pretended to be associated enterprises to use their logos arbitrarily or forged a name of a Shanghai enterprise. At first, Wenzhou enterprises attempted to ease problems in Wenzhou's shoemaking industry by borrowing the good reputation of Shanghai enterprises. However, production and selling of forged and fake commodities became serious again in the early 1990s. As a result, lots of letters of complaint about quality of leather shoes were sent to Shanghai, drawing attention from the departments concerned. In 1991, *Jiefang Daily* exposed this problem again and held that joint operations of shoemaking enterprises in Wenzhou and Shanghai damaged the good reputation of enterprises in Shanghai. After that, the Shanghai government categorically ordered that joint operations of shoemaking enterprises in Wenzhou and Shanghai be co-approved by industrial and commercial bureaus of both Wenzhou and Shanghai (Liu & Zhang, 1994), which, in fact, made joint operations impossible. At that point, Wenzhou's industry of leather shoes reached a dead end. Lots of shoemaking enterprises were shut down and even the Ma'anchi Desheng Shoe Store, which was active in the leather wholesale and retail industry in Wenzhou, closed down quietly (Hu, 1994a).

The real transformation of Wenzhou's industry of leather shoes started at that point. Its main sign was that most enterprises ended their joint operations and started to give clear indications of their own trademarks (Hu, 1994b). In addition, they began to conduct some equipment investment. Since 1992, some locally famous enterprises of leather shoes appeared and the overall quality of leather shoes was greatly improved. In July 1992, in a unified inspection for shoemaking industries in 28 cities carried out by the Quality and Technology Supervision Bureau of the PRC, the qualified rate of Wenzhou's leather shoes was 77.4%, which was higher than the national average level of 68%. In the 1993–1994 casual inspection of shoes in the urban district, qualified rates of glass strength and whole performance of 1,871 batches of shoe products reached 97% and 76%, respectively. At the same time, at the First Shoe Exposition of China in 1993, ten leather shoe enterprises of Wenzhou won a prize, accounting for 21% of total enterprises that won a prize. Afterward, Wenzhou's industry of leather shoes developed rapidly and favorably. Wenzhou's output of leather shoes reached 55,013,300 pairs in 1994 and 115,069,900 pairs in 1995 with an output value of 2.43 billion yuan, accounting for 7.7% of the total industrial output value. In 1997, in an evaluation conducted by the China Light Industry Council, three shoemaking enterprises of Wenzhou earned the title of "China's Top Ten Shoe Enterprises" and 18 shoemaking enterprises won a mark of "genuine leather". 1999 was the best harvest year for Wenzhou's shoemaking industry, for in addition to the three shoemaking enterprises of Wenzhou with the title of "China's Top Ten Shoe Enterprises", 35 enterprises won a mark of "genuine leather". Meanwhile, the State Administration of Industry and Commerce awarded the title of a "Famous Trade Mark of China" to a trademark of leather shoes, which was one of the first three trademarks in Wenzhou and the fourth trademark among shoe enterprises in China earning this title. In addition, four trademarks of leather shoes in Wenzhou won the title of a "Famous Trade Mark of Zhejiang Province" with the other seven trademarks. Meanwhile, 25 enterprises of leather shoes passed the ISO 9000 quality management system standard. In the second half of 1999, the Wenzhou Municipal Government organized several important activities[5] which further enhanced the reputation of Wenzhou's leather shoes in the market, and started to work at establishing the shoe capital of China. Finally, Wenzhou's leather shoes acquired a completely new outlook and regained market recognition. However, at the same time, enterprises in other regions started to copy brands of some enterprises of Wenzhou, causing some complaints. Under this condition, several well-known enterprises of leather shoes in Wenzhou actively assisted functional departments of the government to investigate and take measure.

Hereafter, Wenzhou's industry of leather shoes grew vigorously with respect to brand creation. In 2000, the trademark of another Wenzhou enterprise of leather shoes won the title of a "Famous Trade Mark of China" (only five enterprises of leather shoes won this title in China) and four enterprises of leather shoes got certification of the first batch of national inspection-free products. In the same year, the output of leather shoes of Wenzhou reached 600 million pairs and its output value was more than 30 billion yuan. In 2001, in the National

---

[5] These activities include the following: On August 8, 1999, the government held the Seminar of Path of Kangnai: A Seminar on the Development Strategy of China's Shoe Industry with the *Economic Daily* in Great Hall of the People, Beijing; on October 8, it organized the Advanced Seminar on Building Wenzhou into the Shoe Capital of China with the *Economic Daily* in Wenzhou; on December 16, it held the Advanced Seminar on Yesterday, Today and Tomorrow of Wenzhou Shoes with the *Zhejiang Daily* in Hangzhou; and on December 16–21, it organized a trade fair of famous shoes of Wenzhou with the China Light Industry Council in Wenzhou.

Footwear Inspection Report published by the National Center for Footwear Quality Supervision and Inspection, the qualified rate of Wenzhou's leather shoes reached 100%. In the same year, four shoemaking enterprises of Wenzhou earned the title of "China's Top Ten Shoe Enterprises" and one enterprise won the title of a "Leading Shoe Master of Genuine Leather" (only two enterprises won this title in China). In September of the same year, the China Light Industry Council formally awarded the title of the "Shoe Capital of China" to Wenzhou by documents.

7.3 Quality decision-making of firms in competitive markets

Most enterprises of leather shoes of Wenzhou chose to produce inferior products at first, but enhanced their product quality and created their own brands with the market-oriented reform. Why is that? In other words, how was a market of substandard goods gradually transformed into a market of standard goods? It seems that it is difficult to answer. Generally speaking, in a competitive market, the price-quality decision of an enterprise should be separated but corresponding. That is to say, an enterprise cannot survive by selling seconds at best–quality prices. However, enterprises of leather shoes in Wenzhou, where property right reform was carried out first, severely twisted their price–quality decisions during the market transition. Obviously, behavioral distortion caused by ambiguous property rights (Zhang & Ma, 1999) cannot be explained here and the only reason is competition distortion resulting from a lack of market structure. Hence, the analysis was based on reverse thinking: the price-quality-separated decision-making of enterprises under structure of a competitive market was confirmed first. That is to say, inferior products cannot get a high price. By further investigation, during the transformation from the planning system into the market system, factors of market structure causing distortion of competitive behavior, namely, prevalence of forged and fake commodities, were studied.

In the process of reform, correction of these factors of market structure automatically corrected competitive behavior.

Let us suppose experience goods in discrete time series $t = \{0, 1, 2, \ldots\}$ and two types of enterprises: Enterprise G (a good enterprise) and Enterprise B (an inferior enterprise). Enterprise G can put effort with a unit cost of c and obtain output of quality products (g) with a possibility of a and output of inferior products (b) with a possibility of $1 - a$. Otherwise, it can put zero-cost effort and obtain output of quality products with a possibility of β and output of inferior products with a possibility of $1 - \beta$. Enterprise B can only put zero-cost effort and obtain output of quality products with a possibility of β and output of inferior products with a possibility of $1 - \beta$, where $1 > a > \beta > 0$. In a market, enterprises fetch a price of pt. Originally, Enterprise G set a price $f_0 \in (0, 1)$. When the profit of an enterprise is 0, it chooses to leave the market and cannot return. In this chapter forged and fake commodities are defined as products which are sold by an enterprise at a lower than accepted quality level in the market at a price of pt.[6] In other words, if

---

[6] Of course, in "Suggestions on Severe Punishment of People Who Sell Forged And Fake Commodities" issued by the National Technology Supervision Bureau in 1989 (forwarded by the General Office of the State Council), six types of forged and fake commodities and eight types of situations regarded as forged and fake commodities were put forward. However, in the eyes of common consumers, products of poor quality are forged and fake commodities, which is interesting. In fact, results of market competition require continuous distribution of quality to cater to consumers requiring different quality levels. It is important that price corresponding to quality should accord with an incremental function relationship. Hence, it is necessary to explain that a product of poor quality bought at a low price cannot be regarded as a forged and fake commodity, which was common among forged and fake commodities in Wenzhou's shoemaking industry. At least in Wenzhou in the late 1980s and the early 1990s, most leather shoes were sold at about 20 yuan, so local consumers understood that 20-yuan leather shoes were not comparable with 200-yuan genuine leather shoes sold in Shanghai, Guangzhou, etc. As a result, there were few complaints about local leather shoes in Wenzhou. However, these inferior shoes were sold in stores in other cities at a price of about 200 yuan, resulting in forged and fake commodities, which is studied in this book.

an enterprise sells inferior goods at best-quality prices by informational disadvantages of consumers, this is called the behavior of forged and fake commodities. Obviously, both types of enterprises may display the behavior of forged and fake commodities.

Each consumer is of Bayesian rationality and knows f_0, but doesn't know types of enterprises. Suppose f_i^i is the belief of a consumer who regards Enterprise j as a G-type enterprise during Period i, $f(f_i^i \mid X)$ is the adjusted belief after $X \in \{g, b\}$ and Enterprise G always inputs Cost c in product production. In addition, suppose $f_t = f^{(k)}(f_t^i \mid X)$ is the belief of a consumer who has conducted k transactions ($X \in \{g, b\}$ during each transaction) with an enterprise that the enterprise is a G-type enterprise. In the market of random assortment, consumers make a decision to maximize expected utility. Suppose the utility of buying quality products is 1 and that of buying inferior products is 0. Consumers can also vote by foot only when the expected utility is lower than Reserved utility u, where $\beta \leqslant u \leqslant 1$. In other words, if there's no G-type enterprise in a market, consumers must leave. At any time, consumers can find out that the price fetched by an enterprise can be converted to other enterprises. At any Period t (except Period 0), consumers can only distinguish G-type enterprises from B-type enterprises and enterprises which just conduct transactions (during the last period) from those which haven't carried out any transaction. Suppose consumers are forgetful. In other words, consumers cannot identify an enterprise which had offered them products, even forged and fake commodities, once they changed to buy products of other enterprises.

$$\text{If } f_0(f_t \mid g) = \frac{a \cdot f_t}{a \cdot f_t + \beta(1 - f_t)},$$

$$\text{and } (f_t \mid b) = \frac{(1-a)f_t}{(1-a)f_t + (1-\beta)(1-f_t)}, \tag{7.1}$$

$$\text{then } \frac{1}{f(f_t \mid b)} - \frac{1}{f(f_t \mid g)} = \frac{(a-\beta)(1-f_t)}{a(1-a)f_t} < 0,$$

where $f(f_t|g) > f(f_f|b)$. In other words, the belief of a consumer who bought forged and fake commodities was lower than that of a consumer who bought quality products. Hence, at the end of Period 0, consumers who bought forged and fake commodities would surely give up the current enterprise to find a new enterprise, for the expectation that a new enterprise is a G-type enterprise which is higher than the first enterprise in accordance with the Bayes Rule:

$$E\left(f_1|f_0\right)=\left(\alpha f_0 + \beta\left(1-f_0\right)\right)\cdot f\left(f_0|g\right)+\left((1-\alpha)f_0+(1-\beta)\left(1-f_0\right)\right)\cdot f\left(f_0|b\right)$$
$$>\left(\alpha f_0 + \beta\left(1-f_0\right)\right)\cdot f\left(f_0|b\right)+\left((1-\alpha)f_0+(1-\beta)\left(1-f_0\right)\right)\cdot f\left(f_0|b\right)$$
$$= f\left(f_0|b\right).$$

Similarly, $E\ (f_1|f_0) < E\ (f_0|g)$. That is to say, a consumer who bought quality products of an enterprise would continue to consume products produced by this enterprise. When $t = 1$, all consumers who bought forged and fake commodities during Period 0 gave up the enterprise chosen by them, all enterprises which produced and sold forged and fake commodities withdrew from the market because of loss of consumers (consumers who bought quality products of an enterprise would continue to consume products produced by this enterprise), and all enterprises that survived during Period 1 offered quality products during Period 0. Therefore, $f_1^i = f_1 = f^{(1)}(f_0|g)$, indicating that consumers' expectation of G-type enterprises in a market is equal to the Bayesian expectation after buying a quality product. Suppose it is the same with Period t, namely, $f_t^i = f_t$,

$$f\left(f_t|b\right)<E\left(f_{t+1}|f_t\right)=\left(\alpha f_t + \beta\left(1-f_t\right)\right)\cdot f\left(f_t|g\right)$$
$$+\left((1-\alpha)f_t+(1-\beta)\left(1-f_t\right)\right)\cdot f\left(f_t|b\right)$$

and

$$f\left(f_t|g\right)>E\left(f_{t+1}|f_t\right)=\left(\alpha f_t + \beta\left(1-f_t\right)\right)\cdot f\left(f_t|g\right)$$
$$+\left((1-\alpha)f_t+(1-\beta)\left(1-f_t\right)\right)\cdot f\left(f_t|b\right).$$

It means that all consumers who bought forged and fake commodities during Period t will give up the enterprise chosen by them during Period $(t + 1)$, while consumers who bought quality products of an enterprise will continue to consume products produced by this enterprise. If this is the same with all consumers, all enterprises that survived during Period $(t + 1)$ were definitely those offered no forged and fake commodity during Period t.

The deduction above shows that enterprises which produced forged and fake commodities will certainly be eliminated through market competition, where rational decision-making of consumers is the most crucial part. In fact, consumers' Bayesian rational decisions mean that once they find out that they were sold forged and fake commodities, they will adopt the grim strategy to give up the producer, which is an important guarantee for removing production and selling of forged and fake commodities. Consequently, G-type enterprises are forced to input effort with Cost c and produce as many quality products as possible for winning more consumers. Thus, it can be seen that there will be no problem about adverse selection in a market with long-term competition and consumers' Bayesian rational decisions, which were shown in articles by Klein & Leffler (1981), Shapiro (1982, 1983), Genesove (1993), and Akelorf (1970) too.[7]

Suppose all enterprises that give the same price p_t to both old and new consumers without discrimination survive during Period t and n_t stands for the market share of each enterprise (namely, the number of consumers). As only $\alpha f_t + \beta(1 - f_t)$ enterprises survive during Period t,

$$\frac{n_t}{n_t + 1} = \alpha f_1 + \beta(1 - f_t), \quad \forall_t \geqslant 0. \qquad (7.2)$$

What needs to be further discussed is whether decision-making of an enterprise can cause global equilibrium, where all enterprises put effort with Cost c and produce as many quality products as possible to win more consumers. Suppose v_t is the discounted present value

---

[7] Genesove (1993) held that one condition of the mechanism of adverse selection

of the maximum expected return of an enterprise since Period t, v_t is the discounted present value of future return of an enterprise putting effort with Cost c in Period t, and v_t is the discounted present value of future return of an enterprise putting zero-cost effort in Period t. If an enterprise doesn't put effort with Cost c in Period t,

$$v_t = p_t + \beta\delta\frac{n_t+1}{n_t} = v_{t+1}^h.$$
(7.3)

The discounted present value of effort with Cost c is

$$v_t = p_t - c + \alpha\delta\frac{n_t+1}{n_t} = v_{t+1}^h.$$
(7.4)

The condition ensuring that producers put effort with Cost c constantly (incentive constraint) is

$$\frac{n_t+1}{n_t}v_{t+1}^h \geqslant \frac{c}{(\alpha-\beta)\delta}.$$
(7.5)

As the market is of perfect competition, the balanced initial discount must be $v_0^h = v_0^l = 0.$[8] Hence, when $t = 0$,

$$p_0^* + \beta\delta\frac{n_1}{n_0}v_1^h = 0 \qquad \left(v_0^l = 0\right)$$

$$p_0^* - c + \alpha\delta\frac{n_1}{n_0}v_1^h = 0 \qquad \left(v_0^h = 0\right).$$

Solution: $p_0^* = -\dfrac{\beta}{\alpha-\beta} \cdot c.$

---

was that the party with information superiority didn't have a pricing right. Otherwise, premium of high-quality products in the market would encourage producers to offer high-quality products for rent. Once they provide low-quality products, their loss will outweigh their gain (Klein & Leffler, 1981; Shapiro, 1982, 1983).

[8] If $v_0^h > v_0^l$, all enterprises must put high effort, confirming the proposition. If $v_0^h = v_0^l$, the initial market will attract more manufacturers to remove the rent.

When $t > 0$, $v_t^h = p_t^* - p_0^*$ in line with Equations (7.3)–(7.5). Therefore,

$$p_t^* = \frac{c}{(\alpha - \beta)\delta} \cdot \frac{n_t}{n_{t+1}} + p_0^* = \frac{c}{(\alpha - \beta)\delta} \big((\alpha - \beta)f_{t-1} + \beta(1 - \delta) \big).$$

It indicates that both sides of a transaction can guarantee mutual cooperation via price signals, where the manufacturer constantly offers quality products, while consumers purchase repeatedly. As $f_t + 1 > f_t$, the price series strictly increased, which further verified the role of price in guaranteeing product quality as proposed by Klein & Leffler (1981).

Furthermore, when $t > 0$, $\frac{n_{t+1}}{n_t} = f_t + \frac{1}{\alpha f_1}$. Thus,

$$p_t^* = \frac{c}{(\alpha - \beta)\delta} \cdot \left(\alpha \frac{f_{t-1}}{f^t} - \beta\delta \right)$$

and when $t \rightarrow \infty, \frac{f_{t-1}}{f^t} \rightarrow 1$. Therefore, the upper limit of p_t^* is $\bar{p} = \frac{\alpha - \beta\delta}{(\alpha - \beta)\delta} \cdot c$

and $1 - u \geqslant p \geqslant c$. Thus, it can be seen that a strictly incremental price series won't completely deprive surplus of consumers, and reliable competition is balanced and stable.

7.4 Market structure and competition distortion during the transition period

Institutional transition is a comprehensive process of institutional changes. However, in the process of gradual reform, not all systems changed at the same time, but some systems changed first, leading to the changes of more systems. In Wenzhou, the property right system is one of the most important systems in leading changes. A vast amount of literature showed that shortage of resources in Wenzhou is an important factor for Wenzhou to greatly develop out-of-system economy first (Zhang & Li, 1990; Jin, 1998). The main reason for out-of-system economy is that the development of private economy first led to the change of objective function of market behavior subjects, forming subjects of benefit (profit) maximization in neoclassical economics. However, rules relating to these subjects of benefit maximization were lagging because of the gradual reform, resulting in prevalence of forged and fake commodities. These systems behind the reform were suitable for the system of traditional planned economy, as public-owned enterprises with blurry property rights in essence cannot form behavior subjects of benefit maximization. As a result, there's no incentive mechanism to offer inferior products for higher profit. However, the strong profit-seeking motive and behavior of private enterprises make enterprises take full advantage of various rents caused by institutional difference for income enhancement. However, unlike the usual view that attributes behavior distortion of private enterprises in gradual reform to loss (or lagging) caused by the market system, this chapter tried to explain the behavior distortion of private enterprises from perspectives of economic and marketing characteristics of transition. Possible marketing characteristics include transition from shortage to surplus, price control and deregulation, deregulation of circulation channels, and effective protection of property rights of immaterial assets. The profit-seeking process of private enterprises leads to the above-mentioned changes of marketing characteristics, which is the internal evolution mechanism of building market transaction credit.

7.4.1 *From shortage to surplus*

According to the analysis above, after buying forged and fake commodities produced by a manufacturer, consumers will give up the manufacturer. Let us suppose the change is of zero cost (for the manufacturer). Its precondition is that manufacturers are fully competitive and consumers are free to buy products produced by different manufacturers. However, under the condition of shortage economy, consumers could not change manufacturers of products optionally because of shortage of supply. In fact, in the system of traditional planned economy, consumers were assigned to purchase limited products. After the reform, this situation was improved and people were allowed to pick out products within a scope. However, on the whole, consumers could not buy anything they wanted optionally. In terms of leather shoes, the national supply in the 1980s was quite limited. For example, in 1981, the national retail sales volume was only 18 million pairs with a turnover of 2.4 billion yuan. By 1985, it increased to 26 million pairs and 4.5 billion yuan, respectively.

If there's shortage of supply, consumers cannot change manufacturers at will. In other words, changing a manufacturer needs costs. For the sake of convenient analysis, let us suppose the cost of changing a manufacturer after buying forged and fake commodities meets $c^s \geqslant (\alpha - \beta)$ $(\alpha f_t + \beta(1 - f_t)) f(f_t | b)$, namely, it is greater than the expected profit increase of changing a manufacturer. Under this condition, consumers won't change the manufacturer immediately after they bought forged and fake commodities. In other words, due to shortage of supply, consumers have higher tolerance for forged and fake commodities.

Suppose v_t^1 stands for the discounted present value of future return of an enterprise which offered forged and fake commodities once during Period t and v_t^0 refers to the discounted present value of future return of an enterprise which never offers forged and fake commodities. If the enterprise which offered forged and fake commodities once during Period t still survives, its discount of return is

$$n_t v_t^1 = n_t \left(p_t - c \right) + \alpha \delta n_{t+1} v_{t+1}^1. \tag{7.6}$$

The discount of return of the enterprise which never offers forged and fake commodities during Period t is

$$n_t v_t^0 = n_t \left(p_t - c \right) + \alpha \delta n_{t+1} v_{t+1}^0 + (1 - \alpha) \delta n_{t+1} v_{t+1}^1. \tag{7.7}$$

The incentive constraint of maintaining input of effort with Cost c of both types of enterprises is

$$n_t c = n_{t+1} (\alpha - \beta) \delta \left(v_{t+1}^0 - v_{t+1}^1 \right). \tag{7.8}$$

When $t > 1$, according to Equations (7.6)–(7.8), balanced price series $\{p_t^{**}\}_{t=1}^{\infty}$ is

$$p_t^{**} - c = \frac{c}{(\alpha - \beta)\delta} \cdot \frac{1}{(1-\alpha)}\left(\left(\frac{1}{\delta} \cdot \frac{n_{t-2}}{n_t} - \alpha \frac{n_{t-1}}{n_t}\right) - \alpha\delta\left(\frac{1}{\delta} \cdot \frac{n_{t-1}}{n_t} - \alpha\right)\right).$$

Similarly,

$$p_0^{**} = -\frac{\beta c}{(\alpha - \beta)\delta}, \quad p_t^{**} = \frac{\beta}{(\alpha - \beta)\delta}\left(\frac{1}{\delta} - 1\right) - \frac{\alpha}{(\alpha - \beta)(1-\alpha)}\left(\frac{1}{\delta} - \alpha\right).$$

When it is balanced and $n_t - n_{t-1} = 0$,

$$p^{**} = \frac{\left(\frac{1}{\delta} - \alpha\right)^2 c}{(1-\alpha)(\alpha - \beta)} + c.$$

Obviously, $p^{**} > c$. Manufacturers have net surplus to maintain their production, leading to a balance. In this balance, results of market competition cannot remove forged and fake commodities automatically.

Of course, the tolerance is not limitless. In fact, this chapter supposed that consumers could tolerate one purchase of forged and fake commodities, which is not inevitable, but convenient for analysis. The more times consumers tolerate, the shorter the supply will be, leading to an increase of significance of results in this chapter.

Of course, manufacturers providing inferior products for a long time cannot survive. However, some manufacturers lower quality of their products because consumers cannot change manufacturers rapidly. The degree and duration of quality lowering depend on consumers' costs for changing a manufacturer, namely, the shortage degree. In the extreme, if a consumer is assigned to a manufacturer and cannot change it (or the changing cost is too high), the manufacturer can offer many forged and fake commodities until the discount of expected return is lower than the reservation utility. In addition, the reservation utility of consumers is low, sometimes even zero, in shortage economy, so it is easy to sell inferior products among these consumers.

In essence, transition from shortage economy to surplus economy or transformation from a sellers' market into a buyers' market greatly enhances selection freedom of consumers. In other words, consumers can change a manufacturer at nearly zero cost. Under this condition, it is a credible threat for a manufacturer to offer inferior products, as the change is effective for consumers. If it becomes a universal strategy for all consumers and the common understanding in the market, market transactions will be formed.

7.4.2 *Monopoly of circulation channels and price regulation*

In the system of traditional planned economy, price is under strict control and enterprises do not have a pricing right. In terms of Wenzhou's leather shoes, private enterprises could set price by themselves. However, in order to sell products via circulation channels of state-owned cooperation, these enterprises had to give up their pricing right. In fact, since the mid-1980s, some state-owned shopping malls in some cities started to subcontract their counters and many Wenzhou people contracted for counters to sell Wenzhou's leather shoes. According to information, types and prices of products sold by contractors were under strict control and contractors had little say in price fluctuation. Once suppliers lost their pricing right in the terminal, they focused on fighting for the pricing right upstream. As we all know, in the early stage of the reform and opening-up, private enterprises originated from rural industrialization, so it was difficult for them to enter urban commercial circulation channels. They mainly relied on special markets in the suburb and rural markets. Therefore, they had no advantage when they negotiated with terminal vendors in cities. In fact, these terminal vendors purchased leather shoes produced by small factories at a low price and sold them in shopping malls at a high price.

In Wenzhou, the average price of a pair of leather shoes in a pedlar's market or a special wholesale market was about 20 yuan. Any local consumer who bought this kind of leather shoes wouldn't compare them with the 150–200-yuan leather shoes produced by state-owned enterprises in Shanghai. However, when terminal vendors put those shoes in state-owned shopping malls, consumers treated them as high-price shoes naturally, leading to complaints about quality. It should be clear that control of circulation made controllers of circulation channels rake in exorbitant profits. In order to operate these counters, all terminal vendors had to pay (both dominant or recessive) high costs. Under price control of terminal vendors, why did inferior products become inevitable?

As confirmed above, in a market of perfect competition, one important guarantee of transaction credit is that price can be sent effectively as a signal indicating product quality. Proposition 1 also shows that a strictly incremental price series is an important guarantee to encourage manufacturers to maintain a good reputation and obtain future price discount. However, once the price is limited within a certain scope, the situation changes. As manufacturers cannot maintain input of sight credit and products are of asymmetric information, adverse selection is irresistible. That is to say, consumers buy products at a fixed price and all products whose (expected) quality is higher than the controlled price will be withdrawn from the market, forming a market of inferior products.

During Period t, the incentive constraint of a G-type enterprise putting effort with Cost c is

$$v_{t+1}^h \geq \frac{c}{(\alpha - \beta)\delta} \cdot \frac{n_t}{n_{t+1}}.$$

In order to maintain the effort with Cost c, Price series $\left(p_t^*\right)_{c-1}^{**}$ should meet

$$p_t^* = \frac{c}{(\alpha - \beta)\delta}\left(\alpha \frac{f_{t-1}}{f^t} - \beta\delta\right)$$

and

$$v_t^h = p_t^* + \frac{\beta}{(\alpha - \beta)} \cdot c. \qquad (7.9)$$

As $\lim_{t \to \infty} = P$, suppose there's limited price p and

$$\tilde{p} < \bar{p} = \frac{(\alpha - \beta\delta)}{(\alpha - \beta)\delta}.$$

It means that there must be t'. When $t > t'$, $p_t^* > \tilde{p}$. Thus, according to Equation (7.9),

$$v_t^h = \tilde{p} + \frac{\beta}{(\alpha - \beta)} \cdot c.$$

Under this condition, during Period $t = t' - 1$,

$$v_{t-1}^h = \tilde{p} - c + \alpha\delta \frac{n_{t'}}{n_{t'-1}} \left(\tilde{p} + \frac{\beta}{(\alpha - \beta)} \cdot c \right),$$

$$v_{t-1}^l = \tilde{p} + \beta\delta \frac{n_{t'}}{n_{t'-1}} \left(\tilde{p} + \frac{\beta}{(\alpha - \beta)} \cdot c \right),$$

and

$$\Delta v_{t'-1} = v_{t'-1}^h - v_{t'-1}^l = \frac{(\alpha - \beta)\delta \tilde{p} + \beta\delta c}{\alpha f_{t'-1} + \beta\left(1 - f_{t'+1}\right)} - c$$

$$< \frac{(\alpha - \beta)\delta p_{t'}^* + \beta\delta c}{\alpha f_{t'-1} + \beta\left(1 - f_{t'-1}\right)}, \quad -c = 0$$

then

$$v_{t'-1}^l > \left(1 + \beta\delta \frac{n_{t'}}{n_{t'-1}}\right) p_{t-1}^* + \frac{\beta c}{(\alpha - \beta)} \cdot \beta\delta \frac{n_{t'}}{n_{t'-1}} > \frac{c}{(\alpha - \beta)\delta} \cdot \frac{n_{t'-2}}{n_{t'-1}} \quad 9$$

If $\tilde{t} = t' - 1$, then for any $t \geqslant \tilde{t}$, $v_t^h < v_t^l$. Therefore, when $t \geqslant \tilde{t}$, a G-type enterprise has no motive to put effort with Cost c. Obviously, the lower the limited price, the earlier a manufacturer will lose its motive to invest costs and improve quality of products.

Interestingly, founders of a few well-known enterprises of leather shoes in Wenzhou were originally salespeople. The fact behind the coincidence is that people who engaged in marketing could grasp opportunities in institutional changes of circulation, and established their circulation channels to control price. Once they had pricing space, their enterprises had an incentive to strive for future price premium, leading to improvement of product quality.[10]

---

[9] Because $v_{t'-1}^l = \left(1 + \beta\delta \frac{n_{t'}}{n_{t'-1}}\right)\tilde{p} + \frac{\beta c}{(\alpha - \beta)} \cdot \beta\delta \frac{n_{t'}}{n_{t'-1}} > \left(1 + \beta\delta \frac{n_{t'}}{n_{t'-1}}\right) p_{t-1}^* + \frac{\beta c}{(\alpha - \beta)} \cdot \beta\delta \frac{n_{t'}}{n_{t'-1}}.$

[10] For example, in Wuhan in the first half of the 1980s, the founder of Aokang engaged in footwear operations and gradually established an easily controlled

7.4.3 *Property rights, brands, and tradability*

Due to the discount of expected return of the enterprise during the first period, $n_t v_t = n_t (p^*_t - c) - a\delta^{n_{t+1}} v_{t+1}$, which is equivalent to

$$n_t v_t = \frac{n_{t-1}}{(\alpha - \beta)_\delta} \cdot c. \qquad (7.10)$$

It is a variable increasing over time and its internal impetus is increasing consumers. Good transaction records of the manufacturer lead to a good reputation (brand value). In other words, during the first period, the enterprise put effort with Cost c to improve product quality, getting zero return in this period because of information asymmetry of products. Similarly, product quality of this period will affect expectation of consumers in the next period. In this sense, if the input of an enterprise can lead to more discount of future income in return, it is still profitable. If a manufacturer follows this idea since the first period, its reputation and brand can be formed gradually. Of course, the cost of maintaining the reputation is equal to Cost c. However, an important presupposition is that the future expected income is of no risk and the market return is stable. The presupposition supposes that there's a market with tradable property rights (brands) and any future expected income can be realized through a market of property rights. Therefore, the future income of manufacturers can be considered in current decision-making. Tradable property rights offer a good insurance mechanism for manufacturers, so that manufacturers can cash their income at any time without affecting their decision-making.

If there's a brand transaction with possibility of $\rho \in (0, 1)$ in each period and the possibility of a new G-type enterprise is f_0, the Bayesian

---

selling network. In the second half of the 1980s, he returned to Yongjia to take on an enterprise via the established selling network. Originally, the enterprise invested lots of capital for technological development. Its leather shoes are of high quality and have constantly won the market, creating a good reputation for the enterprise.

belief of the current manufacturer as a G-type enterprise during Period t is

$$f_t^m = (1-\rho)f_t + \rho f_0. \tag{7.11}$$

The market share of the manufacturer during each period is $n_t = \frac{n_{t-1}}{\alpha f_t^m + \beta(1-f_t^m)}$, where $t > 0$. Hence, according to the analysis above, there's balanced price series $\{p^m\}_{t=0}^m$, meeting the incentive constraint of effort with Cost c and:

$$p_t^m = \begin{cases} p_t^* & t = 0 \\ \dfrac{c}{(\alpha - \beta)\delta}\big((\alpha - \beta)f_{t-1}^m + \beta(1-\delta)\big), & t > 0 \end{cases}$$

As $f_t \geq f_0$, $f_t^m = (1-\rho)f_t + \rho f_0 \leq f_t$.

When $t > 0$,

$$\frac{c}{(\alpha - \beta)\delta}\big((\alpha - \beta)f_{t-1}^m + \beta(1-\delta)\big) \leq \frac{c}{(\alpha - \beta)\delta}\big((\alpha - \beta)f_{t-1} + \beta(1-\delta)\big) = p_t^*.$$

Thus, it can be seen that tradability of brands leads to the reduction of equilibrium market price, which is conducive to improvement of consumers' welfare. Reduction of equilibrium price caused by transfer of property rights can be regarded as discounting of future income risks. The different risk preference of different people leads to different prices of the same expected income. Tradable property rights (brands) mean that proprietary rights of a manufacturer are allocated to people who have the lowest risk discount of future expected income. Therefore, in the model, we only needed a simple (fixed) discount ratio for future expected income. However, if property rights are not tradable, especially if reputation of an enterprise cannot be included in price, the result may be invalid. If property rights of an enterprise are not tradable, it means that the enterprise cannot realize risk-free cashing of its future income through the market of property rights. Under this condition, cashing of future income is not equivalent to self-management of an enterprise. Generally speaking, the longer an enterprise operates, the higher its risk expectation of its future income. During transition economy in China, private property rights cannot be clearly protected by the constitution and there's no effective market for property rights of enterprises. All of these greatly enhance subjective risks of enterprise owners (private owners). Some people hold that as private property rights cannot be clearly protected by the constitution, the discount rate of future income of private owners will increase, reducing the importance of future income in decision-making and restricting the manufacturer's behavior (Zhang & Ma, 1999). However, if the future income is definite, no theory holds that discount factors of individuals (standing for personal patience) will change. In fact, what really reduces consideration of future expectation by private owners is huge risks of future expected income under uncertain protection of property rights.

In terms of risks of future income with non-tradable property rights, the discount factor is a variable relating to time, namely, $\delta_t \in (0, 1)$, where $\delta = \dfrac{d\delta}{dt} < 0$ and $\lim\limits_{t \to \infty} \delta_t r = 0$. There must be t'. When $t \geqslant t'$, $\delta_t \leqslant \delta^T = \dfrac{c}{(\alpha - \beta)v_t} \cdot \dfrac{n_{t-1}}{n_t}$; when $t < t'$, $\delta_t \leqslant \delta^T = \dfrac{c}{(\alpha - \beta)v_t} \cdot \dfrac{n_{t-1}}{n_t}$. Obviously, when $t \geqslant t'$, $v \leqslant \dfrac{c}{(\alpha - \beta)\delta^T} \cdot \dfrac{n_{t-1}}{n_t}$. For $t - 1$, $v_{t-1}^l \geqslant v_{t-1}^h$ when $t > t'$. When $t = t' - 1$ and $t > t'$, the manufacturer has no motive to put effort with Cost c for quality improvement.

T depends on the declining rate of t of δ, namely, the fear degree of a manufacturer about risks of future return. Obviously, the sooner a manufacturer loses confidence in the future income, the earlier it will give up inputting costs for quality improvement. Simply put, as a manufacturer's reputation results from quality improvement belonging to specific assets, there will be huge risks if it is non-tradable. On the one hand, the reputation helps manufacturers gain more earnings. On the other hand, it will cause more loss once there's an accident. Hence, manufacturers often accumulate some good reputation initially and then "withdraw capital as long as they clean up", which will obviously lead to more forged and fake commodities in the market.

7.5 Research conclusions and policy implications

During transition economy, the establishment of market credit is progressive. However, this progressive process doesn't depend on the market system and construction of its effective execution system, but on phenomena derived from gradual evolution of characteristics of the whole economic system.

To put it simply, first, subjects of micro-systems of exclusive property rights form market behavior subjects seeking benefit maximization, but various market characteristics originating from the planning system lead to specific constraint conditions for these behavior subjects, leading to specific behavior of benefit maximization. It should be clear that though supply behavior of public-owned enterprises does not seek benefit maximization, its constraints can also lead to distortion of behavior. For instance, output assessment of economic men can cause output maximization, resulting in reduction of quality of products, especially service products. The significance of subjects of micro-systems of exclusive property rights is that they provide tension for distortion constraints breaking the market. Though the breaking process is accompanied by dishonest behavior, competition will surely lead to establishment of market credit in a good marketing environment, which may be not proper for public-owned enterprises.

Second, change of consumers' selection space indicates change of their dependency on specific manufacturers and change of effects of consumers' interests on manufacturers' behavior. Obviously, in shortage economy (where consumers are assigned to specific manufacturers), consumers have no choice and manufacturers can reduce product quality to deprive all surplus of consumers, if the price is controlled. Planned economy causes long-term shortage of consumption goods. That is to say, consumers have no choice and manufacturers don't have to invest to improve their product quality. With the increase of investment in production of consumption goods, an increasing number of products are supplied, which greatly expands consumers' selection space. As a result, if a manufacturer offers inferior products, it will lose its consumers. A paradox is that manufacturers can offer inferior products because of shortage, but these products enhance consumers' selection space, restricting quality of products provided by these manufacturers. Obviously, the vast number of private enterprises leads to sufficient competition in the market and transformation from shortage economy into surplus economy. In surplus economy, a large number of enterprises have to focus on building a good reputation and brands to attract more consumers.

Third, the formation of a pricing right allows manufacturers with a good reputation to constantly obtain premium of future price, which induces manufacturers to put effort and improve the quality for more consumers on a profitable premise. Price regulation (mainly refers to the upper limit of price) can lead to quality reduction as compensation. In addition, price regulation is often related to shortage sectors which are associated with access regulation. Hence, access regulation often causes supply shortage at first, leading to price increase. However, price regulation can further result in quality reduction. Therefore, both access regulation and price regulation lead to deficiency of market credit. In the process of in-depth reform, deregulation and creation of an effective competitive environment are the guarantees of building market credit.

Fourth, tradability of reputation (brands) can greatly reduce risks of future income, motivating manufacturers to create good quality and credit. Reputation (brands) is specific assets depending on enterprises, so tradability of brands corresponds to effective protection and tradability of property rights of enterprises. The trade can be comprehensive and is not limited to transfer of property rights. In the planning system, private property rights are inhibited and even attacked. Though in the course of transition, private property rights are gradually recognized and protected on the whole, the slow process directly leads to risky decisions of owners of private enterprises. Due to lack of effective protection of property rights, risks of expected income increase rapidly, which further leads to increasingly little consideration of expected income. As a result, manufacturers do not have a strong impetus to develop a good reputation. However, tradability of property rights and brands of enterprises can greatly reduce uncertainty of the expected return. A market transaction is equivalent to an insurance mechanism of the expected return, so that manufacturers can cash their future income depending on their reputation at any time. Therefore, enterprises are more likely to build a good reputation (brand).

Last but not least, with respect to the function of the government, much literature involving market credit stressed the important role of the government in establishing market credit. In terms of quality change of Wenzhou's leather shoes, both the media and the public strongly recognize the role of the government in this process. It cannot be denied that establishment and maintenance of the public order of a market cannot do without the government. However, it is not accurate that the government is an important support mechanism for the establishment of market transaction behavior because of it. It only indicates severe functional deficiency of the government in the traditional system. Before effective change of market characteristics as mentioned above, the government's contribution to establishment of market credit was limited. For example, in the late 1980s, the government organized a quality course and an industry association and introduced measures to deal with the considerable forged and fake commodities in Wenzhou. However, afterward forged and fake commodities prevailed again, indicating little effect of these measures. Of course, in the late 1990s, after enterprises started to pay attention to product quality, as an organizer, the government put forward measures to propagandize the new image of Wenzhou's products and raise the prestige of Wenzhou's products, which played an active role in enhancing quality of leather shoes and even other products of Wenzhou.

Chapter **8**

Family Culture and Regional Economic Development in Wenzhou

In China's social and economic transition period, Wenzhou embarked on a path of industrialization and marketization characterized by the development of family industry and professional market, gaining an economic first-mover advantage and achieving outstanding performance. In 1978, the total GDP of the whole city was only 1.32 billion yuan, which increased to 82.5 billion yuan by 2000, and the average annual growth rate was as high as 15.6% according to comparable prices. At the same time, millions of Wenzhou people created Wenzhou streets, Wenzhou villages, and Wenzhou cities throughout the country and throughout the world. The rise of Wenzhou model has aroused widespread concern in academic circles. When people study the origin of Wenzhou model, they mostly analyze the unique location factors and the stock of old system in Wenzhou. In fact, Wenzhou model is no longer just a regional economic phenomenon in a special spatial sense. Wenzhou model is closely related to Wenzhou people, which cannot be explained simply by location or institution. In order to further analyze and study the origin of Wenzhou model and the motive for Wenzhou's economic development, it is necessary for us to introduce the new variable of culture and analyze Wenzhou model from the angle of Wenzhou's humanistic spirit. Wenzhou is located on the border between Zhejiang and Fujian. The origin of local residents is complex, the dialects are numerous, and the local rural residents live in a large number of ethnic groups. Clan conflicts have been frequent in history. At the same time, in the process of industrialization and marketization in recent years, most of Wenzhou's private enterprises have had a very strong family system. It can be said that in the cultural factors that influence the economic development of the Wenzhou region, the family culture factor is also prominent.

Regarding the influence of family culture on economic development, we conducted a preliminary analysis in 1990–1997. At the same time, with the development and evolution of the enterprise organization, in the 1990s, the enterprises in Wenzhou were mainly family-owned enterprises or family enterprises, and the scale was small. Therefore, for those who were anxious for the development of private enterprises in Wenzhou, most of them believed that family culture restricted further development of enterprises. From this point of view, many people put forward the suggestion to promote the family business to get rid of the family system and establish the modern enterprise system. This view was also in tune with the thoughts of some of the officials who were eager to show their achievements, and had thus become almost a mainstream view of the family business problem in society.

What is different from many others is that we believe that it is reasonable for Wenzhou's private enterprises to exist in the form of family enterprises on the basis of a large number of case analysis and in-depth research. The reason why most of Wenzhou's private enterprises adopt the family system is mainly that the product structure dominated by "small commodities" makes the role of economies of scale less obvious. So the size of the business is small, and ownership does not need to spread beyond the family; the enterprise has not existed for long, the operator is still basically the entrepreneur, and most companies' life cycles are unlikely to be long enough to solve the problem of leadership transition. Companies tend to die out in a generation (automatic termination, transfer, or bankruptcy). The family system not only satisfies the uniformity of the decision-making but also the consistency of the behavior required by the enterprise. Moreover, because of the natural self-restraint and self-sacrifice spirit among family members, the family system saves more management fees and brings the benefits of cooperative game to enterprises, especially in the initial stage of enterprise compared to the "capital democracy" based on legal laws and Nash bargaining equilibrium. Therefore, we should treat the proposal of "out of the family system" of private enterprises with caution, not to mention the need to advocate or create a fuss. The relationship between culture and economy is not static, antagonistic, and fragmented. Therefore, this chapter discusses Wenzhou model from the perspective of the interaction between family culture and Wenzhou's regional economic development.

8.1 Restoration of rural family management and family culture

The family system is the most basic social structure of our society. Therefore, family culture is also a family-based culture, which is connected by blood and kinship. Family culture is an important part of traditional Chinese culture. Since ancient times, China has had the theory that "the foundation of a country is built at home". The country is an expansion of home. Similarly, in the Confucian culture that dominates traditional Chinese culture, family ethics is also extended to social ethics. Therefore, the family and family culture have deeply influenced the social structure and the behavior pattern of Chinese people. Fei Xiaotong calls the family-centered relationship in rural China a "differential order pattern". In our traditional society, Lu Zuofu pointed out that as far as agriculture is concerned, an agricultural operation is a family. As far as business is concerned, there are shops outside and families inside. As far as industry is concerned, a number of textile machines are installed in a family, that is, a factory. As far as education is concerned, the old school hall was in one's own family, and the teaching house was in the family.

As far as politics is concerned, a Yamen[1] is often a family. When an official comes, it is a family. The influence of family culture on Chinese society can be seen from this.

---

[1] Yamen is a place of work for government institutions in ancient China.

Wenzhou is located in the south of Zhejiang Province, surrounded by mountains on three sides and facing the sea. It has long been inconvenient for transportation and the environment is closed. Therefore, the local regional culture has a strong traditional color. Especially in the vast rural areas where the clan concept is very strong, clan conflict is frequent. Since Wenzhou is located on the border of Zhejiang Province and away from the political center, the government has weak control over the local area, so the role of the folk clan organizations in the rural society is very strong. The rulers of the past dynasties also believed in the expression "A family becomes a city, and a city becomes a nation", and consciously used the clan organization to strengthen the control of the countryside without affecting the government's rule. However, as an informal social group, strong clans tend to lead to excessive reinforcement of group identity. Once one of the children of the clan has a conflict with the children of another family, it is often associated with the sense of honor of the clan, thus intensifying the conflict between the clans. Even when there is conflict between husband and wife, brother-in-law or sister-in-law, women will often say, "You're the one who bullied my family? " As a result, a small squabble can easily lead to a vicious conflict between families or clans. Cangnan county has always been a region with intense clan conflicts, especially in the south of the Yangtze River. According to the 1925 Pingyang County Annals Local Records, the people living in south of the Yangtze River like fighting, often because of trivialities. That is, each is armed with a knife, and the person killed would be reported to the official for inspection. The conscript laborers were abetted to go to the countryside, and the property and house were all gone. The murderer would be at large with a vexatious suit for several years and the case would not be closed. The case was settled by money per household no matter whether rich or poor. The officials turned a blind eye. The place was weakened by every fight. Poor politics and enlightenment worsened the case.

After the founding of the People's Republic of China, due to the change of rural social structure, the rural collective ownership changed the economic pattern of the traditional family's small production.

The economic base on which family culture depends for its survival changed, and at that time the control of ideology was relatively strict. As a result, the concept of family was once diluted, and the family and clan culture also tended to decline. Clan conflicts are also less frequent than in the past. However, due to thousands of years of historical accumulation of traditional culture, the family, household, and clan concepts in people's minds have long been deeply rooted. Therefore, the influence of family culture has not disappeared completely, and farmers' preference for family production has not been eliminated. As early as 1957, many farmers in Wenzhou took to the practice of "the fixing of farm output quotas for individual households with each on its own". On October 13, 1957, *People's Daily* reported the following: "the fixing of farm output quotas for individual households with each on its own" contracts "three fixing" of the land in the commune (contracted worker, contracted output and package cost) to the production team and then to the members of each household; redividing the plot of land in the commune into small plots would determine the yield, fertilizer, and amount of work required for each plot. Generally with the "division of fields by labor" method, it is contracted to each household members for decentralized management.

The members are fully responsible for the output of the contracted land, the overproduction part is rewarded, and the reduced output is compensated. In the spring of 1957, in Yongjia county, there were more than 200 communes implementing the "the fixing of farm output quotas for individual households with each on its own". By the summer of 1957, there was a trend of "the fixing of farm output quotas for individual households with each on its own" in various counties of Wenzhou. A total of about 1,000 agricultural communes, including 178,000 members (about 15% of commune farmers), implemented the "wrong" approach. The practice, which was criticized and corrected at the time by the powerful intervention of the government, reflected the farmers' yearning for the restoration of family business. Meanwhile, although the control of social ideology was very strict at that time, in fact, after 1955, every family in Cangnan county began to reestablish the family tree. From then on until the end of the 20th century, reestablishment of the family tree was almost never stopped.

Like most rural communities across the country, Wenzhou's traditional rural economy is a semi-self-sufficient small-scale peasant economy. The family in a traditional rural community is not only a basic living unit and population reproduction unit but also a basic production unit, education unit, and social security unit. After the reform and opening-up, when the family contract system that originated in Fengyang, Anhui Province, spread to Wenzhou, it soon got the response from Wenzhou farmers who had already had the experience of "the fixing of farm output quotas for individual households with each on its own". The main position of family economy in rural economy was reestablished. Due to the restoration of the family business mode as the economic foundation of traditional family culture, the traditional family culture in the rural areas of Wenzhou was rejuvenated. According to the record of Qiaotou Annals, in the early 1980s, almost all the major families of Qiaotou town revised their family trees (see Table 8.1).

Table 8.1. Statistics on the time of revision of the family tree of major families in Qiaotou town in the early 1980s.

Year	Surname (number of volume)	The clan of reestablished family tree (number)
1980	Zheng (4), Zhou (2)	2
1981	Ye (Gulian and other villages, 6), Ye, (Jiangshan village, 1), Chen (Qiaotou and so on, 3), Li (3), Wang (1)	5
1982	Chen (Huangbao, 1), Jin (5), Zhan (8), Huang (3), Zhu (1), Shan (2), Pan (1), Wu (1)	8
1983	Sha (1), Zhou (10), Xiang (1), Yang (1)	4

Notes: It is based on the information collected from pp. 40–41 of the 1989 edition of Qiaotou Annals.

In addition to the reestablishment of the family tree, the revival of family culture was also reflected in activities such as sacrificial ancestor worship and rehabilitation of the ancestral hall. There is an existing farmland of 799.62 mu in Hantian village, Tangxia town, Ruian City, with a mountain area of 149 mu and a water area of 102 mu. It is a typical plain village. At the end of 1999, there were 1,135 households and 4,752 people in the whole village. Among the 36 families in the village, a majority of them were Han family members who lived in the Xiyang natural village, Chen family of Qianan, and Cao family of Dongyang. The three surnames account for more than 85% of the village's population, and all have ancestral halls and genealogy. After 1980, during the Qingming Festival every year, they would go to the cemetery to hold a ceremony to worship their ancestors (Chen, 2000). Until 1989, the whole town of Huangtian of Yongjia county (now renamed Huangtian town) rebuilt 33 clan ancestral halls. Some of these ancestral halls were newly built, some were rebuilt on old abandoned ancestral halls, and some were rebuilt through the collective public housing by the original production brigade. Some even had a glimpse of the phrase "the production brigade" next to "some ancestral temple". In many rural areas of Wenzhou, the ancestral halls and temples of the farmers have replaced the original communal houses and become the public places of the rural community. Every year, these places carry out traditional cultural activities such as singing and acting, which attract men and women, old and young. Some also regularly hold the adult ceremony for the youth of the clan every year. Some regularly hold ancestral hall wine activities in the first month of the year. Chenjibao, a town in Cangnan county, formerly known as Xiabaochen, is divided into three administrative villages: East Chen, West Chen, and South Chen. The current population is about 3,000, among them, East Chen is 355, West Chen 240, and South Chen 249. Chen is the clan with the most population in Cangnan county, and according to history, several large clan conflicts in Cangnan county were almost always related to the Chen surname. Chenjiabao is also one of the four settlements of Chen, so Chenjiabao was almost always involved in the conflicts between Chen and people of non-Chen surnames. According to the legend, there were three families in Chenjiabao: the eldest branch, the second branch, and the third branch. The third branch was divided into east third branch and west third branch. In the distribution of the three administrative villages, the east third branch of East Chen village accounted for the most number of people, followed by second branch; the eldest branch of West Chen village accounted for the most, followed by the west second branch; the west second branch of South Chen village accounted for the most, about two thirds, followed by the eldest branch.

In general, the eldest branch in Chenjiabao is the most powerful, followed by the third branch. On the second and third days of the Chinese New Year, it is the time to have an ancestral temple meal for people surnamed Chen. Although the ancestral hall can place more than 100 tables at one time, it has to be separated because of its large population. On the second day of the Chinese New Year, it is feast time for the eldest branch and on the third day, the other branches. When eating an ancestral hall meal, most of the non-local children surnamed Chen come to the get-together with their own dishes. This kind of ritual actually serves to strengthen the clan identity of the juniors of the same family. In recent years, due to the influence of economic development and population migration, the scale of local ancestral hall meal has also been reduced, and people only eat an ancestral hall meal on the second day of the first month. It can be seen from the situation of Chenjiabao that, on the one hand, the rural family culture has been revitalized due to the restoration of the rural family's operation mode and the change of rural social structure. On the other hand, due to the development of rural industrialization and urbanization, the rural population has a tendency to move toward cities or market towns. In recent years, the family and clan culture in Wenzhou rural areas has been gradually fading due to the change of the distribution pattern of the peasants living together.

Of course, we should also be aware that the family and clan culture is rooted in the soil of national culture, so its influence cannot be eliminated in the short term. Generally speaking, all families advocate bringing glory on one's ancestors, being law-abiding, helping the poor and the needy, and keeping harmonious relations with the neighbors. For example, Zhang's Taifu Zhang Zijun's Family instructions stress the following: "Reading and cultivation will be handed down from generation to generation in a family; diligence and thrift make a family flourish; forbearance and tolerance set up a home; guard home against theft and adultery; whoring and gambling dissipate a family fortune; violence and ferocity destroy a family. Don't be jealous; don't listen to the words of sow discord. Don't do a deed of indignation; do not secure personal gain from public interest." It also pointed out that "Lack of talent rather than want is the cause of trouble; blind expansion rather than poor industry is the cause of problem; no ambition rather than aging is where the problem lies; making friends with the evil rather than the want of friends is the cause of the trouble" (*Chronicles of Zhang's History in Cangnan*). It can be seen that most of the values in clan culture are not in conflict with social values. Even from a certain point of view, clan culture has quite positive social functions in poverty relief, mutual aid and friendship, social security, and so on. However, it is undeniable that the concept of family clan is after all a kind of clan culture, and its values and goals are, after all, quite different from the goal of social welfare. So in the new situation, although the concept of clan and family in rural areas of Wenzhou shows signs of fading out, if the government is to relax its vigilance and control, it is likely that there will be a group conflict among different surnames, which will seriously endanger social stability. As in the early 1990s, the clan armory in the south of Cangnan county began to emerge again. In 1990, there were 22 cases of various armed clans fighting in Jiangnan, injuring 10 people. In 1991, there were more than 50 signs of armed fighting, and as a result of the timely suppression, there were only 2 real formations of large-scale armed clan conflict with two people killed and 10 wounded.

The "August 16" incident occurred on August 16, 1992. The cause of the incident was a family marriage dispute between a male youth surnamed Lin in Shanbei village and a young woman surnamed Chen in Gongxi village. However, such a family dispute eventually led to a large-scale armed clan conflict between the Chen and Lin. The conflict involved 23 villages in Xinan township, Wangli town, and other townships, involving more than 2,000 people. The Cangnan County Committee and relevant departments were informed of the matter in advance and sent a working group stationed in time. But both sides still deceived the working group, and started 4 battlefield wars at a appointed time, using detonators, saber, throwing knives, powder shotguns, and other weapons, causing 5 people to die and injuring 18 others (6 were seriously injured). After the crime, the two sides not only refused to report the case but also hid the respective murderers. As for the victims' families, they dealt with each other through private consultations, so that the public security department could not investigate the perpetrators according to law. Since then, the relevant departments of Cangnan county have strengthened the management of the area, and with economic development, people are also busy with business, and the clan conflict has been alleviated in recent years.

8.2 Family culture and rural household economy

Modern new institutional economics holds that an institution plays a decisive role in economic development and is a precipitate of human behavior in history. People's accustomed practices (or habits) and standardized behaviors are the main manifestations of the system. They are all closely related to specific cultural patterns and social processes (Zhang, 1992). Therefore, when we study the causes of Wenzhou model or Wenzhou economic development, as a family culture which has a profound influence on the behavior of Wenzhou farmers, it is a factor that cannot be ignored. It can be said that because of the influence of family culture, family industry has become one of the most important characteristics of Wenzhou model in the early stage of marketization and industrialization.

8.2.1 Family industry and affiliated operation

If we study the history of Wenzhou industrial organization, we can find that it has two origins. First, it is the family factory that originated from the planned economy period to solve the employment problem of children. Second, as far as the countryside is concerned, the underground family factory originated from farmers.

As the labor department had long stopped hiring, the employment of residents had been stagnant, and a large number of voluntary private factories emerged. By 1968, the number had surged to 471, employing 18,100 people, including 307 unapproved and unlicensed organizations (Wenzhou Military Administration Production Office, 1995). The second spurt was in 1974–1976. As the employment problem was more prominent, many people had set aside factories and products to support the employment of their children. According to the statistics of the urban industry and trade system at that time, there were 211 family-run factories and 27,695 employees in the CPC Wenzhou Committee, 1995. At the same time, due to the slow development of state-owned and large collective enterprises, there was also a large space for development of underground family factories in Wenzhou. In 1970, Chen Qingyao, a farmer in Maqiaoren, learned that the necessary "alternating current contactor dynamic and static contact" of the coal mining operation in some coal mine in Anhui was in short supply. So he promised to supply the product and copied it on a white paper and brought it back to Wenzhou. Chen Qingyao came back to Liushi and secretly invited a technician of Wenzhou Yongjiu Lock Factory for guidance, and the first batch of products was successfully copied at home. Since then, the low-voltage electrical appliances had been made in Liushi. Similar occurrences were experienced in the automobile and motorcycle distribution industry in the Hantian village, Tangxia town, and Rui'an City. In 1972, seven friends in the same village, Chen Anjing, Chen Qigan, Chen Xishou, Han Zhisong, Han Laosan, Han Qisheng, and Han Yongwang (some are brothers of the same clan) each invested 300 yuan and set up a factory. Because the policy of the time absolutely prohibited private factories, but encouraged students to study and work in agriculture, and encouraged them to run schools and factories, they then attached the factory to the village-run Hantian Primary School, and named it the Ruian Tangxia People's Commune Hantian School Five Seven Stationery Factory. After the establishment of the factory, it successively produced chemical chess, wood chess, and abaci, causing profits and losses, but ultimately bringing about a state of destitution. It wasn't until September 1973 that Chen Anjing bought a contract of 6,500 yuan for a steering lamp instrument, at the cost of a 10% kickback. Since then, the factory began to produce auto and motorcycle accessory products, and continued to profit. After 1975, Hantian School May 7th Stationery was renamed May 7 Electrical equipment Factory, and the number of workers increased to more than 100, most of them from Kantian village. These former farmers or farm children gradually became skilled workers in production practice. Therefore, when the policy of the Party began to allow farmers to become professional households and key households in the sense of that time in 1982, 40 or 50 workers left the factory immediately and went home to run family workshops. As a result, the Kantian village automobile-motorcycle industry began to spread to the neighboring village with family as a unit (Chen, 2000).

These private enterprises laid a foundation for the development of private enterprises in Wenzhou. But under the constraints of the time, these small private enterprises were often considered to be competing with state-owned and large collective enterprises for raw materials, competing for energy and market, and as a model of capitalism, they were repeatedly rectified. Therefore, although there was sign of emergence of industrial organization at that time, extremely strong institutional constraints inhibited their further development.

In the early stage of the reform and opening-up, in the market environment of the seller, Wenzhou farmers with greater mobility easily got many profit opportunities. However, due to the state's strict control of private commercial activities, there was still no legal status for individuals to engage in commercial activities. There was a need to solve the contradiction that collective economy has legal status but no productive incentive, family management has interest incentive but no legal status. On the premise of not violating the original public-owned system as far as possible, Wenzhou farmers made Pareto improvement on the system. In the 1980s, under the influence of agriculture, many rural enterprises in Wenzhou turned into workshops, or group and even individual operations. In 1980, Jinxiang Brigade Stationery Factory, a village enterprise with more than 40 people in Cangnan county, decided to adopt the method of "decentralized production, centralized management" because there was no profit. Under the premise of maintaining the name of the collective factory, they implemented a unified name for the factory, unified bank account, unified tax payment, unified commission, and unified management fee. Economically independent accounting was applied internally. Later, people called this method "affiliated operation within a year". Farmers in the whole town competed to imitate, and more than 2,500 family households emerged, forming an industrial community centered on aluminum plastic signs and handicraft production.

The so-called affiliated operation refers to that individuals or consortium operators who have not obtained independent economic legal status for various reasons, affiliated to collective or state-owned enterprises and in name of the affiliated enterprises, are engaged in production and operation activities. The basic approach was as follows: the affiliate needs to consult with the affiliated company. After obtaining the consent, they would be provided with a service by the affiliated unit and the management fee would be charged. The service content of the unit was generally "three representations and three lending", namely, issuing the unified invoice, keeping an account, and levying the national tax, and lending letter of introduction, blank contract, bank account to the affiliate. Families or consortia that did not have independent legal person status thus gained legal status and carried out production and business activities. They borrowed the name of the unit, signed contracts, purchased raw materials, and promoted products all over the country.

The amount of money transferred to the bank account of the unit that was affiliated would be deducted by about 7.5%–8% from the amount. (5% was for industrial and commercial taxes, 2% was the income tax, 0.5%–1% was the management fee of the affiliated enterprises, and for a small number of enterprises that were affiliated at the village level, plus 2.5% of the collective accumulation.) The amount after deduction belonged to the affiliate (Huang, 1986). Although the specific conditions in each place for affiliated operation would be slightly different, they were basically the same.

Until 1983, although the state had greatly relaxed its control over the way agricultural production was operated, there was still no legal authorization for private entry into the industrial sector. Industry and commerce committees were afraid to issue permits, the banking sector was afraid to set up accounts for them, and a large number of family factories and farmers engaged in the production and marketing of products were denied the recognition and support of the government. Although many Wenzhou people had long worked outside, it was easier to find profit-making market opportunities in the seller's market environment at that time. However, due to the lack of economic legal status, they had no official seal, letter of introduction, contract, bank account, etc., required by business. The mode of operation effectively solved the problem of market access for private individuals who did not have the right to operate legally at that time. By handing in a certain amount of management fees, individuals bought a pass to enter the market, cross the market entry barriers set by the government in the planned economy period, and individual households began to be engaged in non-agricultural industries legitimately. In addition to the most important outcome of market access, it also had two functions. On the one hand, in the early stage of industrial development, Wenzhou industrial organizations were still in the family factory stage. Their business was unstable and their production was intermittent, and managers did not consider it necessary to take the time to gain legal status in industry and commerce, banks, and other departments. The method of affiliated operation not only had great flexibility but could also save transaction cost. On the other hand, during the planned economy period, the public ownership economy occupied an absolute dominant position, so that people had long formed the value judgment of product quality and socialization degree. The fledgling home factory itself could not compete in technology, quality, and otherwise. Therefore, the use of the form of affiliated operation could also play a role in borrowing the commercial reputation of state-owned and collective enterprises to some extent. In addition, there might be "sail under false colors" in affiliated operation, but with "red hat" it could also play a role in avoiding political risk. So it was not until the early 1990s that many "red hat" companies were reluctant to take off their hats. By the mid-1980s, it was estimated that 62% of the households in Wenzhou were hangers, and in some cases up to 90%. 80% of the streets and district offices were "red hat". By 1988, private employment and private companies were legally recognized, but "red hat" still existed.

In the end of 1988, only 10 out of every 10,000 private enterprises in Wenzhou were legally registered (Paris, 1994). Until the 1990s, when the legal status of private enterprises was established, many of Wenzhou's affiliated enterprises began to take off their hats.

8.2.2 Industrialization and differentiation of rural economic processes

Not only have Wenzhou's rural areas restored the family management of agriculture but many farmers have also incorporated industrial production into family production, and families have shown strong absorptive capacity. By April 1985, the Wenzhou household industry had reached 133,000 households. At the same time, a large number of farmers took the road of prosperity and became "ten thousand yuan households" in the sense of that time. The rapid development of Wenzhou's economy aroused people's general concern.

On May 12, 1985, *Jiefang Daily* published an article titled Village and Township Industry in South Jiangsu and Family Industry in South Zhejiang — 330,000 Wenzhou People engaged in Family Industry. The article first put forward the concept of Wenzhou model in the media, and summarized the characteristics of the development of rural family industry in Wenzhou as follows: It mainly produced small goods. It enlivened circulation channels by farmers and the rural market and relied on a large number of skilled craftsmen and trade experts to open up the road to wealth.

In the beginning of the 1980s, the small-commodity production in Wenzhou rural areas was similar to the outsourcing system in the early western countries. First of all, some people in rural areas with strong mobility, innovative ability, and adventurous spirit differentiated from the farmers and become professional marketers. At that time, the number was more than 100,000, and then it increased to 147,000 by 1986 (Li, 1997). After receiving orders, they assigned the production tasks to each family. The processing fee was charged according to the processing quantity. The production of small commodities such as metal buttons in Huangtian town, Yongjia county, is still maintained in this way. According to our investigation, some businessmen in Huangtian town used this method to produce, and its industry spread to the Shangtang town of Yongjia county, Xialao township, even to the area of Bilian, more than 40 kilometers away. Some rural housewives were also processing these products for Huangtian merchants. This mode of production and management in the outsourcing form combined the modern commodity production with the traditional family production mode, which fully utilized the peasants' spare time. Commodity production in this period was highly integrated with farmers' household production. In the 1980s, in Liushi, Yueqing, there was once a popular "front shop rear factory" family business form. People generally divide their houses into three blocks: the innermost as the living room, the middle as the workshop, and the outermost as the storefront to set up counters.

With the development of rural industrialization, because industrial production could bring much higher economic income than farming, technical content of Wenzhou rural industrial production was low in the early stage of industrialization and the necessary capital quantity required was also very low. Therefore, the surrounding farmers also crossed these not high market barriers, into the industrial field. Because the information channel of farmers is very limited, most of them can only imitate the farmers around. The mutual imitation of a large number of farmers makes Wenzhou rural areas a relatively concentrated industrial cluster with obvious division of labor. At the same time, the convergence of production in the region also made the producers need and rely on centralized trading places. Therefore, a large number of small-commodity markets came into being at this stage. Yang Xiaokai has proved why all transactions were concentrated in one place to improve transaction efficiency, and analyzed the emergence of cities and their hierarchical structures (Yang, 1998). Due to the country's outdated household registration policy, China restricted the process of urbanization, so the rural urbanization in Wenzhou was similar to the construction of a farming city like Longgang.

In the 1980s, Wenzhou's rural industrial production was still in a family workshop stage, but compared with the traditional handicraft industry, the degree of differentiation was much higher. Traditional handicrafts separated the process of production from the process of consumption, but its products were consumed in the community. The Wenzhou rural family industry in the 1980s further divided the consumption of its products from the local community. The purpose was to meet the needs of the unmet consumers in the market, and the relationship between the producers and the consumers occurred through the middleman. By the mid-1980s, the market-oriented production of Wenzhou family enterprises was expanding. At the same time, the expansion of production scale also required the construction of independent factories, and the family had been unable to accommodate the further expansion of industrial production needs.

8.2.3 Family culture and peasant household economic behavior

The industrialization and marketization of the rural areas in Wenzhou was spontaneous in the whole process of gradual reform in China. This has provided a good sample for us to observe and study the behavior of market subjects. As the process of industrialization and marketization was also accompanied by the revival of traditional family culture, the family culture had exerted a great influence on the economic behavior of farmers in the economic transition period.

(1) Industriousness and selfishness: The dual economic personality of the small private enterprises in the family

In rural China, although the collective ownership of rural land negated the peasants' private ownership of the land, it did not substantially change the economic characteristics of the peasants' private ownership of small land.

This is because under the current household contract system, farmers have a long-term right to use their land. After the recent extension of the land contract period, it is stipulated that the land would not change no matter how the number of people changed, which almost recognized the farmers' quasi-ownership of the land. As small private producers, farmers must be characterized by dual economic personality. On the one hand, they are industrious workers. Family is the interest center of people, it is not only the starting point of people's economic behavior but also the destination of its economic behavior. In the interests of the family, farmers would rather invest enormous labor in exchange for small gains in the absence of better profit opportunities. This kind of hard-working spirit makes China produce a characteristic labor-intensive agriculture; also it is because of this spirit that Wenzhou farmers even in the case of very low marginal benefit are willing to increase the input of labor, so as to make the rural household industry in Wenzhou have a tenacious vitality and competitiveness. On the other hand, they are selfish small proprietors, and with the development of commodity exchange, when trading rules are not sound, the selfish family departmentalism idea makes it easy to enrich oneself at others' expense in trading activities. Due to the small size of the family factory, it has the advantages of flexible operation, low cost, low investment, and quick production, which can adapt to the changeable situation of the market and have unique competitiveness. At the same time, due to its small-scale characteristics, the operation objectives and operating behaviors of the family factories tend to be short term, which leads to unfair competition behaviors such as fake, counterfeit products and fraud. In the early stage of industrialization and marketization, the difference between products of family factories was very small, which was more likely to lead to vicious price competition among them, so that the operation had always been trapped in low-grade products from which they could not extricate themselves.

(2) Consanguinity and kinship: The centripetal force of the culture of departmentalism

"When a man gets to the top, all his friends and relations get there with him." In traditional Chinese society, the fate of family members has always been closely related. Similarly, in today's rural community, the blood relationship within a family and household is still the link that keeps family members together in economic life. In the process of rural industrialization in Wenzhou, it can be found that the influence of family and household often exceeds the influence of society, and family and relatives are often the first sources of funds for people to engage in risky business. The success of a person in a certain industry often leads to success of the whole household and even the whole family. Therefore, in Wenzhou rural areas, there are not only many professional families engaged in second and third industries, but also many professional families specializing in the same industry. Especially in the early stage of industrialization and marketization, this kind of economic diffusion with family as the center and the link between blood and kin was more common. Due to the influence of the living pattern of the rural society, the industry is filled with blood relationship. At the same time, it also shows the regional agglomeration of similar industries, which brings about the phenomenon of "cluster". However, this kind of family-oriented culture will also produce strong family centripetal force, which will hinder the cooperation between rural family enterprises and influence the expansion of their operation scale.

Because of their narrow family concept, they adhere to the principle of "keep the goodies within the family", often unwilling to associate with others. Russell once profoundly pointed out, "In China, due to the Confucian concept of loyalty to the family, family career is often successful." But non-individual joint-stock companies are often in trouble because no one has an honest motivation for other shareholders (Russell, 1988). In Wenzhou's rural areas, it is often seen that some farmers run a business together because of the shortage of funds, but after making profits, they finally separated the business because of conflicts of interest and mutual suspicion. This has affected the expansion of rural enterprises in Wenzhou, which has a large number of household businesses all over the country, but only a small number of large ones.

(3) Building houses and tombs: The behavior of farmers' wealth hoarding

In the traditional agricultural society, "thousands of good farmland and houses, many children and grandchildren" was often the ideal family goal of farmers, so the family construction activities after people made money concentrated on buying farmland, building houses, and taking concubines. Although these family values formed in the agricultural society have changed greatly after decades of new socialist culture, after the recovery of the family economy, it has been manifested in people's behavior time and again. Because of the limitation of law and policy, the goal of buying land and taking concubines is impossible, so the private real estate housing allowed by law has become the only family goal that farmers can pursue openly. For many farmers, constructing several beautiful houses is almost the most important family business they have pursued for a lifetime. In recent years, the housing craze in rural Wenzhou is the reflection of farmers' nesting consciousness in investment behavior. Since housing is a sign of wealth, people compare with and imitate each other. Many peasants in Wenzhou not only compare their houses but also keep up with construction of the grim resting places for the deceased. Some even built graves for children only a few years old, causing great damage to the environment. The new graves and the new houses over the mountains have become the characteristic landscape of the Wenzhou countryside.

8.2.4 The development of division of labor economy and the division of rural family structure

With the development of industrialization and specialized division of labor economy, rural economic development will inevitably break through family barriers. With the expansion of business operations and the family workshop production formed in the beginning of the 1980s, it became difficult to meet the needs of further development of production and management in many places. So in the middle of the 1980s, a large number of partnerships emerged in Wenzhou's rural areas.[2]

The transformation of this mode of production marks the gradual differentiation of the functions of Wenzhou rural families. First, commodity production in rural areas began to move away from the family environment and into independent factories. Second, the production function of the family also separated. Farmers used to keep lots of land and grow vegetables to meet their families' needs. In recent years, as a result of specialized production, the family production function has been gradually differentiated. Many farmers no longer grow vegetables, and most of the vegetables they need are transported

---

[2] The partnership was once well intentioned in Wenzhou as a collective enterprise and a socialistic joint-stock company. To date, in the official statistics of Wenzhou City, this partnership and some limited liability companies are still counted in the joint-venture column.

from Wenzhou's urban areas by vendors. As a result, many vegetable's prices in the suburb of Wenzhou are higher than those in the urban area. At the same time, because the family members are often difficult to manage because of ego issues, for many enterprises, in addition to important positions such as finance, for employment of certain general staff, it tends to hire outsiders. In addition, as wives go to work in factories, they have no time to take care of their young children. As a result, the educational function of rural families is gradually degraded, and then transferred to professional educational institutions. At present, almost all of Wenzhou's economically slightly developed villages run nurseries and kindergartens. In recent years, due to a large number of young and middle-aged people going out for business, many of the social security functions previously undertaken by the family, such as old-age care, have also begun to turn to professional institutions.

8.3 Family culture and development of private enterprises

After more than 20 years of development, Wenzhou's private enterprises have made great progress. Some substantial changes have taken place in the characteristics of Wenzhou model, and the industrial organization structure has also changed from a simple family factory in the early stage of industrialization and marketization to a multi-level structure of an individual owner system enterprise, partnership, and corporation. But from each enterprise's intrinsic characteristic, these private enterprises' family system characteristic has not changed. The development of private enterprises in Wenzhou so far shows that not only do the so-called "individual industrial and commercial households" and most of the "private enterprises" completely belong to the household and the family business but most "joint-stock cooperative enterprise" and "shareholding system" companies also retain a strong household and family business sense. Of course, the higher proportion of family enterprises is not unique to Wenzhou, which is not only the characteristic of Wenzhou enterprises, but in fact 80% of enterprises around the world are family-owned enterprises (Galsik, 1998).

However, compared with the rest of the country, the family system in Wenzhou is not obvious because many enterprises in many areas of the country started from state-owned or collective enterprises. Most of Wenzhou's enterprises were the original enterprises founded by the Wenzhou people, which were not only small in scale but also in large numbers, which made them very impressive.

8.3.1 Establishment of family culture and Wenzhou's private enterprises

If we examine the development starting point of Wenzhou's private enterprises, we can find that household and family members play an important role in the establishment of most private enterprises. After all, Wenzhou village's is a society with strong traditional cultural characteristics, so the family culture has exerted a great influence on the rural industrialization. Whether it was the development of the family industry in the early stage of marketization or the establishment of the partnership in the 1990s, the role of household and family was still obvious. The role of family and household is mainly reflected in the following two aspects:

On the one hand, family members are an important source of start-up funds. The process of rural industrialization in Wenzhou was carried out at the same time as the whole economic system. Under the old system, the government did not recognize legitimacy of private industrial activity. Therefore, it was very difficult for farmers and other social individuals to obtain start-up funds from government financial institutions when they were engaged in risky business. After all, industrial and business activities need to cross the barrier of necessary funds, and it was difficult to achieve this purpose on the basis of their own savings. From the practice of rural Wenzhou, it can be found that the start-up funds of peasants engaged in risky business activities were usually obtained from family members or other relatives by blood and kinship. According to Chen (2000), 92% of the 114 households in Hantian village borrowed money from relatives, family members, and friends when they were founded. 84% of households lend money to others. Han Yuming, chairman of Zhejiang Ruiming Auto Parts Co., Ltd. recalled a scene in 1984, "I started out by borrowing 5,000 yuan from my mother-in-law" (Chen, 2000). In addition, from Wang Chunguang's study of Wenzhou's immigrant groups abroad, we can also find that the relationship between relatives and friends was very important for the Wenzhou people to go abroad and establish themselves in foreign countries. People in Wenzhou often smuggled themselves abroad through relatives, and often got the chance to get jobs illegally in three ways: work in workshops and small shops run by relatives and friends; work for other Wenzhou people through introduction by relatives and friends; or do private work in the house where friends and relatives rent to them. In addition, the Wenzhou people raised funds by making private financial forms such as "association".

The so-called "association" refers to a form of mutual economic assistance established with the help of friends and relatives. It is not purely mutual friendship but also a market component. "Association" will be very helpful to people in Wenzhou. The Wenzhou people have been doing business in Paris. When they need money, they raise funds from friends and relatives through "association". If one needs money, one forms an "association" and tells one's friends and relatives and asks them to join. Some people have more friends and relatives and will raise a lot of money through "association". The most obvious effect of the association is to speed up the pace of promoting more Wenzhou people to the position of boss, demonstrating the power of informal relations to help the Wenzhou people enter the market economy (Wang, 2000b). Similarly, the Wenzhou people in Wenzhou and all over the country get start-up funds for industrial and commercial activities through relatives and friends.

On the other hand, the Wenzhou people often learn business experience from relatives, so kinship is an important channel of industry diffusion. In the early stage of industrialization and marketization, Wenzhou farmers also had to face the change of role from farmer to farmer entrepreneur, which is actually the process of farmers learning management experience and industrial production technology. Due to the influence of the social interaction pattern on the peasants, the relatives and friends that often have contact with them become an important source of their new knowledge. After all, regarding the transfer of technology and management experience to the importer, it is a property spillover. In particular, the market iron law of peer-to-peer competition makes it even more so that if you do not have a certain relationship with a relative or friend, generally speaking, he will not pass on to you the relevant business management knowledge and production technology and set up a competitor for nothing. We have learned about it in the process of rural investigation that many rural youths, after graduating from school, often go to relatives' factories or shops to help, or follow them to the docks and run businesses first to learn management experience and necessary market knowledge, in order to operate independently when the conditions are ripe. In fact, this is also the mode by which many Wenzhou rural youth enter the market. It is because of the kinsmen that the time for Wenzhou people to learn market knowledge is greatly shortened, and the cost of market entry is greatly reduced. In June 1986, Cao Qiqi, the senior supply and marketing clerk and the former primary school teacher in Hantian village, led more than 40 supply and marketing clerks to Luoyang City of Henan Province to go forward with great strength and vigor, to participate in the order placing meeting for the national auto parts industry. Some of his peers were mostly blood relatives, roommates, or former students. In the middle of the 1980s, in the early stage of industrialization, it was a shortcut for the farmers who had just come up from the farmland to learn the market experience.

Meanwhile, Chen Dongsheng conducted a questionnaire survey in Hantian village.

In response to the question "kinship and contract, what kind of relationship do you believe in?", 61% of the 114 sample households chose family, and 39% chose contract. This suggests that, in the view of a majority of the villagers in Hantian village, the identity relationship is more important the contractual relationship. In terms of technology, market access, technology transfer, and market expansion, many business owners in Hantian also have a different attitude internally or externally. After a business owner made his fortune in a motorcycle factory, many relatives came to ask for guidance, and the two other shareholders met with the similar circumstances. As a result, the three shareholders reached a tacit understanding: where the relatives of shareholders went to the factory to learn technology, they would be given key positions, so that the old master could carefully teach them; the ordinary worker was forbidden access to technical secrets. Where a relative of a stockholder went to the factory to stock goods and open a shop, the first trip was on credit to him for capital; for common customers, the payment for goods was done when goods were delivered. Over the years, in this way, he helped his three brothers-in-law, and two nephews and a niece make their in production and distribution of automobile products. These people are successful now. Among them, the second nephew Lin learnt technology and management in his factory in 1987. In 1999, the annual output value of Lin's automobile and motorcycle company in Changchun had exceeded 50 million Yuan (Chen, 2000). It can be seen that, under the strong family culture background, farmers' economic behavior pattern has been greatly affected. Especially in the process of entrepreneurship, the support of blood kinship has played an important role in the establishment of private enterprises, which has greatly accelerated the formation of Wenzhou farmer entrepreneurs.

8.3.2 Family culture and the organizational structure of Wenzhou's private enterprises

Wenzhou's private enterprises have grown up in a rich family culture background, and have gradually developed by using the centripetal force of the family. For many people, enterprise is a family business, and the rise and fall of enterprises is also related to the family's honor, and household and family become an important community of shared interests. "If you don't belong to us, there is no guarantee of loyalty." Because of the cohesion of family culture, the trust of non-family members is bound to be reserved. In an economic society, people's rights to assets are not permanent, they are functions protected by themselves through direct efforts, which others attempt to seize, and are protected by the government (Bazer, 1997). Therefore, in order to protect their property rights, people will arrange the key positions with their relatives in order to reduce the cost of supervision in the process of operation. Therefore, in most small family enterprises, the traditional pattern of division of labor between men and women is followed. In general, men are responsible for important foreign business affairs such as supply and marketing, and women are responsible for internal production management or financial management.

For most small businesses, because they produce and manage products that are labor-intensive products that others can easily imitate and replace, some core technologies, customer resources, or financial matters related to the fate of the enterprise are rarely entrusted to outsiders. Even some of the larger companies have obvious familial characteristics. Founded in May 1981, Tingyu Group Company can be called Wenzhou's most typical family business. The company mainly produces high-precision valves, high-tech "online analysis system" instruments, and other products and its output value reached about 300 million yuan in 1998. In the company's organization, Pan Tingyu, the head of the family acts as the chairman of the board of directors, his wife Xu Wenqing as the director of the office, his wife's younger sister Xu Xiaoqing in charge of the general affairs of the office, his eldest daughter Pan Peicong as the general manager, his son Pan Yelei as the vice general manager, the second daughter Pan Peifang as the financial manager, the second son-in-law Lin Xiao as the sales manager, and nephew Shao Jinghai as the purchasing supervisor. The eldest son-in-law Wu Chufan is the general manager of his own father and son company, and is the only major family member who does not hold a position in the company. In addition to the family members, no one outside of the family is in the management of the company (Ma, 1999). It may be a special case where in a company like Tingyu all family members occupy all the key positions, while other family firms may not have all their family members in the same positions. But in general, it is common for key positions to be filled by family members.

In a family business, trust between people is mainly based on kinship. According to the classification of Fukuyama, 1993, it belongs to a low-trust society. A low-trust society based on kinship makes it difficult to create a non-consanguineous private enterprise organization, and it is difficult to avoid the law of "entrepreneurship by the first generation, preserving heritage by the second generation and decline of enterprise by the third generation" for a family business. Therefore, in a low-trust society, small- and medium-sized enterprises dominate the market. This analysis is very relevant to the actual situation of Wenzhou's countryside. It can explain the structure of Wenzhou enterprises from one side, where the small- and medium-sized enterprises are accounted for by 99% of the cultural reasons. Among Wenzhou family businesses, because of the blood and related special cohesion and self-sacrifice of family members of the family for a family business, it makes the enterprise greatly reduce the cost of internal supervision. As a result, small- and medium-sized enterprises throughout Wenzhou, though not modern in organizational form, tend to have strong vitality. The family's resources are limited because they often need to cross the barriers of production factors such as capital. Therefore, even in Wenzhou's rural areas with a strong traditional culture, there are still a large number of non-family partnership enterprises.

But because most partnerships are built on the relationship between relatives and friends. The strong family centripetal force often leads to the external rejection of family members, so the cooperation between non-family members is often difficult to endure because of the trust crisis. In some of the partnership enterprises in Liushi, there have been instances where the major shareholders take turns to manage each other because of mutual distrust. For example, in July 1984, Nan Cunhui and Hu Chengzhong invested 50,000 yuan and founded Yueqing Qiujing Switch Factory. At first, the two men took turns in charge, and by 1991, it was divided into two factories and they managed one factory each. In the second half of the year, they parted ways. Nan Cunhui and Nan Cunfei set up Sino-US Joint-Venture Wenzhou CHINT Electric Appliance Co. Ltd., while Hu Chengzhong and Hu Chengguo established Wenzhou Delixi Electric Appliance Limited Company. Later, Chint and Delixi both become cross-regional national township enterprise groups.

8.3.3 The attempt of Wenzhou's private enterprises to go out of the family system

Depending on their own characteristics, Wenzhou family enterprises have their unique advantages. They play an important role in reducing the transaction cost and improving the system under the condition that the market is underdeveloped and the degree of institutionalization is low. At the same time, it cannot be denied that they also have inevitable limitations. Especially in the fierce market competition, the limitation of resources within the family limits the further development of enterprises. One of the most prominent ones is that the shortage of human resources will directly affect the development of enterprises. Therefore, in order to cope with the increasingly fierce market competition, to retain the core talents of the enterprise and to seek further development, at the end of 20th century, some large private enterprises in Wenzhou began to try to establish modern enterprise system in order to get rid of the restriction of the family system.

Initially, the modern enterprise system tried to spread the stock right to the people outside the family and change the ownership structure of the enterprise. In the process of enterprise development, there must be a large number of people outside the family to join, and with the further development of the enterprise, some key technical personnel and management talents will play increasingly important roles in the enterprises. For these people, despite the prospect of rising wages, many still felt like they were senior workers. At the same time, with their increasingly prominent role in the enterprises, their appeal to other enterprises gradually increased, and the possibility of other enterprises promising various conditions to poach people increased. Therefore, if enterprises did not take measures to retain talents, the key talents of enterprises would be lost. However, for some key managers, because of the nature of their work, there was asymmetric information, and it was difficult for enterprises to supervise their work performance effectively. Even if they wanted to supervise, the cost of supervision was very high. Therefore, it was necessary to encourage them for a long time objectively, and it was an effective incentive method to give certain shares.

In 1991, when Nan Cunhui set up Chint, the equity was basically confined to the family. In addition to himself, Nan Cunfei, his brother was the general manager, his brother-in-law was the deputy general manager, and his nephew also owned shares. But a non-family member as the technical vice general manager had an earlier stake in the company, which reached more than 10 million yuan in 1999. Since 1995, two incorporated companies and six limited liability companies had been formed within Chint Group, and the shareholding structure had begun to spread. In particular, the two companies had dozens of shareholders. For share values, there were tens of thousands of yuan for less, and millions of yuan for more (Ma, 1999). Since then, one of the incorporated companies was to be listed on the stock market after a trial operation. However, the executive body of Chint still had a strong family characteristic, and even in the ownership structure, the total shares of the family members still constituted the majority. Similarly, under the pressure of competition, other companies were also trying to expand their shares outside the family. The Great Wall Group Company in Liushi was founded by six brothers including Ye Xiangyao and Ye

Xiangtao in 1988, namely, the former Great Wall Electrical Components Factory in Yueqing county. In 1993, it was renamed Zhejiang Great Wall Switch Factory, and in 1995 it was named "Zhejiang Great Wall Electrical Appliance Group". In 1997, it became a nationwide non-regional enterprise group. The group's assets amount to 800 million yuan with annual output value of 2 billion yuan in 2000. In addition, the group also has 500 sales companies across the country. Maybe it's the impact of the traditional Chinese heritage equalization system whereby the shares of the company have been divided among the six brothers, each accounting for 1/6. In the past, the company's marketing network was using the agent system formed in the early 1990s. The sales company under the agency did not have a stake in the Great Wall. Therefore, their demand for supply to the group company was often unrestrained but failed to settle with the head office in time. In the long run, it might be uncontrolled. Under the pressure of competition, in order to attract some marketing talents, the company decided to reform the property right of the enterprise, break the closed property right structure of the past, and expand its shares outward. On the one hand, the company set up a marketing network in all parts of the country, and set up a first-level sales company at the provincial level. On the other hand, some of the sales people outside the family have been absorbed into the board through share expansion. Four of the original six shareholders have entered the new board with two remaining out, bringing in seven new directors. At the same time, the company is seeking among non-family members the general manager and is preparing to restructure its management. In this regard, several shareholders believe that the current enterprises are doing well, the annual income is still okay, and the funds are not in short supply; they worry that the expansion of the stock will cause enterprise disorder. General Manager Ye Xiangtao said, "our generation has made the business very well, the family is very united, but is it okay to leave it to the next generation? If the enterprise is purely familial, the equity is still so concentrated, and the equity is not expanded, this enterprise is a relatively good enterprise in our hands, but by the next generation, the enterprise will have no vitality and its life will not be long. Therefore, it is necessary to make a big adjustment on the ownership structure. For us, we have set up this enterprise, but with the cultural structure and management level of our generation, it is difficult to adapt to the fierce market competition. We have completed our historical task at this stage, and if the enterprise is to expand and develop further in the next stage, our ability and knowledge structure will not adapt. After struggling, we should push the enterprise to society. We shall let more talented people join us start a second venture." Chairman Ye Xiangyao said the Great Wall was no longer the property of a person or a family, and that those who are competent are needed by the Great Wall. Otherwise, those incompetent have to leave their positions and let those qualified to do the job (Zhang, 2001).

Family members often find it hard to trust non-family members because of the family culture's external exclusion. As a result, top managers in family businesses often rarely hire outside staff. But in recent years, in order to further develop, some enterprises not only break the closed structure confined to the family in the ownership structure but also try to break through the monopoly of the family members in the governance structure. Founded in 1990, Tianzheng Company is a rising star in Wenzhou's low-voltage electrical industry. The company was first founded by Gao Tianle and Gao Tianfang, two brothers, the former as chairman, the latter as general manager. Later, Gao Tianfang operated a hotel business in Suzhou independently, and Gao Tianle became the chairman and general manager of the company with absolute holding power. The deputy general manager of the company is the brother-in-law with small shares. In the course of enterprise development, Gao Tianle realized that it was difficult to adapt to the needs of enterprise development and market competition only by himself and a few family members. In 1996, he made an open offer for general manager at 300,000 yuan a year in the newspaper, and chose Hu Zhongsheng, who had served as general manager in state-owned enterprises. The company has also successively launched management, technical personnel, and the backbone of ordinary employees to stake in, raising tens of millions of yuan, so that the company's shares are relatively decentralized. As a family business, it is always a little uneasy to ask an outsider to be the general manager of the company, which means to give the entire property of the company to someone outside the family. Therefore, it is not easy to be able to take this step. For this reason, some enterprises have to use some abnormal means to make the reorganization of enterprises proceed. Xinhua Co., Ltd. was the leading manufacturer of low-voltage electrical appliances in Liushi. The chairman and general manager of the company was Zheng Yuanmeng. The company's board of directors had a total of 4 shareholders; in addition to Zheng himself, two were Zheng's wife's uncles and one was Zheng's brother-in-law. In terms of age, Zheng himself was already in his 50s, and the remaining three directors had long been unable to work properly. But the company's major decision-making power, especially the personnel rights, was still in the hands of the majority of the board members outside Zheng.

In face of fierce market competition, Zheng realized that the company had to be reorganized. To this end, from March to June, 1995, the company held a 3-month extraordinary board of directors meeting. In order to force other shareholders to accept the demand for the withdrawal, he adopted every possible means, tough and soft, but they still didn't help. In the end, he had to say, "if you do not withdraw, I will" and that's what led to this reorganization. As a result, one of the other three directors withdrew completely and two of them withdrew half and transferred the shares to the company's four middle managers. After the reorganization, Zheng Yuanmeng retained the post of chairman and awarded the post of general manager to one of the new shareholders, Huang Suifei, who had a college degree. However, despite the fact that Xinhua carried out a restructuring of the ownership structure of the enterprise in an unusual way, it granted the post of general manager to non-family members. However, since the governance structure of the reformed Xinhua Company was still based on "rule by man" rather than "rule by law", the deterioration of the relationship between Zheng and Huang finally resulted in the withdrawal of Huang Suifei from Xinhua Company (Ma, 1999).

It can be seen that in order to eliminate the negative impact of the family system, Wenzhou's private enterprises should not rely solely on changing the ownership structure or hiring non-family members as general managers to solve the problem. Therefore, it was necessary to bring innovation into the enterprise system and form a check and balance mechanism which can effectively restrict the power of the manager, so that the ownership and the management right can be truly separated.

8.4 System innovation and regional economic development

Since Wenzhou's marketization and industrialization are only more than 20 years old, and the history of most private enterprises has not existed for long, most private enterprise owners are often very young, generally in their 30s and 40s. Therefore, many enterprises are not very urgently in need of the replacement of corporate leadership. However, the replacement of leadership and the change of the ownership structure of the enterprise become imminent when the enterprise encounters a new situation of the age structure in companies such as Xinhua company, in which it is difficult to adapt to the new pressures of market competition. Therefore, the company's motivation and pressure for being out of the family system will increase greatly. However, whether a company has shaken off the negative impacts of the family system is not simply dependent on whether there are non-family members, or whether it has hired a general manager who is a non-family member. The key is to see whether the final decision is made by family members. Especially for a few family businesses that have just hired a non-family general manager, it's hard to take this step. As a result, it is often difficult to let the general manager decide all the business.

To a certain extent, the size of the enterprise is increasing under the entrepreneur's control. The stronger the entrepreneur's control, the larger the enterprise's scale can be. Otherwise, the enterprise can only be engaged in small-scale management. For a majority of Wenzhou's private enterprises, the enterprises are controlled by the owners themselves, and the ownership and management rights are highly unified, so there is basically no problem of supervision cost to the operators. Of course, in this case, due to the limitations of their own quality, most enterprises are unable to grow big. With the expansion of the scale of the enterprise and the increase of the management personnel, the family's centripetal force and the self-sacrificing spirit of the family members in the period of starting a business can no longer meet the needs of the development of the enterprise. Simply hiring a competent non-family general manager to run the business will not solve the problem because in this way, it is inevitable for the family shareholders to feel uneasy about the new manager and always feel that the supervision cost is very high; for the employed general manager, he often feels that everything is restrained and supervised. Wenzhou's Tianzheng, Xinhua, Delixi, and even Chint have all hired non-family general managers, but in the end, apart from Tianzheng, most of them parted ways on bad terms. Therefore, Wenzhou's private enterprises still need to have certain conditions to complete the transition to modern enterprises.

On the one hand, it needs the development of the factor market, especially capital market and manager market. The biggest problem of employing non-shareholder managers is that their management and performance are examined and supervised. Under the principal–agent system, because of the difference of the target function between the manager as an agent and the owner as the principal owner, there is a difference between the two in the interest relationship. Therefore, there must be an agent who does not pursue the principal's target interest maximization as its action orientation. Because the performance of an enterprise depends not only on the operator's actions but also on many uncertain factors. The problem of information asymmetry exists between the operator and the owner, and the proprietor's management performance is difficult to assess effectively, and the moral hazard problem of the enterprise manager is inevitable. When there is a fully developed market for managers, the performance of managers can be chosen by the market, and the market selection itself is an effective supervision of managers. However, due to the short time of marketization in the country, Wenzhou has been listed first in the whole country, but the shortage of entrepreneurs is still outstanding. In a seller's market environment with insufficient supply of entrepreneurs, it is not only difficult for enterprises to select managers but the cost is also very high. Even if the manager is chosen, it is difficult to guarantee the operation performance of the enterprise due to the lack of effective market environment supervision. As a result, some private enterprises in Wenzhou have taken the step of hiring a general manager who is not a member of the family, but in the end they have to return back to the situation is which the chairman of the board works as their own general manager. To some extent, this has affected the transformation of Wenzhou's private enterprises to modern public companies.

From the point of view of the capital market, the liquidity of capital can promote the diversification and decentralization of the ownership structure under the condition of the well-developed capital market, which also provides a good institutional environment for the transformation of the family business. However, due to the fact that private enterprises in Wenzhou grew up in the process of transition from planned economy to market economy, the capital of enterprises depended on self-accumulation and private financing. The clear individual property right was not only beneficial to the development of the enterprise but also restricted the expansion of the enterprise capital and the further development of the enterprise. The Securities Law, which came into effect on July 1, 1999, allows private enterprises to go public. In order to further develop, some private enterprises with better performance in Wenzhou are also actively striving for the opportunity of stock listing. It is believed that the shareholding system transformation of Wenzhou's private enterprises will also promote their own transformation to modern enterprises.

On the other hand, the transformation of Wenzhou's private enterprises also needs innovation of the internal system. For shareholders, the biggest obstacle to giving up management is fear of asset security. Without effective checks and balances, they are afraid to leave their property to outsiders. Generally speaking, the chairman and general manager of Wenzhou's private enterprises are mostly family members. They are either held by one person or by family members through division of labor, and from the nature of the family system, there is no essential difference between the two. Therefore, whether or not to establish a modern enterprise system which is convenient for effective control and suitable for the needs of modern market competition has become the key to determine whether enterprises can realize the transition from traditional family enterprises to modern enterprises. In the reform of the corporate shareholding system, Tianzheng company is a relatively successful enterprise in the Wenzhou joint-stock system. Since the beginning of 1997, Tianzheng group has raised nearly 50 million yuan and absorbed more than 80 new shareholders, and changed the original shareholding structure. The main idea of the expansion is that, under the premise of guaranteeing the initial investor's absolute control, they will mainly encourage major managers to participate in the stock market, and focus on absorbing the technical and managerial personnel of the middle and higher levels, and selecting and developing the shares of ordinary employees. The shares are set at 10,000 yuan per share, with a large proportion, with an olive-shaped structure with "big in the middle and small on two ends" shares. At the same time, it reconstructs the corporate governance structure. After the reorganization, the governance structure of the group company was composed of shareholders, board of directors, board of supervisors, and the management team with the president as the core. This formed a power, decision-making, operating, and supervising system with sound functions, norms of conduct, strong restraint, coordination, and mutual checks and balances. As a result of the restructuring, the number of actual investors in a group company reached 89, exceeding the limit of 2–50 shareholders of a limited liability company stipulated in the Company Law. To this end, Tianzheng organized 48 investors with shares of less than 300,000 yuan to set up a staff stockholding board. The board was registered with the civil affairs department, obtaining the status of corporate legal person and electing 5 directors to form a board of directors. The whole board participated as a major shareholder in the shareholders' meeting of the group limited company.

In this way, the number of nominal shareholders was reduced to less than 50, which is in line with the registration requirements of the Company Law and the related business administration. At the same time, the company hired a professional manager with a high salary, and formed the company management team, wholly responsible for the company's daily production management activities. The board of directors becomes a special decision-making body. The board of directors had 11 directors, 2 of whom were managers and 4 were external non-shareholder directors who were experts. The board of supervisors would be elected by the general meeting of shareholders, consisting of seven supervisors, including 5 internal supervisors and 2 external supervisors. The board of supervisors had an audit office. The whole board of supervisors had the functions of "legislation" similar to the people's congress (namely, the development of rules and regulations), the audit supervision of the audit bureau, and the inspection and disposal functions of the discipline inspection commission. Due to the establishment of a relatively perfect internal corporate governance structure, the company initially realized separation of ownership and management which is the most difficult step for the family enterprises.

In short, for most of the family businesses in Wenzhou, the succession of business leaders is not very urgent due to their small size or short business existence. So there is no need for a rush to transform. With the development of the enterprise, when the control of the start-up business leadership is difficult to control, this need will become urgent. Wenzhou's current economy has transitioned from the buyer's market in the transition period to the seller's market in the mature stage. The competition between enterprises has also transitioned from the initial simple price competition to the present quality competition, brand competition, image competition, and formal management competition. The organizational structure of an enterprise has also changed from a simple family factory to a multi-level structure which is based on the family factory and coexists with the partnership and the company. Under the intense market competition pressure, there must be some family enterprises transformed to non-family enterprises. At the same time, because of the implementation of the family-planning policy in the country, in the future environment of the one-child family, the interpersonal relationship of the family will gradually fade. On the contrary, that of students, friends, and other non-blood relations will be further strengthened. It can be predicted that the structural transformation of Wenzhou's private enterprises will take place sooner or later. Therefore, enterprises should prepare for the transition to the modern enterprise system as soon as possible, design the transfer mode of enterprise management power in time, and lay a foundation for the further development of enterprises in the future. At the same time, we should realize that the family enterprise is not a backward symbol, and any enterprise system has its strength as well as its weakness. As long as it is guaranteed by a reasonable system, under certain conditions, family enterprises can also have their own unique advantages and generate good economic performance. Therefore, any problem should be analyzed specifically, and we can't simply say that we have gone out of the family business. On the contrary, we should fully believe that rational entrepreneurs will face market competition and make reasonable system choices for their own enterprises.

Bibliography

Adlakha, H K. Chinese civil society and the anatomy of Wenzhou model. *The Asian Scholar*, 2004(4).

Akerlof, G. The market for "lemons": Qualitative uncertainty and the market mechanism. *Quarterly Journal of Economics*, 1970, 84.

Alan, P L. Wenzhou model and China's modernization. *Asian Survey*, 1992(8).

Bazer, Y. *Economic Analysis of Property Rights*. Shanghai: Shanghai Sanlian Bookstore & Shanghai People's Publishing House, 1997.

Braudel, F. *Civilization materielle, economie et capitalisme*. Gu, L & Shi, K. trans. Beijing: SDX Joint Publishing Company, 1993.

Cai, K. Analysis on Wenzhou humanistic spirit. *Journal of Zhejiang Normal University (Social Science Edition)*, 1999(2).

Cai, K. Investigation of political participation of Wenzhou's private entrepreneurs. *Journal of National School of Administration*, 2000(3).

Chandler, A D, Jr. *Strategy and Structure: Chapters in the History of the American Industrial Enterprise*. Cambridge: MIT Press, 1969.

Chandler, A D, Jr. The Visible Hand: *The Managerial Revolution in American Business*. Chong, W. trans. Beijing: Commercial Press, 1997.

Chandler, A D, Jr. *The Economics of Scale and Scope: The Dynamics of Industrial Capitalism*. Zhang Y, *et al*. trans. Beijing: China Social Sciences Press, 1999.

Chang, Z. Abandoning the South Jiangsu model — reports on privatization of township enterprises at South Jiangsu. *Economic Observer*, 2001-05-07.

Chayanov, A. *Peasant Economic Organization*. Xiao, Z. trans. Beijing: Central Compilation Press, 1996.

Chen, D. The influence of village family culture on the auto motor parts industry of Hantian village. *Wenzhou Forum*, 2000(4).

Chen, D & Xiao, L. *Song of Wenzhou: The Wenzhou People Who Dare to Be the First in the World.* Beijing: Guangming Daily Press, 2000.

Chen, L. Views on the professional market. *Zhejiang Journal of Social Sciences,* 1996(5).

Chen, Q, *et al. Zhengdao Taixing.* Beijing: China Economic Publishing House, 1998.

Chenery, H B & Elkington, H. *Structural Change and Development Policy.* Beijing: Economic Science Press, 1991.

Chu, X. Family business research: A topic of modern significance. *Chinese Social Sciences,* 2000(5).

CPC Wenzhou Committee. A report on urgent research issues (1978) //Yu, X, *et al. A Brief History of Wenzhou Industry.* Shanghai: Shanghai Academy of Social Sciences Press, 1995.

Davis & North. Theory of institutional change: Concepts and reasons//Coase, A & North *et al. Property Rights and Institutional Changes.* Shanghai: Shanghai Joint Publishing Press, 2000.

Dong, F & Zhao, R, *et al.* Investigation of Wenzhou's rural commodity economy and exploration of the path for China's rural modernization. *Economic Research,* 1986(6).

Douglass, C N & Robert, P T. *The Rise of the Western World: A New Economic History.* Li, Y & Cai, M. trans. Cambridge: Cambridge University Press, 1999.

Du, R. Interpretation of Wenzhou Economic Mode. *China Economic Times,* 2000-07-05.

Expert Group on China's Reform and Development Report. *The Experience of Growth: A Case Study of China's Excellent Large Enterprises.* Shanghai: Shanghai Far East Press, 1999.

Fan, G. Two reform modes and two reform costs. *Economic Research Journal,* 1993(1).

Fang, M. *Institutional Transition and Development Path of Zhejiang Province.* Hangzhou: Zhejiang People's Publishing Housing, 2000.

Fang, M, *et al. Institutional Changes and Development Track of Zhejiang Province.* Hangzhou: Zhejiang People's Publishing House, 2000.

Fei, X. A journey to Wenzhou. *The Outlook,* 1986 (20–22).

Fei, X. *Earthbound China.* Beijing: Peking University Press, 1998.

Feng, X. Influence and integration power of traditional culture: Comparison between Jiangsu model and Wenzhou model II. *Economic Izvestia,* 2000(12).

Feng, X. Marketization: Evolution path of local modes. *China Rural Survey*, 2001(1).

Fewsmith, J. *The Logic and Limits of Political Reform in China*. Cambridge: Cambridge University Press, 2013.

Fite, G C & Reese, J E. *An Economic History of the United States*. Shenyang: Liaoning People's Publishing Housing, 1981.

Galsik, K. *The Propagation of Family Business*. Beijing: Economic Daily Press, 1998.

Gao, B & Zhang, J. *Wenzhou: The Shoe Capital of China*. Beijing: China Light Industry Press, 2002.

Ge, L & Xie, L. *Institutional Innovation in the Process of Marketization: Economic Research on Zhejiang Rural Joint Stock System*. Hangzhou: Zhejiang People's Publishing House, 2000.

Genesove, D. Adverse selection in the wholesale used car market. *Journal of Political Economics*, 1993, 101(4).

Guo, Z. Characteristics, reasons, effects and revelations of Wenzhou regional characteristic scale economy. *Zhejiang Academic Journal*, 1997(5).

Hörner, J. Reputation and competition. *CARESS Working Paper*, 1999.

Hu, W. Today, stand up with head high: A revelation about the development of Wenzhou's shoemaking industry (I). *Wenzhou Daily*, 1994-01-03(2)a.

Hu, W. Today, stand up with head high: A revelation about the development of Wenzhou's shoemaking industry (II). *Wenzhou Daily*, 1994-01-05(2)b.

Huang, J. Wenzhou's affiliated operation and its perfection. *Zhejiang Journal of Science*, 1986(5).

Huang, Z. *Small Peasant Family and Social Development in Yangtze River Delta*. Beijing: Zhonghua Book Bureau, 2000.

Jiang, Y. *The Feelings of Wenzhou: People Won't Forget Them*. Beijing: Guangming Daily Press, 2000.

Jiangsu Provincial Bureau of Statistics. *Jiangsu Provincial Statistical Yearbook (1998)*. Beijing: China Statistics Press, 1998.

Jin, X. Transformation of the "Zhejiang Model" and market innovation. *Zhejiang Academic Journal*, 1998(1).

Jin, X. The reform path of the coexistence of various institutional changes and the gradual transformation. *Journal of Zhejiang University (Humanities and Social Sciences)*, 2000a(4).

Jin, X. Free up the mind, frictional cost and institutional transformation: Wenzhou model and reform experience of Zhejiang. *Zhejiang Social Sciences*, 2000b(5).

Jin, X & Ke, R. Research on the factors hindering cooperation, institutional loopholes and reform in the share cooperation system//Jin, X. *Organizational Innovation and Regional Economic Development*. Hangzhou: Hangzhou University Press, 1998.

Jin, X, Zhang, J & Zheng, Y. *Organizational Innovation and Regional Economic Development*. Hangzhou: Hangzhou University Press, 1998.

Ke, R. Wenzhou cangnan cotton yarn trade and division of labor. *Tianze Luncong*, 1998a(1).

Ke, R. A few problems during the development of private enterprises: Analysis of transaction fees — Empirical investigation from Wenzhou model. *Zhejiang Social Sciences*, 1998b(2).

Ke, R & Zhong, H. *Modernization Process of Family Business: Hope Group Co., Ltd. Investigation*. National Body Reform Seminar. "Reform and Development Report" Special Case, 1998.

Kihlstrom, R & Riordan, M. Advertising as a signal. *Journal of Political Economy*, 1984, 92.

Klein, B & Leffler, K. The role of market forces in assuring contractual performance. *Journal of Political Economy*, 1981, 81.

Kong, J. Marketization and property right system: Theoretical analysis of transition process. *Economic Research Journal*, 1994(6).

Kreps, D, *et al*. Rational cooperation in the finitely repeated prisoners' dilemma. *Journal of Economic Theory*, 1982, 27.

Kuznets, S. *Modern Economic Growth: Rate, Structure, and Spread*. Beijing: Beijing Institute of Economics Press, 1998.

Li, D. *The Mystery of Wenzhou*. Beijing: Reform Press, 1997.

Li, D. *The Riddle of Wenzhou: The Successful Model of China's Poverty Alleviation*. Beijing: Guangming Daily Press, 2000a.

Li, D. *The Son of Wenzhou: The Man of Reform and Opening Up*. Beijing: Guangming Daily Press, 2000b.

Li, D. *The Tan of Wenzhou: Theoretical Sparks in the Practice of Reform and Opening Up*. Beijing: Guangming Daily Press, 2000c.

Li, H. *New Leap-forward of Wenzhou*. Shanghai: Shanghai Academy of Social Sciences Press, 1996.

Li, H. *Modernization and Wenzhou's Development*. Beijing: Science Press, 2000.

Li, J. Origin of the "autonomy" spirit: Difference and similarities between Wenzhou's folk "autonomy" and Shunde's local "autonomy". *Economic Izvestia*, 2000(12).

Li, M. "Relative loss" and "chain effect": Analysis and thinking of the contemporary immigration wave of Wenzhou region. *The Study of Sociology*, 1999(5).

Li, Q. *China's Jews: Mysterious Wenzhou People*. Beijing: Economic Daily Press, 1999.

Lin, B, *et al*. *Series of Wenzhou Model*. Nanning: Guangxi People's Publishing House, 1987.

Lin, B. *Wenzhou Dialogues Related to Wenzhou Model*. Nanning: Guangxi People's Publishing House, 1990.

Liu, X. A brief discussion on contemporary clan fighting in Southern Zhejiang. *A Sociological Study*, 1993(5).

Liu, X & Zhang, Z. Vigilant quality standard: One review on Wenzhou's quality standard. *Wenzhou Daily*, 1994-08-04(1).

Luo, W. The prospect of professional market is not optimistic. *Zhejiang Social Sciences*, 1996(5).

Ma, H. Investigation of ten-thousand yuan household of Yueqing county. *Rural Work Communications*, 1985(9).

Ma, J. The development of Wenzhou stock cooperation system//*Manual on the Practice of Shareholding Cooperative System* (internal issue), 1993a.

Ma, J. The market economy and joint-equity cooperative enterprise in Wenzhou. *Wenzhou Forum*, 1993b(S).

Ma, J. Research on the development of Wenzhou's joint-stock partnership. *Zhejiang Academic Journal*, 1994(2).

Ma, J. Reflections on the system innovation and management innovation of private enterprises in Wenzhou. *Economic Research Data*, 1999(12).

Mantoux, P. *The Industrial Revolution in the Eighteenth Century: An Outline of the Beginnings of the Modern Factory System in England*. Yang, R, Chen, X & Wu, X. trans. Beijing: The Commercial Press, 1983.

Miao, Z. The choice of reform strategy in institutional change. *Economic Research Journal*, 1992(10).

Milgrom, P & Roberts, J. Price and advertising signals of product quality. *Journal of Political Economy*, 1986, 94.

National Bureau of Statistics. *China Statistical Yearbook* (*1998, 1999, 2000*). Beijing: China Statistics Press, 1998, 1999, 2000.

Nelson, P. Information and consumer behavior. *Journal of Political Economy*, 1970, 78.

Nelson, P. Advertising as information. *Journal of Political Economy*, 1974, 81.

Nolan, P & Dong, F. *China's Marketing Strength: Competitiveness of Small Business and Argument about Wenzhou*. London: Zed Books Ltd, 1990.

Noldeke, G & Samuelson, L. Learning to signal in markets. *MEMO*, 1994.

North, D C. *The Rise of the Western World*. Beijing: Huaxia Publishing House, 1999.

Owen. *Trip to Wenzhou: Talk about Wenzhou from All Walks of Life*. Beijing: Guangming Daily Press, 2000.

Pallis. Local enthusiasm and state reform: Wenzhou model in the eyes of a foreign scholar. Wei, G. trans. *Literature and Information of the Party School of Shanghai Municipal Party Committee*, 1994(4).

Pan, S & Luo, D. Private finance and economic development. *Journal of Financial Research*, 2006(4).

Parris, K. Local initiative and reform: The Wenzhou model of development. *The China Quarterly*, 1993(6).

Peng, S. *Relations and Trust: A Native Study of Chinese Interpersonal Trust, China Sociological Yearbook, 1995–1998*. Beijing: Social Sciences Literature Press, 2000.

Rothschild, M & Stiglitz, J. Equilibrium in competitive insurance markets: An essay on the economics of imperfect information. *The Quarterly Journal of Economics*, 1976, 90.

Russell. *The Theory of Power*. Shanghai: Oriental Press, 1988.

Sang, J. Look to South Jiangsu for township enterprise, look to Wenzhou for household industry, 330,000 Wenzhou people engaged in household industries. *Jiefang Daily*, 1985-05-12.

Scheibe, H N, Vatter, H G & Faulkner, H U. *American Economic History of Nearly a Hundred Years*. Beijing: China Social Sciences Press, 1983.

Schmalensee, R. A model of advertising and product quality. *Journal of Political Economy*, 1978, 86.

Shapiro, C. Consumer information, product quality, and seller reputation. *Bell Journal of Economics*, 1982, 13(1).

Shapiro, C. Optimal pricing of experience goods. *Bell Journal of Economics*, 1983, 14(2).

Sheng, H. *Transitional Economics in China*. Shanghai: Shanghai Joint Publishing Press, 1994.

Shi, J. The modernization and development mode of Zhejiang. *Zhejiang Social Sciences*, 1999(3).

Shi, J. Historical institutional analysis: Observation from perspectives of personalized transaction and impersonal transaction. *Zhejiang Social Sciences*, 2004(2).

Shi, J. Solution for financial risks in Wenzhou. *Finance and Economics*, 2012(4).

Shi, J & Luo, W. *Study on the Modernization Process of Zhejiang Province 1978–1998*. Hangzhou: Zhejiang People's Publishing House, 2000.

Shi, J & Zheng, B. Thoughts on the "10th Five-Year Plan" economic and social development of Zhejiang Province. *Zhejiang Economics*, 2000(3).

Spence, M A. Job market signaling. *The Quarterly Journal of Economics*, 1973, 77.

Stigler, G J. *The Organization of Industry*. Chicago: Chicago University Press, 1983.

Stiglitz, J E & Andrew, A W. Credit rationing in markets with imperfect information. *American Economic Review*, 1981, 71.

Tang, R & Chen, L. Review of *Wenzhou model*. *Reform*, 2000(4).

Tetsushi, S, Hu, D & Keijiro, O. From inferior to superior products: An inquiry into the Wenzhou model of industrial development in China. *MEMO*, 2002.

Wang, C. Flowing social network: The behaviors of Wenzhou people in Paris and Beijing. *The Study of Sociology*, 2000a(3).

Wang, C. *Wenzhou People in Paris: An Immigrant Group's Cross-Social Construction*. Nanchang: Jiangxi People's Publishing House, 2000b.

Wang, C, *et al*. Wenzhou people in Paris: A unique social integration method. *Social Sciences in China*, 1999(6).

Wang, D. General theory of institutional innovation. *Economic Research Journal*, 1992(5).

Wang, X. Family system and rural industrial development: Comparative study of rural areas in Guangzhou and Wenzhou. *Chinese Social Sciences Quarterly*, 1996(2).

Wang, X. *Cultural Tradition and Economic Organization*. Dalian: Northeast University of Finance and Economics Press, 1999.

Wang, X & Zhu, C. *Private Enterprises and Family Economy of China's Rural Region: Investigation of Xiangdong Village, Cangnan County, Zhejiang.* Taiyuan: Shanxi Economic Press, 1996.

Wen, J. *The Spring of Wenzhou: Spring Breeze of the Third Plenary Session of the Eleventh CPC Central Committee.* Beijing: Guangming Daily Press, 2000.

Wenzhou Military Administration Production Office. Investigation of the basic situation of street enterprises (1968), city archive 51-18-33//Yu, X, *et al. A brief History of Wenzhou Industry.* Shanghai: Shanghai Academy of Social Sciences Press, 1995.

Wenzhou Municipal Bureau of Statistics. *Wenzhou Municipal Statistical Yearbook* (*1999*). Beijing: China Statistics Press, 2000.

Wilinsky, A. Retail trade concentration due to consumers' imperfect information. *Bell Journal of Economics,* 1983, 14.

Williamson. The transaction cost economics. *Study Materials for Economic Workers,* 1988, 87.

Wilson, C. The nature of equilibrium in markets with adverse selection. *Bell Journal of Economics,* 1980, 11.

Wu, X. The discussion of the rural commercial economy of developed Wenzhou. *People's Daily,* 1986-08-06.

Xiang, B. Escape, unity and expression of "Zhejiang village". *China Social Sciences Quarterly,* 1998(1):22.

Xiang, B. *Community across the Border—the Life History of "Zhejiang Village" in Beijing.* Beijing: SDX Joint Publishing Company, 2000.

Xiang, G. *View the Turn of the Century Through Wenzhou.* Beijing: Huaxia Publishing House, 1998.

Xiao, L. *The Secrets of Wenzhou-seeking the Best Combination.* Beijing: Guangming Daily Press, 2000.

Xie, J & Ren, B. *A Study on Private Economy in Wenzhou: Analysis of Wenzhou Model Based on Private Economy.* Beijing: China Industry and Commerce Press, 2000.

Xie, L. *Study on Zhejiang Private Economy.* Hangzhou: Zhejiang People's Publishing House, 2000.

Xie, S. Economic analysis of forged and fake commodity. *Economic Research Journal,* 1997(8).

Xu, F, *et al.* The basic pattern and practical experience of South Jiangsu model. *Economics Information,* 1997(11).

Xu, J, Zhang, Y & Zhang, L. Analysis of the evolution of Wenzhou private enterprise system. *Social Science Front*, 2001(1).

Xu, M. Political economics on the occurrence and development of Wenzhou model: Some related problems of the transition economics. *Journal of Shenzhen University (Humanities & Social Sciences)*, 1999(3).

Yan, S. The growth and construction of China's economy. *Keiso Shobo*, 1992(190).

Yang, R. On conflicts and coordination between the mode of institutional change and the objective of institutional choice in China. *Economic Research Journal*, 1994(5).

Yang, R. The three-stage theory of the transformation of institutional changes in China. *Economic Research Journal*, 1998(1).

Yao, X & Luo, W. *Comparative Economic System Analysis*. Hangzhou: Zhejiang University Press, 1999.

Ye, J. Credit in the field of economics: A literature review. *Chinese Social Sciences Review*, 2003, 2(2).

Yi, X. An analysis of the obstacles to the sustained and rapid development of Wenzhou rural industry. *China Rural Economy*, 2001(3).

Yu, B. Political, economic, social: Re-investigation of Wenzhou model. *Rural Economy and Society*, 1988(2).

Yu, G. From Wenzhou model to "one system more manifestations". *Ta Kung Pao*, 1992-01-28.

Yuan, E. *Wenzhou Model and Path to Prosperity*. Shanghai: Shanghai Social Sciences Press, 1987.

Yuan, F, *et al*. *Social Restructuring in China*. Beijing: China Social Press, 1998: 30.

Zhang, J. The Chinese rural informal financial sector after the reform: Case study of Wenzhou. *Chinese Social Sciences Quarterly*, 1997(3).

Zhang, J, *et al*. The self-revolution of a family enterprise. *China Economic Times*, 2001-04-26(5).

Zhang, M. Investigation of Wenzhou's "Second Entrepreneurship". *The Study of Sociology*, 1996(4).

Zhang, R. Comparative method shall be used for research of Wenzhou model. *Comparison of Economic and Social Institutions*, 1986a(2).

Zhang, R. Characteristics and reasons of Wenzhou model. *Zhejiang Academic Journal*, 1986b(3).

Zhang, R. A few theoretical understanding questions of Wenzhou model. *Zhejiang Academic Journal*, 1988(5).

Zhang, R. Wenzhou model: New changes of functionalities of enterprises, market and government. *Zhejiang Academic Journal*, 1994(3).

Zhang, R. Private enterprises need to innovate again. *China's Rural Economy*, 2000(8).

Zhang, R & Li, H. *A Study on the Wenzhou Model*. Beijing: China Social Sciences Press, 1990.

Zhang, S. On institutional equilibrium and institutional reform. *Economic Research Journal*, 1992(6).

Zhang, S. Theoretical reflections on Wenzhou model: A review on "Historical Institutional Analysis of Wenzhou Model" by Shi Jinchuan. *Zhejiang Social Sciences*, 2004(2).

Zhang, W & Ma, J. The property right foundation of malignant competition. *Economic Research Journal*, 1999(7).

Zhang, W. *Enterprise Theory and Reform of Chinese Enterprises*. Beijing: Peking University press, 1999.

Zhang, W. *Property Rights, the Government and Reputation*. Beijing: SDX Joint Publishing Company, 2001.

Zhang, X. On equilibrium and evolution of institution. *Economic Research Journal*, 1993(9).

Zhang, X. *The Information Mechanism of Private Financial Contracts*. Beijing: Social Sciences Academic Press, 2016.

Zhang, Y. *Economic Development and Institutional Change: Economic Analysis of Institution*. Beijing: China Renmin University Press, 1992.

Zhao, S & Zhu, Z. *Advance and Fission*. Hangzhou: Zhejiang University Press, 2000: 70–74.

Zhao, W. *Modern Industrial Society and the Selection of Economic System*. Beijing: China Social Sciences Press, 1994.

Zhao, W. The Wenzhou power. *Economic Izvestia*, 1999(11).

Zhao, W. Regional opening — unique Chinese pattern and development trend. *Zhejiang Academic Journal*, 2001(2).

Zhao, W & Deng, Q. Corporate mergers and acquisitions. *Zhejiang Academic Journal*, 1999(6).

Zhao, W & Huang, X. External constraints: The major obstacles in the promotion of two Chinese regional industrialization modes. *China Industrial Economics*, 1997(11).

Zhejiang Provincial Reform Commission. Manual on the practice of shareholding. *Cooperative System*, 1993(11).

Zhejiang Provincial Bureau of Statistics. *Zhejiang Provincial Statistical Yearbook* (*1999, 2000*). Beijing: China Statistics Press, 1999, 2000.

Zheng, Y. *The Road of Wenzhou*. Beijing: Guangming Daily Press, 2000.

Zhong, H & Ke, R. *Competition, Motivation and Externality: Investigation of Huawei Technologies Co., Ltd*. Reform and Development Report of National Body Reform Research Institute, 1998.

Zhou, Q. Enterprises in the market: A special contract between human capital and non-human capital. *Economic Studies*, 1996(6).

Zhou, X. Tradition and transition: Social mentality of Chinese farmers— comparative study of Zhouzhuang township, Kunshan and "Zhejiang village" in Beijing. *Chinese Social Sciences Quarterly*, 1996(2).

Zhou, X. The function innovation of Wenzhou local government//*Institutional change and Economic Development: A Study of Wenzhou Model*. Hangzhou: Zhejiang University Press, 2001: 340–341.

Zhu, C. Regional cultural characteristics of rural residential houses in Wenzhou: A case study of Cangnan county. *A Sociological Study*, 1996(5).

Zhu, K. Rural culture and Wenzhou cultural household economy. *Zhejiang Social Sciences*, 1997(5).

Zhu, K. Evolvement of industrial cluster in the period of economic transformation: A preliminary study of Wenzhou regional economy. *China Rural Observation*, 1999(3).

Zhu, K. Ethnic culture and villager autonomy: A survey of village level democratic election in Cangnan county, Zhejiang Province. *China Rural Observation*, 2000(4).

CPSIA information can be obtained
at www.ICGtesting.com
Printed in the USA
BVHW041908230520
580197BV00010B/12